Archbishop Marcel Lefebvre

D1553607

THEY HAVE UNCROWNED HIM

From Liberalism to Apostasy
The Conciliar Tragedy

ANGELUS PRESS
2915 FOREST AVENUE,
KANSAS CITY, MISSOURI 64109

ANGELUS PRESS
2915 FOREST AVENUE
KANSAS CITY, MISSOURI 64109
PHONE (816) 753-3150
FAX (816) 753-3557
ORDER LINE 1-800-966-7337
WWW.ANGELUSPRESS.ORG

ISBN 0-935952-05-5
First Printing–August 1988
Second Printing–November 1988
Third Printing–November 1992
Fourth Printing–September 2003

Printed in the United States of America

God's plan is to "sum up everything in Christ" (Col. 1:16-17), that is to say, to bring back all things to one sole head, the Christ. Pope St. Pius X took this same expression of St. Paul as his motto: *Omnia instaurare in Christo–to re-establish, to restore all in Christ*: not only religion, but civil society.

–*Archbishop Marcel Lefebvre*

Table of Contents

Part III
The Liberal Conspiracy of Satan
Against the Church and the Papacy

Part IV
A Revolution in Tiara And Cope

Preface to the American Edition

The Angelus Press is pleased to offer to the English-speaking reader this masterpiece of Archbishop Lefebvre, *They Have Uncrowned Him*. In this book, he points out the deep roots of the evils of our times, especially in the Church. The cancer, or better "the AIDS,"[1] which is destroying the defenses of the Church from within, has a name. Archbishop Lefebvre gives it its proper name: Liberalism. On December 8, 1977, he had already said: "...the fruit that the Devil presents to the modern world to deceive it, is Liberty." Liberty of man, set up as an absolute, is indeed the cause of the weakening of faith in many, and even, oftentimes, the loss of faith.

We, in America, may have some difficulties understanding this. We have seen the Church grow and multiply wonderfully before the Council, under a regime of liberty. The Popes themselves, Leo XIII and Pius XII in parti-cular, acknowledged this wonderful growth. We are therefore surprised when Liberalism is accused of being the poisonous seed in the Council and the cause of the post-conciliar disaster. We would be tempted to relativize and say: this may be true in France, where Liberals have fought against the Church violently during the Revolution of 1789, and throughout the whole of the nineteenth century. Freemasons have openly designated the Church as their target to destroy in Europe. But here, it is not the same!

Such an attitude would lack clear-sightedness. The main difference is that throughout the Middle Ages, Christ

---

1 The expression is used by His Grace.

reigned in Europe, but was unknown in America. From its beginnings, the majority of the settlers were non-Catholic, and thus America has never been a Catholic country. When the enemies of Christ set up to spread their poisonous doctrine in Europe, they attacked the Church even with violence. Their goal was to *destroy the Catholic City.* In America, there was no Catholic City to destroy!

We must heed the words of the Popes. "If the Catholic religion is honored among you, if it is thriving, if it is ever-growing, that has to be attributed entirely to the divine fruitfulness enjoyed by the Church."[1] This growth is thus not a fruit of Liberalism, but rather of the grace of Our Lord spreading through the dedication of missionaries, priests, nuns and fervent faithful; it is a fruit of the traditional Catholic liturgy which attracted many souls by its beauty and universality. Moreoever, the Pope continues: "It (the Church) would produce still more fruits if it enjoyed, not only freedom, but the favor of the laws too, and the protection of the civil authorities."[2] Thus, Liberalism is far from being the cause of the Church's growth in America before the Council. Neither is it the cause of the temporal success of America: it is rather to be found in the natural virtues of its citizens, in the sense of initiative and leadership of hard-working people.

But Liberalism is certainly the cause of what we see today: the complete dissolution of the forces of our country! Is not abortion promoted under the pretext of the false "liberty of women to do what they want with their own body?" Are not "gay-rights" promoted under the same pretext of false liberty? Is not Liberalism what is weakening America's stand against Communism? And in the Church, is it not Liberalism in the clergy that caused so few priests to remain faithful to the Mass of their ordination when the New Mass came in?

"What we need is to come back to the spirituality of the Martys!" said Father Schmidberger. How true this is! The Martyrs understood that man is not first, but God is first

---

1 Leo XIII, *Longinqua Oceani,* 6 January 1895.
2 Ibid.

and must be given pride of place in our life, in our families, in our countries: "Seek ye therefore first the Kingdom of God and His justice, and all these things shall be added to you."[1] Fidelity to Our Lord Jesus Christ is a good even greater than our own life. The true Faith is a treasure that we must not only keep for ourselves, but give to all around us: parents to children, priests to faithful, and citizens to their fellow citizens! The Liberals, so-called Catholics, are ashamed of the Faith; the Martyrs have given their blood for it. "Whosoever shall confess Me before men, him shall the Son of man also confess before the Angels of God... But he that shall be ashamed of Me and of My words, of Him the Son of man shall be ashamed, when He shall come in His majesty."[2]

In order to have the courage and the zeal to confess Our Lord Jesus Christ, one must have a strong conviction, a strong faith. Liberalism, as Archbishop Lefebvre explains masterfully in this book, weakens this conviction and leads to its complete destruction. Let us come back to the spirituality of the first American Martyrs!

To sum up this whole book in one word, the Liberals do not understand the first and greatest commandment: "Thou shalt love the Lord thy God with thy whole heart, and with thy whole soul, and with thy whole mind."(Mt. 22:37.) The Liberals would say: how can this be love, if it is commanded? For them the law is opposed to liberty, to love. A Law of Love is incomprehensible for them! But Our Lord Jesus Christ's Law is a Law of Love! It is true love, because we have the psychological liberty not to love God (we CAN reject Him);[3] it is a Law because we are duty-bound to love Him (we are NOT ALLOWED to reject Him)! God is the *Summum Bonum,* the Supreme Good. His Goodness attracts powerfully our love; but His Supremacy im-

---

1 Matt. 6:33.
2 Lk. 12:8 and 9:26.
3 This psychological liberty is not even a necessary condition for the love of God; it is rather an imperfection due to the fact that we do not yet see Him "face to face," in His Infinity, as He is! In Heaven, this imperfection no longer exists: the saints love God with a love that is above liberty: they cannot not love Him! O perfect bond of Charity, that is made permanent and necessary!

poses on us a duty to love Him. Every created thing, compared to the Creator, is like nothing: a finite thing compared to the Infinite is as nothing. This is why Our Lord says to the young man thirsting for perfection: "God alone is Good!"[1] That is: God alone is worthy to be loved; everything else is as dust in comparison: "Vanity of vanities and all is vanity."[2] Thus the Church teaches us to pray: "May Thy holy mysteries, O Lord Jesus, produce in us a divine fervor, whereby having tasted the sweetness of Thy most dear Heart, we may learn to despise earthly things and love those of Heaven!"[3] Now the Liberals have taken away this prayer: they no longer want to despise the things of the earth! True liberty is always in regard to inferior things; false liberty is in regard to superior realities. Liberals, wanting to be free from God, become slaves to earthly things! In one word, the Liberals reject God's Supremacy, they relativize it, and set up a new absolute: Liberty!

May the Immaculate and humble Virgin Mary help us always to acknowledge that Divine Supremacy of her Son, and that if there is anything good in us, in our families or in our country, it all comes from the Divine Goodness, from her Son, Who, with the Father and the Holy Ghost, reigns for ever and ever! May we acknowledge this reign here below, in our life, in our families and in our countries, so that we may share it in eternity, with all the Saints!

Father François Laisney

June 10th, 1988
Feast of the Sacred Heart of Jesus

---

1 Matt. 19:17.
2 Eccle. 1:2.
3 Postcommunion of the Feast of the Sacred Heart.

Preface

The idea behind this work made its first appearance at some conferences on Liberalism made for the seminarians at Ecône. The purpose of the conferences was to enlighten the understanding of these future priests about the most serious and the most harmful error of modern times, and to permit them to pass a judgement consistent with the truth and with the faith on all the consequences and manifestations of atheistic Liberalism and of liberal Catholicism.

The liberal Catholics convey the liberal errors to the interior of the Church and in the associations which are still a little bit Catholic. It is very instructive to re-read the teachings of the Popes on this subject and to ponder the vigor of their condemnations.

It is valuable to recall the approbations given by Pius IX to Louis Veuillot, the author of that admirable book, The Liberal Illusion, *and by the Holy Office to the book of Dom Felix Sarda y Salvany,* Liberalism Is A Sin.

And what would these authors have thought, if they had ascertained, as we have today, that Liberalism reigns as master at the Vatican and in the episcopates?

Hence, the urgent necessity for future priests to know this error. For the liberal Catholic has a false conception of the act of faith, as Dom Sarda well shows.[1] Faith is no longer an objective dependence on God's authority, but a subjective feeling, which as a result respects all the errors and especially the religious errors. In his chapter XXIII, Louis Veuillot shows clearly that the fun-

---

[1] Chapter VII.

damental principle of 1789 is religious independence, the secularization of Society, and finally religious liberty.

Father Tissier de Mallerais, Secretary General of the Priestly Society of Saint Pius X, encouraged by the Superior General, has had the inspiration to complete and to organize this set of conferences and to publish them, so that this very timely teaching can benefit others as well as the seminarians.

And while this work was being completed, the most abominable manifestation of liberal Catholicism was being performed at Assisi, a tangible proof that the Pope and those who approve of him have a false idea of the faith, a modernist notion, which is going to shake the whole edifice of the Church. The Pope himself declares this in his allocution of December 22, 1986, to the members of the Curia.

With the purpose of keeping and protecting the Catholic faith from this plague of Liberalism, this book seems to me to have come at the right time, becoming an echo of the words of Our Lord, "He that believeth and is baptized will be saved, but he that believeth not shall be condemned" (Mk. 16:16). It is this belief that the Word of God incarnate has demanded of all if they want to be saved. It is this that cost Him his life and then that of all the martyrs and witnesses who have professed it. With religious Liberalism, there are no more martyrs, or missionaries, but only rummage-sale dealers in religion, around the peace-pipe of a purely verbal peace!

Far be from us this Liberalism, grave-digger of the Catholic Church.

Following Our Lord, let us carry the standard of the Cross, the only sign and the only source of Salvation.

May Our Lady of Fatima, on the seventieth anniversary of her apparition, deign to bless the propagation of this book, which echoes her predictions.

† Marcel Lefebvre

Ecône, January 13, 1987
On the Feast of the Baptism of Our Lord

Author's Introduction

Where are we going? What will be the end of all the present-day bewilderments? It is not a question so much of wars, of atomic or ecologic catastrophes, but above all of the revolution on the outside and on the inside of the Church, of the apostasy in short which is winning over entire peoples, formerly Catholic, and even the hierarchy of the Church right up to its summit. Rome seems to be submerged into a complete blindness; the Rome of all times is reduced to silence, paralyzed by the other Rome, the liberal Rome that occupies it. The sources of divine grace and faith are drying up, and the veins of the Church are coursing everywhere in her the mortal poison of naturalism.

It is impossible to comprehend this profound crisis without taking into consideration the central event of this century: the Second Vatican Council. My feelings with regard to that are well enough known, I believe, so that I can express from the outset the essence of my thoughts: without rejecting this Council wholesale, I think that it is the greatest disaster of this century and of all the past centuries, since the founding of the Church. In this, I am doing nothing but judging it by its fruits, making use of the criterion that Our Lord gave us.[1] Now when Cardinal Ratzinger is asked to show some good fruits of the Council, he does not know what to answer.[2] And whereas one day I was asking Cardinal Garrone how a "good" council had

---

1 Matthew 7:16.
2 Joseph Cardinal Ratzinger, *Interview on the Faith*, Fayard, Paris, 1985, pp. 45-48.

been able to produce such bad fruits, he replied to me, "It is not the Council, it is the means of social communication."[1]

It is there that a little bit of reflection can help common sense: if the post-conciliar age is dominated by the revolution in the Church, is this not very simply because the Council itself introduced it? "The Council, this is 1789 in the Church," declared Cardinal Suenens. "The problem of the Council was to assimilate the values of two centuries of liberal culture," says Cardinal Ratzinger. And he explains himself: Pius IX, by the Syllabus, had rejected without appeal the world sprung from the Revolution, by condemning this proposition: "The Roman Pontiff can and should reconcile and adapt himself to progress, Liberalism, and with modern civilization."[2] The Council, Cardinal Ratzinger says openly, was a "Counter-Syllabus" by bringing about this reconciliation of the Church and of Liberalism, notably by *Gaudium et Spes*, the longest conciliar document. The Popes of the nineteenth century, indeed, did not know how to discern, it seems, what there was of Christian truth, and therefore capable of assimilation by the Church, in the Revolution of 1789.

Such an affirmation is absolutely dramatic, especially when voiced by representatives of the magisterium of the Church! Indeed what was, essentially, the Revolution of 1789? It was the naturalism and the subjectivism of Protestantism, reduced to juridical norms and imposed on a society still Catholic. From this you have the proclamation of the rights of man without God; from this, the exaltation of the subjectivity of each one at the expense of objective truth; from this the placing onto the same level of all the religious "faiths" before the Law; from this, in short, the organization of society without God, outside Our Lord Jesus Christ. One sole word describes this monstrous theory: *Liberalism.*

Alas, it is there that we truly touch on the "mystery of iniquity."[3] From the day after the Revolution, the devil raised up on the inside of the Church men filled with the

---

1 Interview of February 13, 1975.
2 *Syllabus*, prop. 80. Denz. 1780.
3 2 Thess. 2:7.

spirit of pride and of novelty, posing as inspired reformers who, dreaming of reconciling the Church with Liberalism, attempted to bring about an adulterous union between the Church and the principles of the Revolution! How indeed can Our Lord Jesus Christ be reconciled with an accumulation of errors that are opposed so diametrically to His Grace, to His Truth, to His divinity, to His universal kingship? No, the Popes were not mistaken when, supported by tradition and assisted by the Holy Ghost, they condemned with their supreme authority and with a remarkable continuity the great liberal Catholic betrayal. "In such a case, how did the liberal sect succeed in imposing its views in an ecumenical council? How did the union, against nature, between the Church[1] and the Revolution give birth to the monster, whose incoherences now fill with fright even its most ardent supporters? It is to these questions that I will do my best to respond in these chapters on Liberalism, by showing that once having penetrated into the Church, the poison of Liberalism leads to apostasy as a natural consequence.

"From Liberalism to apostasy"—such is the theme of these chapters. To be sure, to live in a time of apostasy has in itself nothing of an exalting nature! Let us ponder nevertheless that all the times and all the centuries belong to Our Lord Jesus Christ: *Ipsius sunt tempora et sæcula,* the paschal liturgy has us say. This century of apostasy, without doubt in a different way from the centuries of faith, belongs to Jesus Christ. On the one hand, the apostasy of the great number manifests the heroic fidelity of the small number; it was like this at the time of the prophet Elias in Israel, when God preserved only seven thousand men, who did not bend the knee before Baal.[2] Let us therefore not bend the knee before the idol of the "cult of man,"[3] "established in the sanctuary and sitting as if it were God."[4] Let us remain Catholics, adorers of the only true God, Our Lord Jesus Christ, with His Father and the Holy Ghost!

1 Or rather of the men of the Church, or the external apparatus of the Church.
2 3 Kings 19:18.
3 Expression of Paul VI.
4 2 Thess.2:4.

On the other hand, as the history of the Church bears witness, every age of crisis prepares an age of faith and, in fidelity to tradition, a true renovation. It is up to all of you to contribute to this, dear readers, by humbly receiving what the Church has transmitted to us, right up to the eve of Vatican II, through the words of the Popes, and what I pass on to you in my turn. It is this steadfast doctrine of the Church that I have received without any mental reservation; that is what I impart to you without reserve: *quam sine fictione didici, sine invidia communico.*[1]

---

1 Wisdom 7:13.

Part I

Liberalism:
Principles and Applications

Chapter I

The Origins of Liberalism

"If you do not read, you will sooner or later be traitors, because you will not have understood the root of the evil."

Father Paul Aulagnier,
September 17, 1981.

It is with these words that one of my colleagues recommended to the seminarians the reading of good books on Liberalism.

Indeed it is not possible to understand the present crisis of the Church, or to know the true character of the people in present-day Rome, or to find out the proper attitude to take *vis-à-vis* the events, without investigating the causes. In order to achieve this, it is necessary to go back into history and discover the primary cause in that Liberalism condemned by the Popes for the past two centuries.

Our Light: the Voice of the Popes

We will set out then from the origins, as the Sovereign Pontiffs do, when they denounce the confusions that are at hand. Now, always while indicting Liberalism, the Popes look farther into the past. All of them, from Pius VI to

Benedict XV, take the crisis back to the struggle waged against the Church in the sixteenth century by Protestantism, and to the naturalism of which this heresy was the cause and the propagator.

The Renaissance and Naturalism

Naturalism is found beforehand in the Renaissance, which, in its effort to recover the riches of the ancient pagan cultures, and of the Greek culture and art in particular, came to glorify man, nature, and natural forces to an exaggerated degree. In exalting the goodness and the power of nature, one devalued and made disappear from the minds of men the necessity of grace; the fact that humanity is destined for the supernatural order, and the light brought in by revelation. Under a pretext of art, they determined to introduce then everywhere, even in the churches, that nudism—we can speak without exaggeration of nudism—which triumphs in the Sistine Chapel in Rome. Without doubt, looked at from the point of view of art, those works have their value; but they have, alas, above all a carnal aspect of exaltation of the flesh that is really opposed to the teaching of the Gospel: "For the flesh covets against the spirit," says Saint Paul; "and the spirit militates against the flesh."[1]

I do not condemn this art if it is kept in secular museums, but I do not see in it a means of expressing the truth of the Redemption, that is to say, the happy submission of restored nature to grace. My judgment will certainly be different on the baroque art of the Catholic Counter-Reformation, especially in the countries that resisted Protestantism: the baroque will still call on chubby angels, but this art, that is very much of movement and of sometimes pathetic expression, is a cry of triumph for the Redemption, a chant of victory for Catholicism over the pessimism of a cold and hopeless Protestantism.

Protestantism and Naturalism

Speaking precisely, it can seem strange and paradoxical

---

[1] Galatians 5:17.

to qualify Protestantism as being naturalism. There is nothing in Luther of this exaltation of the intrinsic good of nature, since, according to him, nature is incurably fallen and concupiscence is invincible. Nonetheless the excessively nihilistic look that the Protestant casts onto himself results in a practical naturalism: by dint of depreciating nature and exalting the force of *faith alone*, one relegates divine grace and the supernatural order to the domain of abstractions. For the Protestants, grace does not operate a true interior renewal; baptism is not the restoring of an habitual supernatural state; it is only an act of faith in Jesus Christ, who justifies and saves. Nature is not restored by grace, it remains intrinsically corrupt, and faith obtains from God nothing more than this: He throws over our sins the modest cloak of Noah. From then on, the whole supernatural organism that baptism has just added to nature by taking root in it, all the infused virtues and the gifts of the Holy Ghost, are reduced to nothing, brought back as they are to that lone frenzied act of faith—confidence in a Redeemer who spares only to withdraw far from His creature, leaving an ever so colossal abyss between man, permanently miserable, and the thrice-holy transcendent God. This *pseudo-supernaturalism,* as Father Garrigou-Lagrange-Garrigou-Lagrange, Father Reginald calls it, in the end leaves man, although redeemed, to the mere strength of his natural virtures; he collapses fatally, in *naturalism,* so well do the opposite extremes join up! Jacques Maritain well expresses the naturalist outcome of Lutheranism:

> Human nature will only have to reject as a vain theological accessory the cloak of a grace that is nothing for it, and to take back onto itself its faith-confidence,[1] in order to become that nice emancipated beast whose unbroken infallible progress delights the universe today.[2]

And this naturalism will be applied especially to the civic and social order: grace being reduced to a fiduciary sentiment of faith, the Redemption now consists only of an individual and private religiosity, without a hold on the public life. The public order, economic and political, is

---

1 Faith reduced to no more than a mere confidence that one is "saved."
2 *Trois Réformateurs,* p. 25.

therefore condemned to live and to develop itself outside
Our Lord Jesus Christ. At the extreme, the Protestant will
look for the criterion of his justification in the eyes of God
in his economic success; it is in this sense that he will glad-
ly inscribe onto the door of his house this sentence of the
Old Testament: "Honor God with thy goods, give Him the
first-fruits of all thy revenues, and then thy granaries will
be abundantly filled and thy cisterns will overflow with
wine."[1]

Jacques Maritain has some good words on the
materialism of Protantism, which will give birth to
economic Liberalism and to capitalism:

> Behind Luther's appeals to the Lamb who saves, be-
> hind his outbursts of confidence and his faith in the par-
> don of sins, there is a human creature who raises up his
> head and who arranges his affairs very well in the mud
> where he is immersed by the fault of Adam! He will
> manage in the world, he will follow the thirst for power,
> the imperalist instinct, the law of this world which is his
> world. God will be only an ally, a mighty one.[2]

The result of Protestantism will be that men will attach
themselves more to the goods of this world and will forget
the eternal goods. And if a certain Puritanism comes to exercise an exterior supervision over public morality, it will
not impregnate men's hearts with the truly Christian spirit,
which is a supernatural spirit, called *primacy of the spiritual*.
Protestantism will be led necessarily to proclaim the emancipation of the temporal from the spiritual. Now it is
precisely that emancipation that one will find again in
Liberalism. The Popes then had good reason to denounce
this naturalism of Protestant inspiration as the origin of the
Liberalism that disrupted Christianity in 1789 and 1848.
Thus, Leo XIII says:

> This audacity of faithless men, which threatens civil
> society every day with more serious destruction, and
> which stirs up anxiety and trouble in all minds, has its
> cause and its origin in those poisoned doctrines which,
> spread out in these latest times among the peoples like

---

1 Proverbs 3:9-10.
2 Op. cit., pp. 52-53.

seeds of vices, have borne very malignant fruits in their season. Indeed you know very well, Venerable Brethren, that the cruel war that has been declared since the sixteenth century against the Catholic Faith by the innovators, aimed at this goal of turning aside all revelation and overthrowing the whole supernatural order, in order that access may be opened up to the discoveries or rather the frenzies of unaided reason.[1]

And, closer to our time, Pope Benedict XV:

> Since the first three centuries and the origins of the Church, in the course of which the blood of Christians fertilized the entire earth, one can say that the Church never was in such a danger as that which showed itself at the end of the eighteenth century. It was then indeed that a philosophy in delirium, a prolonging of the heresy and the apostasy of the Innovators,[2] acquired a universal power of seduction over minds and brought about a total bewilderment, with the settled purpose of ruining the Christian foundations of society, not only in France, but little by little in all the nations.[3]

Birth of Political Naturalism

Protestantism had set up a very harsh attack against the Church and caused a deep tearing of Christianity in the sixteenth century, but it did not succeeed in penetrating the Catholic nations with the venom of its political and social naturalism, until this secularizing spirit had reached the academics, and then those so-called "Philosophers of the Enlightenment."

In reality, philosophically, Protestantism and juridical positivism have a common origin in the nominalism of the decadent Middle Ages, which led as well to Luther, with his purely extrinsic and nominal idea of the Redemption, as to Descartes, with his idea of an unintelligible divine law submitted to the purely arbitrary decisions of God's will. All of Christian philosophy, however, affirmed with Saint Thomas Aquinas the unity of the eternal divine law and of

---

1 *Quod apostolici*, December 28, 1878.
2 The Protestant reformers.
3 Letter *Anno jam exeunte*, March 7, 1917.

the natural human law: "The natural law is nothing except a participation in the Eternal Law by the rational creature,"[1] writes the Angelic Doctor. But with Descartes, a break is already made between the divine right and the natural human right. After him the academics and the jurists will not be long in practicing the same separation. Thus, Hugo Grotius (1625), summed up by Paul Hazard:

> But divine right? Grotius tries to safeguard it. What we have just said, he declares, would take place even if we should grant—what cannot be conceded without a crime—that there is no God, or that human affairs are not the object of His solicitude. Since God and Providence exist without any doubt, we have here a source of right, in addition to that which emanates from nature. "This natural right itself can be attributed to God, since the divinity has willed that such principles exist in us." The law of God, the law of nature..., continues Paul Hazard, this double formula, it is not Grotius who invented it, the Middle Ages knew it already. Where is its character of newness? How does it happen that it is criticized, condemned by the doctors? For whom does it create a stir? The novelty consists in the separation of the two terms, which they try to insinuate; in their opposition, which they tend to assert; in an attempt at conciliation as an afterthought, which by its mere self supposes the idea of a rupture.[2]

The jurist Pufendorf (1672) and the philosopher Locke (1689) completed the secularization of the natural right. The philosophy of the Enlightenment imagines a "state of nature" that has no more to do with the realism of Christian philosophy and that culminates in the idealism with the myth of the *good savage* of Jean-Jacques Rousseau. The natural law is reduced to a cohesion of sentiments which man has of himself and which are shared by the majority of men; the following dialogue is found in Voltaire:

B. What is the natural law?
A. The instinct that makes us feel justice.

---

1 Ia IIæ 91, 2.
2 *La crise de conscience européenne*, Paris, Fayard, 1961, 3rd part, chapter 3.

B. What do you call just and unjust?
A. What appears as such to the entire world.[1]

Such an outcome is the fruit of a reason that has lost its way, that in its thirst for emancipation from God and His revelation has likewise burned the bridges connecting it with the simple principles of the natural order, which the supernatural divine revelation recalls and the Magisterium of the Church confirms. If the Revolution separated the civil power from the power of the Church, that is, at root, because it had already for a long time been separating faith and reason for those who adorned themselves with the name of philosophers. It will not be out of place to recall what Vatican Council I teaches on this subject:

> Not only can faith and reason never be in disagreement, but they mutually lend themselves support as well; since right reason demonstrates the foundations of the faith and, illuminated with the light of faith, devotes itself to the knowledge of the divine things while faith, for its part, frees and protects reason from errors and teaches it with a multi-faceted learning.[2]

But the Revolution took place precisely in the name of the *goddess Reason*, of reason deified, of the reason that sets itself up as the supreme norm of truth and falsity, of good and evil.

Naturalism, Rationalism, Liberalism

You can now catch a glimpse from this of how much all these errors overlap one another: Liberalism, Naturalism, finally Rationalism, which are only complementary aspects of what must be called the *Revolution*. There, where right reason, illuminated by the Faith, sees only harmony and subordination, the deified reason hollows out abysses and raises up walls: nature without grace, material prosperity without the searching for eternal goods, the civil power separated from the ecclesiastical power, politics without God or Jesus Christ, the rights of man against the rights of God, and, finally, freedom without truth.

---

1 Voltaire, Dialogues philosophiques, l'A.B.C. 1768, *Quatrième entretien, De la loi naturelle et de la curiosité,* quoted by Paul Hazard, op. cit.
2 Constitution *de fide catholica "Dei Filius,"* Denziger 1799.

It is in that spirit that the Revolution happened; it was being prepared for more than two centuries already in people's minds, as I have tried to show you. But it is only at the end of the eighteenth century that it succeeded and bore its decisive fruits: its political fruits, due to the writings of the philosophers, the encyclopedists, and of an unimaginable activity of Freemasonry,[1] which in a few decades had penetrated and set up cells in the whole ruling class.

Freemasonry: Propagator of these Errors

With what precision, with what clear-sightedness the Sovereign Pontiffs denounced this enterprise. Pope Leo XIII exposes it in *Quod apostolici* already quoted, and again in the Encyclical *Humanum genus* of August 20, 1884, on the sect of the Freemasons:

> In our time the instigators of evil seem to have formed a coalition in an immense effort, under the impulse and with the help of a Society spread out in a great number of places and skillfully organized the Society of the Freemasons.

> In their vigilant solicitude for the salvation of the Christian people, Our predecessors had very quickly recognized this principal enemy at the moment when, coming out of the darkness of an occult conspiracy, it sprang forth to the attack in the full light of day.

Leo XIII then mentions the Popes who had already condemned Freemasonry: Clement XII, in the Encyclical, *In Eminenti*, of April 27, 1738, brought excommunication against the Freemasons; Benedict XIV renewed this condemnation in the Encyclical, *Providas*, of March 16, 1751; Pius VII with the Encyclical, *Ecclesiam*, of September 13, 1821, particularly denounced the *Carbonari*; Leo XII with his Apostolic Constitution, *Quo graviora*, of March 13, 1826, unmasked in addition the secret society, *L'Universitaire*, which was attempting to pervert the youth; Pius VIII with his Encyclical, *Traditi*, of May 24, 1829; Pius IX, in his consistorial

---

1 1517: revolt of Luther, who burned the Bull of the Pope at Wittenberg; 1717: foundation of the Grand Lodge of London.

allocution of September 25, 1865, and the Encyclical, *Quanta cura*, of December 8, 1864, spoke in the same way.

Then, deploring how little the governments were taking into account these very serious warnings, Leo XIII reports the dreadful progress of the sect:

> It results from this that, in the lapse of a century and a half, the sect of the Freemasons has made unbelievable progress. Using at the same time boldness and cunning, it has invaded all the ranks of the social hierarchy and is beginning to seize a power, in the bosom of the modern States, which is equivalent to sovereignty.

What would he say now, when there is no government that does not comply with the decrees of the Masonic lodges![1] And it is now for the assault on the hierarchy of the Church that the Masonic spirit, or Masonry itself, rises up with ranks closed. But I will come back to that.

What is then the Masonic spirit? Here you have it declared in a few words from the mouth of Senator Goblet d'Aviello, member of the Grand Orient of Belgium, speaking on August 5, 1877, at the lodge of the Philanthropic Friends of Brussels:

> Say to the neophytes that Masonry... is above all a school of vulgarization and a finishing school, a sort of laboratory where the great ideas of the age come to be combined and affirmed in order to spread out in the secular world in a tangible and practical form. Tell them, in a word, that *we are the philosophy of Liberalism.*

It is enough to tell you, dear readers, that even if I do not always name it, Freemasonry is at the center of the topics of which I am going to speak to you in all the following chapters.

---

1 Even the communist countries should not be excepted, since the communist party is a pure Masonic society, with the sole difference that it is perfectly legal and public.

Chapter II

The Natural Order and Liberalism

"Liberty is not at the beginning, but at the end. It is not at the root, but in the flowers and the fruits."

Charles Maurras

There is a work that I recommend particularly to those who want to have a concrete and complete outline of Liberalism, in order to be able then to prepare exposés on Liberalism, intended for people who are little conversant with this error, with its ramifications, and who are accustomed to "think liberal," even among Catholics attached to tradition. There are often those who do not realize the depth of the penetration of Liberalism in all of our society, in all of our families.

It is easily recognized that the "advanced Liberalism" of a Giscard d'Estaing in the years around 1975 brought France to socialism; but it is believed in all good faith that the *"liberal right"* can deliver us from totalitarian oppression. Some well-meaning people do not know really whether they should approve or find fault with the *"libera-*

lization of abortion," but they would be ready to sign a petition to liberalize euthanasia. In actual fact, everything that carries the label of *liberty* has been, for two centuries, surrounded with the halo of prestige that surrounds this word that has become sacrosanct. And, nonetheless, it is by this word that we are perishing; it is Liberalism that is poisoning civil society as well as the Church. Therefore, let us open this book of which I am speaking to you: *Liberalism and Catholicism* by Father Roussel, published in 1926; and let us read that page which depicts Liberalism very concretely (pp. 14-16), adding to this a little commentary:

> The Liberal is a fanatic for independence; he extols it
> to the point of absurdity, in every domain.

So there you have a definition. We are going to see how it is applied, what are the liberations that Liberalism insists on.

1. The independence of the true and of the good in regard to being: this is the relativistic philosophy of mobility and of becoming. The independence of the intelligence with regard to its object: being sovereign, the reason does not have to submit itself to its object; it creates it; whence the radical evolution of truth; relativistic subjectivism.

Let us emphasize the two key words: subjectivism and evolution.

Subjectivism means introducing freedom into the intelligence, whereas on the contrary the nobility of the intelligence consists in submitting itself to its object, that is, in the *adæquatio* or conformity of the thinking subject with the known object. The intellect works like a camera; it must fit with precision the intelligible touches of reality. Its perfection consists in its fidelity to the real. It is for this reason that the *truth* is defined as *the conformity of the intellect with the thing.* Truth is that quality of thought by which it is in accord with the thing,with that which is. It is not the intellect that creates the things; it is the things that impose themselves onto the intellect, such as they are. Therefore the truth of what is affirmed depends on that which *is;* it is an objective thing. The person who is searching for the truth has to renounce himself, to renounce any construction of his own mind, to renounce any idea of "inventing" the truth.

On the contrary, in subjectivism, it is the reason that constructs the truth: we have the submission of the object to the subject! The subject becomes the center of all things. Things are no longer what they are, but what I think. In such a case, man disposes of truth according to his own taste. This error will be called *idealism* in its philosophical aspect, and *Liberalism* in its moral, social, political, and religious aspect. As a consequence, the truth will be different according to individuals and social groups. The truth is then necessarily shared. No one can claim to have it exclusively in its wholeness; it is made and it is sought after without end. It can be guessed how contrary that is to Our Lord Jesus Christ and to his Church.

Historically, this emancipation of the subject in relation to the object (to that which is) was brought about by four persons. **Luther,** at first, refused the magisterium of the Church and kept only the Bible. Since he rejected every created intermediary between man and God, he introduced the *free investigation,* starting with a false notion of Scriptural inspiration: individual inspiration! Then **Descartes,** followed by **Kant,** systematized subjectivism: the intellect is closed up on itself, and it knows only its own thought. This is the "cogito" of Descartes, the "categories" of Kant. Things themselves are unknowable. Finally, **Rousseau:** emancipated from its object, having lost common sense, the subject is left without defense faced with *the common opinion.* The thought of the individual is going to be dissolved into the public opinion, that is to say in what everyone or the majority thinks; and this opinion will be created by the techniques of group dynamics organized by the media, which are in the hands of the financiers, the politicians, the Freemasons, etc. By its own impulse, intellectual Liberalism falls into the *totalitarianism* of thought. After the rejection of the object, we are seeing the evanescence of the subject, which is thus ripe for undergoing all forms of slavery. Subjectivism, by exalting freedom of thought, results then in the crushing of thought.

The second mark of intellectual Liberalism, we have mentioned, is *evolution.* By rejecting the submission to the real, the Liberal is drawn to reject the immutable essences of things; for him there is no nature of things, there is no stable human nature ruled by definitive laws set down by the Creator. Man is in perpetual progressive evolution; the man of yesterday is not the man of today; one collapses into relativism. What is more, man himself creates himself; he is the author of his own laws, which he has to refashion incessantly according to the sole inflexible law of needed progress. Then it is evolutionism, in all realms: biological (Lamarck and Darwin), intellectual (rationalism and its myth of the indefinite progress of human reason), moral (emancipation from the "taboos"), political-religious (emancipation of societies with regard to Jesus Christ).

The crest of evolutionary delirium is reached with **Father Teilhard de Chardin** (1881-1955), who affirms, in the name of a pseudo-science and a pseudo-mysticism, that matter becomes spirit, that nature becomes the supernatural, that humanity becomes the Christ: a triple confusion of an evolutionist monism irreconcilable with the Catholic faith.

For the faith, evolution is death. They speak of a Church that evolves, they want an evolving faith. "You must submit to the living Church, to the Church of today," they were writing to me from Rome in the mid seventies, as if the Church of today should not be identical to the Church of yesterday. I answered them, "Under those conditions, tomorrow it will no longer be what you are saying today!" Those people have no concept of truth, of being. They are Modernists.

2. *The independence of the will in regard to the intellect: an arbitrary and blind force, the will must not at all be concerned with the judgements of reason; it creates the good just as reason brings forth the true.*

In a word, it is the arbitrary: "*Sic volo, sic jubeo, sit pro ratione voluntas!*—Thus I will, thus I order, let my will be my reason!"

3. *The independence of the conscience with regard to the objective rule, and to the law; conscience sets itself up as the supreme rule of morality.*

According to the Liberal, law limits freedom and imposes onto it a constraint which is first of all moral: the obligation; and finally physical: the sanction. The law and its constraints run counter to human dignity and to conscience. The Liberal confuses liberty and license. Now Our Lord Jesus Christ is the living Law, being the Word of God; from there we can gauge once more how deep the opposition of the Liberal towards Our Lord is.

4. *The independence of the anarchical powers of feeling with regard to reason: this is one of the characteristics of romanticism, the enemy of the primacy of reason.*

The romantic takes pleasure in brewing up slogans; he condemns violence, superstition, fanaticism, integrism, racism, because of what those words conjure up in the imagination and in the human passions. And in the same spirit, he makes himself the apostle of peace, of liberty, of tolerance, of pluralism.

5. *The independence of the body in regard to the soul, of the animal nature in regard to reason—this is the radical overthrowing of human values.*

They exalt sexuality, they sacralize it. They reverse the order between the two ends of marriage (procreation and education on the one hand, allaying of concupiscence on the other) by determining for it as a primary end carnal pleasure and "the self-fulfillment of the two spouses" or the two "partners." That will be the destruction of marriage and of the family; this is without mentioning the aberrations which transform the sanctuary of marriage into a biological laboratory or which reduce the infant not yet born to a lucrative ingredient in cosmetics.[1]

6. *The independence of the present with regard to the past, whence the contempt for tradition and the morbid love of novelty under the pretext of progress.*

This is one of the causes that Saint Pius X attributes Modernism to:

---

1 Cf. *Fideliter* No. 47.

The remote causes seem to Us capable of being reduced to two: *curiosity* and *pride*. Curiosity, by itself, if it is not wisely regulated, suffices to explain all the errors. This is the opinion of our predecessor Gregory XVI, who wrote: "It is a lamentable spectacle to see how far the wanderings of human reason go once the spirit of novelty is given way to."[1]

7. *The independence of the individual in regard to all of society, all natural authority and hierarchy: independence of children vis-à-vis their parents, of woman with regard to her husband (women's liberation); of the worker in regard to his employer; of the working class towards the bourgeois class (class struggle).*

Political and social Liberalism is the reign of individualism. The basic unit of Liberalism is the individual.[2] The individual is supposed to be an *absolute subject of rights* (the "Rights of Man"), without there being a question of duties which bind him to his creator, to his superiors, or to his fellow-creatures, or, above all, of the *Rights of God.* Liberalism makes all the natural social hierarchies disappear; but in doing this, in the end it leaves the individual alone and without defense in regard to the crowd of which he is only an interchangeable element, and which swallows him up entirely.

The social doctrine of the Church, on the contrary, affirms that society is not a shapeless mass of individuals,[3] but an arranged organism of coordinated and hierarchically arranged social groups: the family, the enterprises and trades, then the professional corporations, finally the State. The corporations unite employers and workers in the same profession for the protection and the promotion of their common interests. The classes are not antagonistic, but naturally complementary.[4] The law called *Le Chapelier* of June 14, 1791, by prohibiting the associations, killed the corporations which had been the instrument of social peace since the Middle Ages. This law was the fruit of liberal individualism, but instead of "freeing" the workers,

1 Encyclical *Pascendi*, September 8, 1907.
2 Daniel Raffard de Brienne, *Le deuxième étendard*, p. 25.
3 Cf. Pius XII, Christmas Radio Message to the entire world, December 24, 1944.
4 Cf. Leo XIII, Encyclical *Rerum novarum*, May 15, 1891.

it crushed them. And when, in the nineteenth century, the assets of the liberal bourgeoisie had crushed the formless mass of workers who had become the proletariat, a way was found, at the initiative of the socialists, to regroup the workers in trade unions. But the trade unions only made the social war worse by extending the factitious opposition of capital and proletariat to the scale of all of society. It is known that this opposition, or "class struggle," was at the origin of the Marxist theory of dialectical materialism: so that a false social problem created a false system: communism.[1] And now, since Lenin, the class struggle has become, by means of communist usage, the privileged weapon of the communist revolution.[2]

Let us then hold on to this undeniable historical and philosophical truth: Liberalism leads by its natural propensity to totalitarianism and to the communist revolution. It can be said that it is the soul of all the modern revolutions and of the Revolution itself in short.

---

1 Cf. Pius XI, Encyclical *Divini Redemptoris*, March 19, 1937, #15.
2 Ibid. #9.

Chapter III

Our Lord Jesus Christ and Liberalism

"The truth will make you free!"
Our Lord Jesus Christ

A fter having explained that Liberalism is a revolt of man against the natural order conceived by the Creator, which leads to the individualistic, egalitarian, and con-centration-camp-like city, it remains for me to show you how Liberalism also grapples with the supernatural order which is the plan of Redemption—that is to say, how final-ly Liberalism has for its purpose to destroy the reign of Our Lord Jesus Christ, as much over the individual as over the city.

With regard to the supernatural order, Liberalism proclaims two new kinds of independence which I will now explain.

1. *The independence of reason and of science in regard to faith: this is rationalism, for which reason, sovereign judge and measure of truth, is self-sufficient and rejects any foreign domination.*

This is what is called **rationalism.**

Liberalism here wishes to free reason from the faith, which imposes dogmas on us, formulated in a definitive way, to which the intellect has to submit itself. The simple hypothesis that certain truths can go beyond the capacities of reason is inadmissible. Dogmas therefore must be constantly re-submitted to the test of reason and science because of the scientific progresses. The miracles of Jesus Christ, the supernatural elements in the lives of the saints have to be reinterpreted, demythologized. It will be necessary to carefully distinguish between the *"Christ of faith,"* a construction of the faith of the Apostles and of the primitive communities, and the *"Christ of history,"* who was only a mere man. You can grasp how much rationalism is opposed to the divinity of Our Lord Jesus Christ and to the divine revelation!

I have already explained how the Revolution of 1789 was accomplished under the sign of the goddess of Reason. Already in 1751 the frontispiece of the *Encyclopedia* of Diderot represented the picture of the crowning of Reason. Forty years later, the deified Reason became the object of a public religious cult:

> On the 20th *brumaire*,[1] three days after some priests, the metropolitan bishop Gobel at their head, became "unpriested" before the Assembly, Chaumette proposed to solemnize that day when "reason had regained her empire." They hastened to put such a noble idea into effect, and it was decided that the Cult of Reason would be celebrated in a splendid way at Notre Dame of Paris, which was specially adorned by the solicitude of the painter David for this occasion. At the top of a mountain of papier-mâché, a small Greek temple sheltered a pretty dancing lady, who was very proud of having been promoted to Goddess of Reason; groups of young girls crowned with flowers were singing hymns. When the festival had been completed, remarking that the representatives were not a great number, they left in a proces-

---

1 November 10, 1793. The French Revolution, in its will to cut everything from the past, tried a whole new system of counting dates: the weeks disappeared to give place to "décadies" (of ten days: everything had to be decimal!), the months were renamed, the years were no longer counted from Our Lord Jesus Christ, but rather from the French Revolution. This system lasted only a few years.

sion with Reason, to go to visit the national Convention, whose President embraced the goddess.[1]

But this overly radical rationalism did not please Robespierre. When, in March 1794, he had knocked down the "exaggerated ones,"

> It seemed to him that his all-powerfulness should be founded on some high-mindedly theological foundations and that he would put a crowning touch onto his work by establishing a Cult of the Supreme Being, of which he would be the high priest. On the 18th floréal, Year II,[2] he gave a speech "on the relations of religious and moral ideas with the republican principles, and on the national holidays," on which the Convention voted its impressions. He affirmed in it that "the idea of the Supreme Being and of the immortality of the soul" is a continuous recall to justice, and that it is therefore social and republican. The new cult would be that of virtue. A decree was voted in, according to which the French people recognized the two axioms of Robespierre's theology; and an inscription consecrating the fact was to be placed in the front of the churches. A list of the non-working holidays followed, which took up two columns. The first one on the list was that of the "Supreme Being and Nature"; it was decided that it would be celebrated on the 20th prairial.[3] Thus was the celebration: beginning in the garden of the Tuileries where a gigantic pyre devoured in its flames the monstrous image of atheism, while Robespierre was pronouncing a mystical discourse, after which the crowd chanted hymns fit for the occasion, it continued with a parade up to the Champs-de-Mars, where all the people in attendance followed a chariot draped in red, drawn by eight oxen, loaded with ears of wheat and foliage, among which there sat enthroned a statue of Liberty.[4]

The very incoherences of rationalism, the "variations" of this "religion within the limits of simple reason,"[5] sufficiently demonstrate their falseness.

---

1 Daniel-Rops, *The Church of the Revolutions*, p. 63.
2 May 7th, 1794.
3 June 8th, 1794.
4 Daniel-Rops, op. cit., p. 64.
5 A work of Kant, 1793.

2. *The independence of man, of the family, of the professions, above all of the State, with regard to God, to Jesus Christ, to the Church; this is, according to one's point of view, naturalism, laicism, latitudinarianism (or indifferentism)... from this you have the official apostasy of the peoples pushing away the social kingship of Jesus Christ, failing to recognize the divine authority of the Church.*

I will illustrate these errors by means of a few considerations:

Naturalism maintains that man is limited to the sphere of nature and that he is in no way destined by God to the supernatural state. The truth is completely different: God did not create man in the state of pure nature. God constituted man at the outset in the supernatural state: God, says the Council of Trent, had formed the first man *"in the state of holiness and of justice."*[1] That man was deprived of sanctifying grace was the consequence of original sin, but the Redemption maintains God's design: man remains destined to the supernatural order. To be reduced to the natural order is for man a *violent state* that God does not approve of. Here is what Cardinal Pie teaches, showing that the natural state is not in itself bad, but that it is the removal from the supernatural order which is bad:

> You will teach, then, that human reason has its own power and its essential competence; you will teach that philosophical virtue possesses a moral and intrinsic goodness that God does not disdain to remunerate, in individuals and in peoples, by certain natural and temporal rewards, at times even by some loftier favors. But you will also teach and you will prove, by arguments inseparable from the very essence of Christianity, that the natural virtues, that the natural lights, cannot lead man to his last end, which is the heavenly glory.
>
> You will teach that dogma is indispensable, that the supernatural order in which the very Author of our nature has established us, by a formal act of his will and of his love, is obligatory and unavoidable; *you will teach that Jesus Christ is not optional and that outside his revealed law there does not exist, there will never exist, any philosophical*

---

1 Denzinger 788.

and peaceful golden means where anyone, a chosen soul or a vulgar soul, can find the repose for his conscience and a just rule for his life.

You will teach that it is important not only that man does the good, but that it is important that he does it in the name of the faith, by a supernatural impulse, without which his acts will not attain the final goal that God has indicated for him, that is to say, the eternal happiness of heaven...."[1]

Thus, in the state of humanity concretely willed by God, society cannot be constituted or exist outside Our Lord Jesus Christ: this is the teaching of Saint Paul:

It is in Him that all things have been created, those that are in the heavens and those that are on the earth all has been created by Him and for Him. He is before all things, and all things subsist in Him.[2]

God's plan is to *"sum up everything in Christ,"*[3] that is to say, to bring back all things to one sole head, the Christ. Pope Saint Pius X took this same expression of Saint Paul as his motto: *"Omnia instaurare in Christo,"* to re-establish, to restore all in Christ: not only religion, but civil society:

No, Venerable Brethren—it must be recalled energetically in these times of social and intellectual anarchy, when everyone sets himself up as a teacher and a legislator,—society will not be built other than as God has built it. Society will not be built up, if the Church does not lay the foundations and direct the construction; no, civilization is no longer to be invented, or the new city to be built, in the clouds. It has been, it is; it is Christian civilization, it is the Catholic city. It is a question only of setting up and continually restoring it upon the natural and divine foundations against the ever reborn attacks of an unhealthy Utopia, of revolt, and of impiety: *"omnia instaurare in Christo."*[4]

Mr. Jean Ousset, in his masterpiece, *Pour qu'Il règne,*[5] has some excellent pages on naturalism, in its second part

---

1 Cardinal Pie, bishop of Poitiers, Works, T. II, pp. 380-381, quoted by Jean Ousset, *Pour qu'Il règne, p. 117.*
2 Colossians 1:16-17.
3 Ephesians 1:10.
4 Letter on the Sillon, *Notre charge apostolique,* of August 25, 1910, PIN. 430.
5 *"So That He May Reign."*

entitled "*The Oppositions Made to the Social Kingdom of Our Lord Jesus Christ*"; he takes up three categories of naturalism: a "naturalism aggressive or clearly displayed" which denies even the existence of the supernatural, i.e. that of the rationalists (cf. above); then a moderated naturalism which does not deny the supernatural but refuses to grant it preeminence, because it holds that all religions are an emanation from the religious sense : this is the naturalism of the Modernists; finally there is the inconsequent naturalism, which recognizes the existence of the supernatural and its very divine preeminence, but considers it to be an "optional matter"—this is the practical naturalism of many lax Christians.

Laicism is a political naturalism: it contends that society can and should be constituted and that it can subsist, without taking into account at all God and religion, without considering Jesus Christ, without recognizing the rights of Jesus Christ to reign, that is to say, to inspire with His doctrine all legislation of the civil order. As a consequence the laicists want to separate the Church from the State: the Church would be reduced to the common law of all associations before the State, and no account whatsoever would be taken of its divine authority and of its universal mission. From then on there would be instituted an instruction and even an education that are "public," at times even obligatory, and lay, that is to say, atheistic. Laicism is State atheism without the name!

I will come back to this error, proper to the Liberalism of today, which enjoys the favor of the declaration on religious liberty of Vatican II.

Indifferentism proclaims that the profession of one religion or of another by man is indifferent. Pius IX condemns this error: "*Man is free to embrace and to profess the religion which, led by the light of his reason, he has judged to be true*" (*Syllabus*, condemned proposition number 15); or: "*Men can find the path of salvation in the worship of any religion*" (number 16); or again: "*One can indeed hope for the eternal salvation of all those who do not find themselves at all in the true Church of Christ*" (number 17).

It is easy to guess the rationalist or modernist roots of these propositions. To this error is added *the indifferentism of the State* on religious matters: the State poses as a principle that it is not capable (agnosticism) of recognizing the true religion as such, and thus that it has to concede the same freedom to all the cults. It would agree to grant to the Catholic religion, if need be, a *de facto* precedence, because it is the religion of the majority of the citizens. But to recognize it as *true*, that would be, it says, to want to re-establish theocracy; this would be in any case to attribute to the State a competence that it does not have, it asserts, to ask it to judge on the truth or the falsity of a religion.

Bishop Pie (not yet a Cardinal) ventured to expose this profound error, as well as the Catholic doctrine on the social Reign of Our Lord Jesus Christ, to the emperor of the French, Napoleon III. In a memorable interview, with a true apostolic courage, he gave the prince a lesson on Christian law, on what is called *the public law of the Church*. With this famous conversation, I will finish this chapter.

It was on March 15, 1856, Father Théotime of Saint Just tells us, from whom I am borrowing this quotation.[1] To the Emperor, who was boasting of having done for religion more than the Restoration itself,[2] the bishop replied:

> I am eager to render justice to the religious tendencies of Your Majesty, and I know how to recognize, Sire, the services that you have rendered to Rome and to the Church, particularly during the first years of your government. Has not the Restoration perhaps done more than you? But let me add that neither the Restoration, nor you, have done for God what should have been done, because neither the one nor the other of you has raised His throne again, because neither the one nor the other of you has disavowed the principles of the Revolution whose practical consequences nonetheless you are fighting, because the social gospel on which the State inspires itself is still the declaration of the rights of man, which is nothing else, Sire, than the formal denial of the Rights of God.
>
> Now, it is the right of God to govern over the States as over individuals. There is nothing else that Our Lord

---

1 Father Théotime of Saint Just, *The Social Kingdom of Our Lord Jesus Christ According to Cardinal Pie*, Paris, Beauchesne, 1925, (2nd edition), pp. 117-121.

2 The *Restoration* indicates the restoration of the monarchy by Louis XVIII, after the French Revolution and the First Empire. This Restoration had, alas, consecrated the liberal principle of the freedom of the cults.

came to look for on earth. He must reign here by inspiring the laws, by sanctifying the morals, by enlightening
education, by directing the councils, by ruling over the
actions of the governments as over those of the governed.
Everywhere where Jesus Christ does not exercise this
rule, there is disorder and decadence.

Now, I have the right to tell you that He is not reigning among us and that our Constitution is not that of a
Christian and Catholic State—far from that. Our public
law indeed establishes that the Catholic religion is that of
the majority of the French, but it adds that *the other forms
of worship have the right to an equal protection.* Is this not
tantamount to proclaiming that the Constitution equally
protects truth and error? Well! Sire, do you know what
Jesus Christ answers to governments who make themselves guilty of such a contradiction? Jesus Christ, King of
heaven and earth, replies to them, "And I too, governments who succeed one another by overturning one
another, I also grant you an equal support. I have conceded this protection to your uncle the emperor; I have
given the same patronage to the Bourbons, the same
defense to Louis-Philippe, the same shelter to the
Republic; and to you likewise the same protection will be
granted."

The emperor stopped the bishop: "But yet, do you
believe that the age in which we are living admits of that
state of things, and that the moment has come to establish
that exclusively religious reign that you ask of me? Do
you not think, Your Excellency, that that would be to let
loose all the evil passions?"

Sire, when the great political men like Your Majesty
raise the objection to me that the moment has not come, I
can only yield, because I am not a great political person.
But I am a bishop, and as a bishop I reply to them, "The
moment has not come for Jesus Christ to rule,—well!
Then the moment has not come for the government to endure."[1]

To close these two chapters on these aspects of
Liberalism, I would like to try to emphasize what is the
most fundamental in the emancipation that it proposes to
men, alone or joined in society. Liberalism, as I have ex-

---

1 History of Cardinal Pie, Tome I, Book II, Chapter II, pp. 698-699.

plained, is the soul of all revolution; it is equally, since its birth in the sixteenth century, the omnipresent enemy of Our Lord Jesus Christ, the God incarnate. From that point on, there is no doubt; I can affirm that Liberalism is identified with the revolution. Liberalism is the revolution in all spheres, the radical revolution.

Bishop Gaume wrote some lines on the Revolution, which seem to me completely to characterize Liberalism itself.

If, tearing away its mask, you ask it (of the Revolution): "Who are you?" it will say to you, "I am not what is thought. Many people speak of me, and very few know me. I am neither carbonarism, nor rioting, nor the change from monarchy to republic, nor the substitution of one dynasty for another, nor the temporary disturbance of the public order. I am not the howlings of the Jacobins, nor the furies of la Montagne, nor the battle of the barricades, nor looting, nor arson, nor the agrarian law, nor the guillotine, nor the drownings. I am not Marat, or Robespierre, or Babeuf or Mazzini, or Kossuth. These men are my sons, they are not I. These things are my works, they are not I. These men and these things are transitory facts, and I am a permanent state.

I am the hatred of all order which man has not established and in which he is not king and God all together. I am the proclamation of the rights of man without care for the rights of God. I am the foundation of the religious and social state upon the will of man instead of the will of God. *I am God dethroned and man in His place. This is why I am called Revolution, that is to say, overthrow....*"[1]

---

1 Bishop Gaume, *The Revolution, Historical Researches*, Lille, Secrétariat Société Saint Paul, 1877, Tome I, p. 18, quoted by Jean Ousset, *Pour qu'Il règne*, p. 122.

Chapter IV

Does the Law Oppress
Liberty?

*"Liberty consists in the fact that, by the
help of the civil laws, we can live more easily according to the prescriptions of the eternal law."*

Leo XIII

I could not give a better summary of the disasters
produced by Liberalism in every domain, such as they are
exposed in the preceding chapter, than by quoting to you
this passage from a Pastoral Letter of bishops dating from a
hundred years ago, but so very up-to-date a century later.

At the present hour, Liberalism is the chief error of the
intellects and the dominant passion of our century. It
fashions an infected atmosphere which envelops the
political and religious world on all sides, which is a
supreme peril for society and for the individual.

An enemy of the Catholic Church as gratuitous as it is
unjust and cruel, it heaps up in a bundle, in an insane disorder, all the elements of destruction and of death, in
order to banish it from the earth.

It falsifies ideas, corrupts judgments, adulterates consciences, enervates characters, inflames passions, subjugates governments, stirs up the governed, and, not content to put out (if that were possible) the torch of revelation, it moves forward, unconsciously and boldly, to extinguish the light of natural reason itself."[1]

The Liberal Principle

But is it possible to discover, among such a chaos of disorders, in an error so multiform, the fundamental principle that explains it all? I have told you, following Father Roussel, "The Liberal is a fanatic of independence." That is it. But let us attempt to state it precisely.

Cardinal Billot, whose theological treatises were the books I studied at the Gregorian University and at the French Seminary in Rome, has devoted to Liberalism a few energetic and luminous pages of his treatise on the Church.[2] He expresses as follows the basic principle of Liberalism:

Liberty is the fundamental possession of man, quite sacred and inviolable, which it is not at all permitted to harm by any coercion whatever. As a consequence, this freedom without limit must be the immovable stone on which all the elements of the relations among men will be organized, the immutable norm according to which all things will be judged from the point of view of the law. Consequently, everything that in a society will have the principle of the inviolate individual liberty as a basis will be equitable, just, and good. All the rest will be iniquitous and wicked. That was the thought of the perpetrators of the revolution of 1789, a revolution whose bitter fruits the entire world still tastes. That is the whole object of the "Declaration of the rights of man," from the first line up to the last. For the ideologues it was the necessary point of departure for the complete rebuilding of society in the political order, in the economic order, and above all in the moral and religious order.[3]

1 Pastoral letter of the bishops of Ecuador to their diocesan faithful, July 15, 1885, quoted by Don Sarda y Salvany, *Liberalism Is a Sin*, pp. 257-258.
2 *De Ecclesia*, Tome II, pp. 19-73.
3 Translation outlined from the Latin text, by Father Le Floch, *Cardinal Billot, Light of Theology*, p.44.

But, you will say, is not liberty a characteristic of intelligent beings? As a consequence, is it not right that the basis of the social order is derived from it? Be careful, I will reply! Of which liberty are you speaking? For this term has several meanings, which the Liberals strain their ingenuity to confuse. Therefore we have to distinguish.

There is liberty and liberty...

Let us then do a little philosophy. The most elementary reflection shows us that there are three kinds of liberty.

1. First, *psychological liberty,* or free will, proper to beings provided with intelligence, which is the faculty of turning one's mind towards such or such a good independently of all interior necessity (reflex, instinct, etc). Free will constitutes the fundamental dignity of the human person, which is to be *sui juris,* to depend on oneself, and therefore to be responsible, which an animal is not.

2. Then we have *moral liberty,* which concerns the use of free will: a good use if the means chosen lead to the obtaining of a good end, a bad use if they do not lead to that. You can see from this that moral liberty is essentially relative to the good. Pope Leo XIII defines it in a way that is magnificent but very simple: moral liberty, he says, is *"the faculty of moving oneself in the good."* Moral liberty is not therefore an absolute; it is all relative to the Good, that is to say, finally to the law. For it is the law, and firstly the eternal law which is in the divine intelligence, then the natural law, which is the participation in the eternal law by the rational creature, it is this law which determines the order put in by the Creator between the ends that He assigns to man (to survive, to multiply, to organize in society, to arrive at his last end, the *Summum Bonum,* which is God) and the means suitable for obtaining these ends. The law is not an antagonist of liberty; on the contrary, it is a necessary help; and that must be said also of the civil laws worthy of that name. Without the law, liberty degenerates into *license,* which is "doing what pleases me." Certain Liberals, making an absolute of this moral liberty, precisely advocate license, the freedom indifferently to do good or evil, to adhere indifferently to the true or the false. But who cannot

see that the possibility of falling short of the good, far from
being the essence and the perfection of liberty, is the mark
of fallen man's imperfection! Moreover, as Saint Thomas
explains,[1] the power of sinning is not a liberty but a ser-
vitude: "He who commits sin is a slave of sin."[2]
On the contrary, guided well by the law, channeled between its priceless guard-rails, liberty attains its end. Here
is what Pope Leo XIII sets forth in this regard:

> The condition of human liberty being such, it needed
> a protection, it needed helps and aids capable of directing
> all its movements towards the good and turning them
> away from evil. Without that, liberty would have been for
> man a very harmful thing. —And first a law, that is to say
> a rule of what must be done or not done, was necessary
> for it.[3]

And Leo XIII concludes his explanation with this admirable definition, which I will call plenary, of liberty:

> In a society of men, liberty worthy of the name does
> not consist in doing everything that pleases us: that
> would be in the State an extreme confusion, a disorder
> that would result in oppression. Liberty consists in this,
> that, with the help of the civil laws, we can live more easi-
> ly according to the prescriptions of the eternal law."[4]

3. Finally there comes *physical liberty,* or liberty of action or liberty vis-à-vis constraint, which is the absence of
external constraint that impedes us from acting according
to our conscience. Well, it is precisely this liberty that the
Liberals make into an absolute; and it is this conception
that we are going to have to analyze and criticize.

Natural Order and Natural Law

But before this, I want to insist on the existence of the
natural order and of the natural law, because the Liberals
will consent to admitting laws, but laws which man himself
has forged, since they reject all order (or ordination, or or-

---

1 Commenting on the word of Jesus Christ in Saint John.
2 Jn. 8:34.
3 Encyclical *Libertas*, June 20, 1888, PIN. 179.
4 Ibid. PIN. 185.

dinance) and all law of which man would not be the author!

Now, that there is a natural order conceived by the creator for mineral, vegetable, and animal nature, and equally for human nature, this is a scientific truth. No scholar would dream of denying the existence of the laws written into the nature of things, and of men. What does scientific research indeed consist in, for which billions are spent? What is it, if not the quest for laws? People speak often of scientific inventions, but this is an error; nothing has been invented, someone has only discovered laws and exploited them. These laws which are discovered, these constant relations between things, are not created by the scholars. It is the same thing with the laws of medicine that govern health, the laws of psychology that rule the fully human act: these laws, everyone is agreed, man does not make them, he finds them already planted in human nature. Now from the moment when it is a question of finding the moral laws that regulate human acts in connection with the great finalities of man, the Liberals then speak only of pluralism, of creativity, of spontaneity, of liberty. According to them, every person or every philosophical school has the power to construct its own proper ethics, as if man, in the rational and voluntary part of his nature, were not a creature of God!

Has then the human soul made itself, or does it make itself? Yet it is obvious that, in spite of all their complexity and all their diversities, souls are tailored on the same model and have the same nature. Whether it is the soul of a Zulu of South Africa, or of a Maori of New Zealand, whether you are talking about a Saint Thomas Aquinas or of a Lenin, you are always dealing with a human soul. Now, a comparison will help you understand what I want to say: nowadays one does not buy a rather complicated device, such as a washing machine, a copy machine, a computer, without asking how to operate it. There is always a law to use, a rule that explains the proper use of this object in order to succeed in making it do its work correctly, to make it arrive at its end, I would say. And this rule was made by him who devised the machine in question, not by the housewife who would consider herself free to play with all the keys and all the buttons! So, all proportions being preserved, there is a similar relation between our soul and the Good Lord! God gives us a soul, he creates it, thus necessarily he gives us laws: he gives us the means to make use of them to arrive at our ends, and above all at our ultimate end, which is God himself, known and loved in eternal life.

"Oh, we do not want that," the Liberals cry out. "It is man who should create the laws of the human soul." Let us not then be surprised that they make of man something out of balance, by means of making him live contrarily to the laws of his nature. Imagine some trees that would withdraw from the laws of vegetation; well, they would die, that is clear! Trees that would stop giving their sap, or indeed birds that would refuse to look for their food because that contingency did not please them... well, they would perish. Not to follow their law, which their natural instinct dictates to them, is death! And notice here that man does not follow a blind instinct like the animals; God has given us this immense gift of reason, so that we may have understanding of the law that rules us, in order that we direct ourselves freely towards the end, but not without applying the law! The eternal law and the natural law, the supernatural law, and also the other laws which derive from the first ones: the human laws, civil or ecclesiastical, all these laws are for our good. Our happiness is in them. Without an order preconceived by God, without laws, liberty would be for man a poisoned gift. Such is the realistic conception of man, which the Church defends as much as it can against the Liberals. It was in particular the honor of the great Pope Pius XII to have been the champion of the natural and Christian order in the face of the attacks of contemporary Liberalism.

To come back from that to speaking of liberty, let us say briefly that liberty cannot be understood without law: these are two realities strictly correlative, which it would be absurd to separate and contrast:

It is absolutely in the eternal law of God that we must

search for the rule of liberty, not only for individuals, but also for human societies.[1]

---

1 Encyclical *Libertas*, PIN. 184.

Chapter V

Beneficial Constraints

*"Do not consider that you are constrained,
but to what you are constrained, if it is to
the good or to the evil."*

Saint Augustine

Liberalism, as I have told you, makes of liberty of action,
defined in the preceding chapter as exemption from all
constraint, an absolute, an end in itself. I will leave to Cardinal Billot the care of analyzing and refuting this fundamental pretension of the Liberals. He writes:

> The fundamental principle of Liberalism is the
> freedom from all coercion whatever it may be, not only
> from that which is carried out by violence and which
> aims only at external acts, but also from the coercion
> which proceeds from the fear of laws and penalties, from
> social dependencies and necessities, in a word, from the
> ties of every nature which prevent man from acting ac-
> cording to his natural inclination. For the Liberals, this
> individual liberty is the good par excellence, the fun-
> damental, inviolable good, to which everything should
> yield, except perhaps what is required for the purely
> material order of the city. Liberty is the good to which all

the rest is subordinated; it is the necessary foundation of all social construction.[1]

Now, Cardinal Billot always says, "This principle of Liberalism is absurd, against nature, and visionary." And there you have the critical analysis that he develops; you will permit me to outline it by commenting on it.

The Liberal Principle is Absurd

This principle is absurd: *incipit ab absurdo*, it begins in absurdity, by pretending that the principal good of man is the absence of every tie capable of hampering or restraining liberty. The principal good of man, indeed, should be considered as an *end:* that which is desired in itself. Now liberty, liberty of action, is only a *means*, is only a faculty that can permit man to acquire a good. It is thus completely relative to the use that one makes of it: good if it is for the good, bad if it is for the evil. It is therefore not an end in itself, it is certainly not the principal good of man.

According to the Liberals, constraint would always be an evil (except to guarantee a certain public order). But it is clear, on the contrary, that, to take an example, prison is a good for the evil-doer, not only to guarantee public order, but for the punishment and amendment of the culprit. Likewise the censorship of the press, which is practiced by the Liberals against their enemies, according to the (liberal?) adage "No liberty against the enemies of liberty," is in itself a good, not only to secure the public peace, but to defend society against the expansion of the venom of error, which corrupts minds.

It must be affirmed therefore that constraint is not an evil in itself, and even that it is, from the moral point of view, *quid indifferens in se*, something indifferent in itself. Everything depends on the end to which it is employed. This is moreover the teaching of Saint Augustine, Doctor of the Church, who writes to Vincent:

> You see now, I think, that we should not consider the fact that one is constrained, but to what he is constrained: whether it is to the good or to the evil. It is not that

---

1 Op. cit., pp. 45-46.

anyone can become good despite himself, but the fear of what he does not want to suffer puts an end to the obstinacy which was posing an obstacle and urges him on to study the truth that he did not know. It makes him reject the falsehood that he was upholding, seek the truth that he did not know; and he reaches the point of wanting what he did not want.[1]

I intervened myself several times at Vatican II to protest against the liberal concept of liberty, which was being applied to religious freedom, an idea according to which liberty would be defined as exemption from all constraint. This is what I declared then:

> Human liberty cannot be defined as a liberation from all restraint, without danger of destroying all authority. Constraint can be physical or moral. Moral constraint in the religious domain is very useful and is found over and over all throughout the Holy Scriptures: "The fear of God is the beginning of wisdom."[2]

> The declaration against constraint, in no. 28, is ambiguous and, in certain aspects, false. What would happen, indeed, to the paternal authority of the fathers of Christian families over their children? To the authority of the teachers in the Christian schools? To the authority of the Church over apostates, heretics, schismatics? To the authority of the heads of Catholic states over the false religions, which bring with them immorality, rationalism, etc?[3]

It seems to me that the first epithet of *absurd* that Cardinal Billot attributes to the principle of Liberalism cannot be better reaffirmed than by quoting Pope Leo XIII:

> Nothing more absurd and more contrary to good sense could be said or imagined than this assertion: Man being free by nature should be exempted from all law.[4]

We might as well say, "I am free, therefore I must be left free!" The underlying sophism is obvious if this is explained: I am free by nature, endowed with free will, thus I am also free from all law, from all constraint exerted by the

1 Letter 93 —*ad Vincentium*— N° 16, PL 33, 321-330.
2 Observation sent to the Secretariat of the Council, December 30, 1963.
3 Oral intervention in the conciliar hall, October, 1964.
4 Encyclical *Libertas*, PIN. 180.

threat of penalties! Unless it is claimed that the laws should
be devoid of all sanction? But that would be the death of
the laws; man is not an angel, all men are not saints!

Modern Spirit and Liberalism

I would like to make a remark here. Liberalism is a very
serious error of which I have related the historical origin
above. But there is a modern spirit which, without being
candidly liberal, represents a tendency towards Liberalism.
It is found from the sixteenth century on among the
Catholic authors not suspected of sympathy with
naturalism or Protestantism. Now there is no doubt that it
is a mark of this modern spirit to ponder thus: "I am free to
the extent that there is no law that comes along to limit
me."[1] Beyond a doubt, every law comes along to limit
freedom of action; but the spirit of the Middle Ages, that is
to say, the spirit of the natural, Christian order of which
we were speaking above, always envisaged the law and its
restraints first as a help and a guarantee of true freedom,
and not primarily as a limitation. A question of emphasis,
you say? I say: No! An essential question that marks the
beginning of a fundamental change of mentality: a world
turned towards God seen as the ultimate end to attain, cost
what it may; a world entirely oriented towards the
Sovereign Good, gives place to a new world centered on
man, preoccupied with man's prerogatives, his rights, his
liberty.

---

1 François Suarez, S.J. (1548-1617), expresses this mind when he writes, *homo continet
libertatem suam—"Man holds his own liberty" in the sense that liberty is previous to
the law. (*De bon. el mal. hum. act.*, disp. XII, sect. V, p. 448,. quoted by DTC XIII, 473.)
A Thomist mind like Leo XIII would not admit this disassociation of two realities
strictly correlative.

Chapter VI

Necessary Inequalities

*"Nature goes forward with actions of auth-
ority and inequality, contradicting at a
right angle the odd liberal and democratic
hypothesis."*

Charles Maurras

An Individualism against Nature

Let us carry on with the analysis of the principle of
Liberalism. It is contrary to nature, says Cardinal Billot,
"in that it pretends that everything should give way to the
good of individual liberty, that social necessities have mul-
tiplied the obstacles to this liberty, and that the ideal
regime for man is that in which the law of pure and perfect
individualism would reign." Now, the author adds, "this
individualism is absolutely contrary to human nature."

You will have recognized the individualistic Liberalism
of Jean-Jacques Rousseau, which we find again at the bottom of all the present-day political thought. According to
Rousseau, men are born free, that is to say, subjected to no
restraint, by nature asocial, created to live alone in the
jungle, where they are happy. The origin of their misfor-
tunes and of inequality resides in the introduction of

private property, which engendered rivalries: a "state of war of all against all." If men group themselves then in society, it is in no way out of a necessity of their nature, but is by the sole decision of their free will, as an emergency exit from that state where man is a wolf towards other men. Society has nothing natural; it is purely conventional in its historical origin and in its constitution: this convention is the "social contract."[1]

This whole theory is refuted in advance, first by Saint Thomas Aquinas, who demonstrates the *social nature* of man, by bringing into evidence the fact that man is the animal most devoid of natural means of subsisting in an autonomous manner when he comes into the world, and this other fact, that men at the adult age cannot satisfy all their needs alone; therefore they have to help one another.[2] I would like to have you read an admirable page from the contemporary political thinker, Charles Maurras (1868-1952), who, following Saint Thomas, authoritatively sweeps away the Rousseauist individualist and egalitarian mythology; it is entitled "protective inequality."[3] It will be sufficient for me here to deliver to you what Leo XIII teaches on this subject in his Encyclical on the origin of political power:

> The important error of these philosophers consists in not seeing what is nevertheless obvious; it is that men do not constitute an uncivilized and solitary race. It is that before any resolution of their will, their natural condition is to live in society.[4]

A Visionary Equality

The egalitarian principle is visionary, Cardinal Billot says, "in the first place because it does not agree in any way with reality: it supposes, at the origin of all society, an initial pact. Where did one see this? It supposes the free entry of each one into society. That is even stronger. It assumes that all men are tailored on exactly the same

1 Cf. Baltasar P. Argos, S.J., *Political Catechism*, Orme Rond, 1981, p. 58.
2 Cf. Saint Thomas, *De Regimine principum*, Book I, Ch. 1.
3 Charles Maurras, *My Political Ideas*, natural politics, p. 17 sq.
4 Encyclical *Diuturnum*, of June 29, 1881, PIN. 97.

model—are exactly *equal*—which is the abstract man, millions of times reproduced without features of individuality. Where is he?" —"*Apply the social contract, if it seems good to you,*" says Taine; "*but do not explain it except to the men for whom it has been fabricated. They are abstract men who are not of any century or of any country, pure entities hatched under the wand of metaphysics.*"[1]

Leo XIII expresses the same judgement in a few concise words which follow the sentence quoted above: "*Add to that that the pact in which they take pride is an invention and an idle fancy.*"[2]

I insist on the fancifulness of this equality, according to which men are born equal, or at least equal in rights: "Men are born and remain free and equal in rights," proclaims the first article of the declaration of the rights of man and of the citizen of 1791. Let us look at what the Popes have thought of this:

Pope Pius VI, first of all, condemning especially article II of this same declaration,[3] goes from that to the principle itself of liberty-equality: he condemns it by calling it "idle fancies" and "words devoid of meaning":

> Where is then this liberty of thought and action that the National Assembly grants to social man as an indefeasible right of nature? Is not this visionary right contrary to the rights of the supreme Creator to whom we owe our existence and all that we possess? Furthermore, can it be ignored that man has not been created for himself alone, but in order to be useful to his fellow creatures? For such is the weakness of human nature that, to preserve themselves, men need the mutual help of one another; and that is why men have received from God reason and the use of words, to put them into a state of claiming the assistance of other people and of helping in their turn those who implore their support. It is therefore nature itself that has brought men together and has gathered them in society. Moreover, since the use that man must make of his reason consists essentially in recog-

---

1 Taine, *The Revolution*, Tome I, Book II, Chapter 2.
2 Loc. cit.
3 "The free communication of thoughts and opinion is one of the most precious rights of man; every citizen then can speak, write, print freely, with the condition that he is responsible for the abuse of this liberty in the cases determined by the law."

nizing his sovereign progenitor, in honoring him, in admiring him, in yielding to him all of his person and all of his being; since from his childhood he has to be subject to those who have superiority of age over him; to let himself be governed and instructed in lessons; to learn from them to regulate his life according to the laws of reason, of society, and of religion; therefore this *equality*, this *liberty* that are so vaunted are for him, from the moment of his birth, only *vain fancies* and *words empty of meaning.*[1]

From this liberty-equality, supposedly native in the individual, will be derived, by virtue of the social contract, the principle of the sovereignty of the people. Sovereignty resides originally in the people and not at all in God or in the natural authorities established by God; Pius VI does not fail to note this consequence.

Pope Leo XIII in his turn condemns the liberal principle of the equality of men, taken up again by the socialists, and carefully distinguishes the equality that men have from their common nature, from the inequality that they have from their diverse functions in society, and that is affirmed by the Gospel:

> The socialists never cease, as we know, proclaiming that all men are by nature equal among themselves; and on this account they claim that no one owes to authority either honor or respect, or obedience to the laws, except to those which they have sanctioned according to their caprice.
>
> On the contrary, according to the Gospel documents, the equality of man rests in the fact that, all having the same nature, all people are called to the same most high dignity of sons of God; and at the same time, one sole and same end being proposed to all, every person must be judged according to the same law and receive the penalties or the reward depending on his merit. Nevertheless, there is an inequality of right and of power that emanates from the very Author of nature, "of Whom all paternity in heaven and earth takes its name."[2]

Leo XIII then recalls the precept of obedience to autho-

---

1 Letter *Quod aliquantulum,* of March 10, 1791, to the bishops of the French National Assembly, PIN.3.
2 Encyclical *Quod Apostolici,* PIN. 71-72.

rities, given by the Apostle Saint Paul: "There is no power
that does not come from God; and those that exist have
been established by God. This is why he who resists authority resists the order willed by God" (Romans 13:2). Then
the Pontiff teaches that the hierarchy which is found in
civil society is not a pure fruit of the will of men, but above
all the application of a divine ordination, of the divine plan:

> For He who has created and who governs all things
> has disposed them, in His provident wisdom, in such a
> manner that the lower ones attain their end by the middle
> ones and these by the higher ones. Likewise, therefore He
> has willed that, in the heavenly kingdom itself, the choirs
> of angels be distinct and subordinated, in the same way
> again, that He has established in the Church different
> degrees of orders with the diversity of functions, in such
> a way that not all be apostles, nor all doctors, nor all pas-
> tors (Rom. 13: 1-7). So has He established in civil society
> several orders different in dignity, in rights, and in
> power, in order that the State, like the Church, form one
> sole body composed of a great number of members, some
> more noble than others, but all of them necessary, the
> ones to the others, and solicitous of the common good.[1]

It appears to me that these texts clearly show the total
unrealism of the fundamental principle of Liberalism, liberty-equality. It is on the contrary an undeniable *fact of nature*
that the individual, at any stage of his life, is precisely not
an interchangeable *individual*, but he is a *member* that is at
the outset a part of a *body* set up without his having a word
to say about it. Within this body, besides, he is subject to
necessary and beneficial restraints. In this body, finally, he
will discover the place that corresponds to his natural or
acquired talents, as well as to his supernatural gifts, being
subject there also to hierarchies and to inequalities that are
still very beneficial. Thus, has God devised it—a God of
order and not of disorder.

---

1 Ibid. no. 74.

Chapter VII

Jesus Christ:
King of the Republics?

*The majority does not make the truth; it is
the truth that should make the majority.*

Unknown

I still have much to say about Liberalism. But I want you to understand well that it is not some personal opinions that I am proposing to you. This is why I am desirous of advising you about papal documents and not about personal sentiments that would easily be attributed to an early formation received at the French Seminary in Rome. Father Le Floch, who was then the superior there, had indeed the reputation of a traditionalist to a very marked degree. Therefore it will be said of me, "He has been influenced by what was told him in the seminary!" Well, I do not deny this influence; even more, every day I thank the good Lord for having given me Father Le Floch as superior and as a teacher. He was accused then of making politics: and God knows whether it is a crime, or the opposite, to make the politics of Jesus Christ and to raise up political men who will use all the legitimate, even all the legal, means in order to drive away from the city the enemies of Our Lord Jesus Christ![1] But, indeed, Father Le Floch never meddled in politics, even in the thick of the plot put together against - *l'Action Française*[2] was misled and condemned *L'Action Française*. His successor, Pius XII, had to lift his sanction. But the harm was done: 1926 marked in France a decisive stage in the "occupation" of the Church by the liberal group, called "liberal Catholic." and of the crisis which ensued at the time when I was a seminarian.

In return, what Father Le Floch constantly spoke to us about was the danger of Modernism, of Sillonism, of Liberalism. And it was by basing himself on the Encyclicals of the Popes that Father Le Floch succeeded in securing in us a firm, solidly supported conviction, founded on the immutable Doctrine of the Church, of the danger of these errors. It is this same conviction that I desire to communicate to you, like a torch that one passes on to his posterity, like a light that will preserve you from these prevailing errors that are more than ever *in ipsis Ecclesiae venis et visceribus*, in the very veins and bowels of the Church, as Saint Pius X used to say.

You will understand therefore that my personal political thought on the government that is best suited to France, for example, is of little importance. Besides, the facts speak for themselves: what the French monarchy had not succeeded in doing, democracy has brought into being: five bloody revolutions (1789, 1830, 1848, 1870, 1945), four foreign invasions (1815, 1870, 1914, 1940), two plunderings of the Church, exilings of the religious orders, suppressions of Catholic schools, laicizations of institutions (1789 and 1901), etc. Still, certain people will say, Pope Leo XIII asked for the "rallying" of French Catholics to the republican regime.[3] (This, by the way, provoked a political and religious catastrophe.) Others moreover criticize this act of

1 It is not because the left-wing bishops indulge in socialist or communist politics that the Church should abstain from delving into politics! The Church has a power, undoubtedly indirect, but real over the temporal domain and over the life of the city. The social reign of Our Lord Jesus Christ is an essential preoccupation of the Church.
2
3 Cf. Encyclical *In the Midst of Solicitudes*, February 16th, 1892, to the bishops and faithful of France.

Leo XIII by qualifying it, as well as its author, as liberal. —I do not believe that Leo XIII was a liberal or, even less, a democrat. No, he simply thought that he was forming a good political combination for the good of religion in France; but it is clear that he was forgetting the irremediably liberal, masonic, and anti-Catholic origin and constitution of French democracy.

The Democratic Ideology

Sprung from the liberal postulate of the individual-king, the democratic ideology then is built up logically: individuals go into their social state by means of a conventional pact: the social contract, which is, says Rousseau, a *"total transfer of every associate, with all his rights, to the whole community."* From that derive:

–the necessary *popular sovereignty:* the people are necessarily sovereign, they have their power only from themselves, and they keep it even after they have elected their governors:

–the illegitimacy of every regime that does not have as a basis the popular sovereignty, or that in which the governors assure them that they receive their power from God.

As a consequence of this, we have, in practice:

–the struggle for the universal establishment of democracy;

–the "crusade of the democracies" against every regime that makes reference to divine authority, which would be called then a "sacral" or "absolutist" régime; in this regard, the treaty of Versailles of 1919, which suppressed the last truly Christian monarchies, was a liberal, precisely Masonic victory;[1]

–the political rule of the majorities, who are supposed to express the sacrosanct and infallible general will.

I would like to repeat, in case it is needed, in the face of this democratism which is now penetrating the Church by means of collegiality, that *the majority does not make the truth:* but without the truth and true justice towards God and our neighbor, what can be built that is solid?

1 Cf. H. Le Caron, *The Plan For World Domination of the Counter-Church,* p. 22.

Condemnation of the Democratic Ideology
by the Popes

The Popes have never ceased condemning this democratic ideology. Leo XIII did this *ex professo* in his Encyclical *Diuturnum*, of which I have already spoken to you:

A good number of our contemporaries, walking in the footsteps of those who, in the last century, bestowed upon themselves the title of philosopher, pretend that all power comes from the people; that, as a consequence, authority does not properly belong to those who exercise it, but only by virtue of a popular mandate, and under the condition that the will of the people can always take back from these trustees the power that it has delegated to them.

This is where Catholics separate themselves from these new teachers; they want to seek in God the right to govern, and they make it derive from Him as from its natural source and its necessary principle.

However, it is important to remark here that, if it is a question of designating those who should govern the republic, this designation can, in certain cases, be left to the choice and to the preferences of the majority, without Catholic doctrine's putting the least obstacle to it. This choice, indeed, determines the person of the sovereign; it does not confer the rights of sovereignty. It is not authority that is established; it is decided only by whom it should be exercised.[1]

Therefore, *all authority comes from God, even in a democracy!*

All authority comes from God. This truth is a revealed truth, and Leo XIII devotes himself to establishing it solidly on Holy Scripture, the tradition of the Fathers, and finally reason: an authority originating from the people alone would not have the power to oblige in conscience under pain of sin:[2] will say in *Pacem in Terris*, that one stirs up in everyone the search for the common good! Authority is above all a moral force.

It is not a man who has in himself or of himself what is

1 PIN. 94.
2

necessary to curb the free will of his fellow creatures by a bond of conscience. God alone, in so far as he is universal creator and legislator, possesses such a power. Those who exercise it need to receive it from Him and to exercise it in His name.[1]

Finally Leo XIII devotes himself to showing the falsity of Rousseau's social contract, which is the foundation of the contemporary democratic ideology.

The Church Does Not Condemn the Democratic Régime

What I want to show you now is that not every democracy is liberal. There is the democratic *ideology*, and there is the democratic *régime*; if the Church condemns the ideology, she does not condemn the régime, that is to say, the *participation of the people in the power*.

Saint Thomas justified the legitimacy of the democratic régime:

> If all have a certain part in the government, by this indeed the peace of the people is preserved. And everyone loves such an organization and looks after preserving it, as Aristotle says in Book II of his *Politics*.[2]

Without preferring democracy, the universal Doctor considers that in the concrete the best political régime is a monarchy in which all the citizens have a certain part of the power, for example in choosing those who govern under the monarchy. This is, says Saint Thomas, "a government that well combines monarchy, aristocracy, and democracy."[3]

The French monarchy of the Old Régime, like many others, was more or less of this type, no matter what the Liberals say. There existed then, between the monarch and the multitude of subjects, a whole order and a hierarchy of multiple intermediate bodies, which made the best of their competent advice in high places.

The Catholic Church, as far as she is concerned, does

---

1 *Diuturnum,* PIN. 96.
2 Ia IIæ, 105, 1.
3 Ibid.

not indicate any preference for this or that form of government; she allows the peoples to choose the type of government best adapted to their own character and to the circumstances:

> Nothing prevents the Church from approving government by one person alone or by several, provided that the government be just and ordered to the common good. This is why, as long as justice is safe, it is not at all forbidden to the peoples to give themselves such or such a political form which will be adapted best to their proper genius or to their traditions or to their customs.[1]

What is a Non-liberal Democracy?

I admit that a non-liberal democracy is a rare species, vanished today; but it is still not at all an idle fancy, as shown by the republic of Christ the King, that of Ecuador of Garcia Moreno in the last century.

Here are the characteristic traits of a non-liberal democracy:

1. First principle. *The principle of popular sovereignty:* first it limits itself to the democratic régime, and respects the legitimacy of a monarchy. Then it is radically different from that of the Rousseauist democracy: the power resides in the people, well and good, but neither originally nor finally. Thus it is from God that power comes to the people, from God as the author and from the social nature of man, and not from the individual-kings. And once those in power are elected by the people, these last do not keep the exercise of the sovereignty.[2]

–*First consequence:* it is not a shapeless multitude of individuals that governs, but the people in established bodies: its heads of families (who will be able to legislate directly in some very small States, like that of Appenzell in Switzerland), its peasants and merchants, industrialists and workers, big and small property owners, military men and magistrates, religious, priests, and bishops; that is, says Mgr. de Ségur, "the nation with all its living forces, established in a genuine representative manner, and capable of

1 Leo XIII, Encyclical *Diuturnum* PIN. 94.
2 Cf. *Diuturnum,* quoted above, and also Mgr. de Ségur, *The Revolution,* p. 73.

expressing its wishes through its true representatives, of freely exercising its rights."[1] Pius XII in his turn carefully distinguished the *people* and the *mass:*

> People and shapeless multitude, or, as it is customary to say, "mass," are two different concepts. The people lives and moves of its own life; the mass is in itself inert, and it cannot be moved except from the outside. The people lives of the fullness of the life of the men who compose it, each one of whom, in the place and in the manner that is proper to him, is a person conscious of his own responsibilities and of his own convictions. The mass, on the contrary, waits for an impetus from outside, plays easily into the hands of whoever exploits their instincts and their impressions, being quick to follow by turns today this flag and tomorrow that other one.[2]

–*Second consequence:* elected governments, even if they are called, as by Saint Thomas, "vicars of the multitude," are such only in the sense that they do for it what it cannot do itself, that is, govern. But power comes to them from God, "from whom all paternity in heaven and on earth draws its name" (Eph. 3:15). The people in power are therefore responsible for their acts first of all before God, whose ministers they are, and only after that before the people, for whose common good they govern.

2. Second principle. *The rights of God* (and those of his Church, in a Catholic nation) are set down as the base of the constitution. The decalogue is therefore the inspirer of all legislation.

–First consequence: the "general will" is null if it goes against God's rights. The majority does not *"make"* the truth; it has to keep itself *in* the truth, under penalty of a perversion of democracy. With reason Pius XII underlines the danger, inherent in the democratic regime, against which the constitution must react: the danger of depersonalization, of massification, and of manipulation of the multitude by pressure groups and artificial majorities.

–Second consequence: democracy is not secular, but openly Christian and Catholic. It conforms to the social

1 Ibid.
2 Radio message for Christmas, December 24, 1944.

doctrine of the Church concerning private property, the principle of subsidiarity, education left to the care of the Church and of the parents, etc...

To sum up: democracy, no less than any other governmental form, must bring about the social reign of Our Lord Jesus Christ. Democracy must, all the same, have a King: Jesus Christ.

Chapter VIII

Liberalism, or Society without God

"Indifferentism is atheism minus the name."

Leo XIII

I am going to try to expose for you here, after having analyzed the principles of political Liberalism, how the movement of generalized laicization, which has now almost entirely destroyed Christendom, has its source in the liberal principles. This is what Pope Leo XIII shows in his Encyclical *Immortale Dei*, in a very classic text that we should know:

The "New Law"

But this pernicious and deplorable taste for novelties, started in the sixteenth century, after having at first upset the Christian religion, soon by its natural propensity passed over to philosophy, and from there to all the levels of civil society. It is in this source that we must find the origin of these modern principles of unrestrained liberty, dreamed up and promulgated among the great upheavals of the last century, like the principles and the bases of a new law, unknown up to then, and on more than one point in disagreement not only with Christian law, but with the natural law. Here is the first of all these principles: all men, from the fact that they are of the same race and of the same nature, are similar and, by this fact, equal among themselves in the practice of life. Everyone depends on himself alone so much that he is not in any way subject to the authority of others: with complete freedom he can think about anything that he wants, and do what pleases him; no one has the right to command others. In a society founded on these principles, the public authority is only the will of the people, which, depending only on itself, is also the only one to command itself. It chooses its agents, but in such a way that it delegates to them not so much the right as the function of power in order to exercise it in its name. The sovereignty of God is ignored, exactly as if God did not exist, or were not at all interested in the society of mankind; or, indeed, as if men, either in particular or in society, owed nothing to God, or as if one could imagine any power whatsoever of which the cause, the force, the authority did not reside quite entirely in God himself.

In this manner, it can be seen, the State is nothing else than the multitude that is master and governor of itself; and from the idea that the people is supposed to be the source of all law and of all power, it follows that *the State does not believe that it is tied to any obligation towards God, does not officially profess any religion, is not bound to search out which is the sole true one among them all, or to prefer one to the others, or to favor one of them most importantly;* but that it has to afford them all equality before the law from the moment when the discipline in the republic does not suffer any detriment from this. Therefore, everyone will be free to make himself a judge of every religious question, everyone will be free to embrace the religion that he prefers, or not to follow any if none of them suits him. From this follow necessarily freedom of all conscience without restraint, absolute freedom to adore or not to adore God, license without limit both to think and to publish one's thoughts.[1]

---

1 PIN. 143.

Consequence of the "New Law"

It being given that the State rests on these principles, which are in great favor today, it is easy to see to what place the Church is unjustly relegated. Indeed, in the places where practice is in agreement with such doctrines, the Catholic religion is put in the State on a basis of equality, or even of inferiority, with societies that are foreign to it. There is no consideration at all taken of the ecclesiastical laws; the Church, which has received from Jesus Christ the order and the mission to teach all nations, sees itself forbidden to have any influence in public instruction. In matters that are of common concern, the heads of State pass arbitrary decrees and on those points display a proud scorn for the holy laws of the Church. Thus, they make the marriages of Christians go back to their jurisdiction; pass laws on the conjugal bond, its unity, its stability; lay their hands on the goods of clerics and deny to the Church the right to possess anything. In short, they treat the Church as if it had neither the character nor the rights of a perfect society, and were simply an association similar to the others that exist in the State. Further, whatever it has of rights, of legitimate power of action, they make this depend on the concession and the favor of the governments.[1]

Ultimate Consequences

...Thus, in this political situation that several favor today, there is a tendency of ideas and of whims to drive the Church completely out of society, or to hold it subjected and chained to the State. The greater part of the measures taken by the governments are inspired by this plan. The laws, public administration, education without religion, the plundering and destruction of the religious orders, the suppression of the temporal power of the Roman Pontiffs, all tends to this end: to strike the Christian institutions to the heart, to reduce the freedom of the Catholic Church to nothing and its other rights to nothingness.[2]

Leo XIII therefore showed that the new law, which is

---

1 PIN. 144.
2 PIN. 146.

that of the liberal principles, leads to *the indifferentism of the State* with regard to religion; that is, he says, *"atheism minus the name,"*[1] and to eliminating the Catholic religion from society. In other words, the objective of the impious Liberals is nothing less than the elimination of the Church, to be reached by the destruction of the Catholic States that support the Church. These States were the bulwark of the faith. Thus, it was necessary to demolish them. And once these bulwarks of the Church were destroyed, once the political institutions that were its protection and the expression of its benevolent influence were suppressed, the Church itself would be paralyzed and prostrate, and with it the Christian family, the Christian school, the Christian spirit, and even the Christian name itself. Thus Leo XIII clearly saw this Satanic plan, woven by the Masonic sects, which is leading today to its ultimate consequences.

Laicizing Liberalism at Work at Vatican II

But the heaped measure of impiety, which had never been attained up to then, was accomplished when the Church itself, or at least what has endeavored to pass for it, adopted at Vatican II the principle of the laicism of the State, or what goes back to the same thing, the rule of equal protection by the State of the adherents of all the cults, by means of the declaration on religious liberty. I will come back to this. But that intimates likewise how far the liberal ideas have penetrated the Church itself right up to its highest spheres. I will return to this also.

In order to recapitulate the logical sequence of the liberal principles up to their extreme consequences for the Church, here is the schema which I joined to my letter to Cardinal Seper on February 26, 1978; it is an enlightening parallel between *Quanta cura* of Pius IX and *Immortale Dei* of Leo XIII:

---

1 PIN. 148.

Leo XIII
Immortale Dei[1]

1) Condemnation of individualist indifferentist rationalism, and of State indifferentism and monism.

"All men are equal among themselves; everyone depends on himself alone so much that he is not in any way subject to the authority of others; with complete freedom he can think about anything that he wants, and do what pleases him..."
"The public authority is only the will of the people... From the idea that the people is considered to be the source of all law... it follows that the State does not consider itself tied to any obligation towards God, does not officially profess any religion, is not held... to prefer any of them to the others..."

2) Consequence: the "right to religious liberty" in the State:
"...but that it should concede to all equality under the law, from the time when the discipline of the republic does not suffer any detriment from this. Everyone therefore will be free to make himself the judge of every religious question, to embrace the religion that he prefers, or not to follow any of them if none of them please him..."

Pius IX
Quanta Cura[2]

1) Denunciation of naturalism and of its application to the State:

"Many today apply to civil society the impious and absurd principle of naturalism, and dare to teach that the best political regime and the progress of civil life demand absolutely that human society be established and governed without any more taking into consideration of religion, as if it did not exist, or at least without making any distinction between the true and the false religions."

2) Consequence: the "right to religious liberty" in the State:
"And against the doctrine of the Holy Scriptures, of the Church, and of the Holy Fathers, they affirm without hesitation that 'the best condition of society is that in which there is not conceded to the Power the duty of restraining the violators of the Catholic religion by legal penalties, except to the degree that public tranquillity demands it...'"
And: "Freedom of conscience and of forms of worship is a

1 PIN. 143-144.
2 PIN. 39-40.

right proper to every man. This right must be proclaimed and guaranteed in every society that is well organized..."

3) Consequences of this "new law":
"It being given that the State rests on these principles, which are in great favor today, it is easy to see to what place the Church is unjustly relegated. Indeed, in that place where practice is in agreement with such doctrines, the Catholic religion is put in the State onto the basis of equality, or even of inferiority, with societies that are foreign to it... In short, they treat the Church as if it had neither the character nor the rights of a perfect society, and was simply an association similar to the others that exist in the State."

3) Consequence of this "new law": harm to the Church:
Pius IX denounces the last "opinion" quoted here in (2) as:

"an erroneous opinion, fatal to the maximum for the Catholic Church and the salvation of souls."

He says no more about it, but adds later on that all that leads to:

"setting religion apart from society."

Beyond a doubt, Vatican II does not affirm the first principle of Liberalism, which I call here individualistic indifferentist rationalism; but, as I will show you, all the rest is there: State indifferentism, the right to religious liberty for all the followers of all religions, destruction of the public law of the Church, suppression of the Catholic States: it is all there, this whole series of abominations finds itself consigned there, and demanded by the very logic of a Liberalism that does not want to say its name but is the poisoned source of all this.

Chapter IX

Liberty of Conscience and of Forms of Worship

> *"Under the seductive name of freedom of cult, they proclaim the legal apostasy of society."*
>
> Leo XIII

It is in his Encyclical *Libertas* that Pope Leo XIII reviews the new liberties proclaimed by Liberalism. I will follow his exposé step by step.[1] This Pope says:

> It is well for us to consider separately the diverse kinds of liberties that are given as the great acquisitions of our age.

The liberty of forms of worship (or liberty of conscience and of forms of worship) is the first: it is, as Leo XIII explains it, claimed as a *moral liberty* of the individual conscience and as a social liberty, a *civil right* recognized by the State.

And first, in regard to individuals, let us examine this

---

1 PIN. 201.sq.

liberty so contrary to the virtue of religion, the liberty of cults, as it is called, a freedom that rests on this principle, that it is permissible for everyone to profess such a religion as pleases him, or even not to profess any. But, all to the contrary, it is indeed there, without any doubt, among all the duties of man, the greatest and the holiest, that which orders man to render to God a worship of piety and of religion. And this duty is only a consequence of the fact that we are perpetually in dependence on God, governed by the will and the Providence of God, and that, having come forth from Him, we must return to Him.

If indeed the individual-king is supposed to be the source of his own rights, it is logical for him to attribute to his conscience a full independence with regard to God and religion. Leo XIII then passes to religious liberty as a civil right:[1]uoted in the preceding chapter, from the Encyclicals *Immortale Dei* of Leo XIII, and *Quanta Cura* of Pius IX, and the following chapter.

Considered from the social point of view, this same liberty requires that the State render no worship to God, or authorize any public cult, that no religion be preferred to another, that *all of them be considered as having the same rights,* even when this people makes a profession of Catholicism.

If indeed society is only a purely conventional collection of individual-kings, it does not owe anything to God either; and the State considers itself exempt from all religious duties. This is manifestly false, says Leo XIII:

Indeed there can be no doubt, that the union of men in society is the work of the Will of God. This is clearly seen in its members, in its form which is authority, in its cause, or in the number and importance of the advantages which it procures for man.[2] It is God who has made man

---

1
2 Note of the Editor: The Pope is here referring to the scholastic concept of the "four causes." For example, in a car the material cause is the steel, plastic and other material of which it is built; the formal cause is its shape and arrangement of its parts; the efficient cause is its builder; the final cause is for the owner to drive safely. The material cause of society is its members; the formal cause is the authority; the efficient cause is the Creator of man's nature; the final cause is all the benefits society brings.

for society and who has joined him to his fellow creatures, in order that the needs of his nature, to which his
solitary efforts could not give satisfaction, can find this in
association with others. This is why civil society, in so far
as it is a society, necessarily has to recognize God as its
principle and its author, and, consequently, render to his
power and to his authority the homage of its worship.
No, neither by justice nor by reason can the State be
atheistic or, what would revert to atheism, have, with
regard to all religions, as is said, the same dispositions,
and grant them indiscriminately the same rights.

And Leo XIII takes care not to neglect a necessary
precision: when one speaks of *religion* in an abstract manner, he is speaking implicitly of *the only true religion*, which
is that of the Catholic Church:

> Since it is necessary then to profess one sole religion
> in society, that one must be professed which is the only
> true one and which is recognized easily, especially in the
> Catholic countries, by the sign of truth of which it carries
> in itself the brilliant expression.

Therefore the State must recognize the true religion as
such and make a profession of Catholicism.[1] The lines that
follow condemn without appeal the pretended agnosticism
of the State, its pretended neutrality in religious matters:

> The heads of State must therefore preserve and protect
> this religion if they intend, as is their obligation, to
> provide prudently and usefully for the interests of the
> community. For the public power was established for the
> usefulness of those who are governed, and although it
> has as its proximate end only to bring the citizens to the
> prosperity of this earthly life, it is nevertheless a duty for
> it not to lessen, but on the contrary, to increase for man
> the faculty of attaining to that supreme and sovereign
> good in which the eternal bliss of men consists, which be-
> comes impossible without religion.

I will come back to these lines, which contain the fundamental principle that regulates the relations of the State
with religion—I always mean the true religion.

---

1 That is, write into the Constitution the principle of this recognition.

*

The Encyclical *Libertas* appeared on June 20, 1888. One
year later, Leo XIII came back to the liberty of forms of
worship in order to condemn it anew in admirable terms
and with a very apostolic zeal, in his Letter to the Emperor
of Brazil.[1] Here are some extracts that show the absurdity
and the godlessness of the liberty of cults, since it necessarily implies State atheism:

> Liberty of forms of worship, considered in its relation-
> ship to society, is founded on the principle that the State,
> even in a Catholic nation, is not bound to profess or to
> favor any cult; it must remain indifferent with regard to
> all and take them all into equal consideration legally. It is
> not a question here of that *de facto* tolerance which, in
> given circumstances, can be conceded to the dissident
> cults, but rather of the recognition granted to them of the
> very rights that belong only to the one true religion,
> which God has established in the world and has desig-
> nated with clear and precise characters and signs, so that
> everyone can recognize it as such and embrace it.
>
> Further, such a liberty indeed places on the same level
> truth and error, faith and heresy, the Church of Jesus
> Christ and any human institution whatever; it establishes
> a deplorable and deadly separation between human
> society and God its Author; it leads finally to the sad con-
> sequences of State indifferentism in religious matters, or,
> what comes to the same thing, its atheism.

Those are words of gold! Those are words that should
be learned almost by heart. The liberty of forms of worship
implies State indifferentism to all religious forms. *Religious
liberty necessarily means State atheism.* For, professing to
recognize or to favor all the gods, the State in fact recognizes none, especially not the true God! That is what we
say when someone presents the religious liberty of Vatican
II to us as a conquest, as progress, as a development of
Church doctrine! Is atheism then progress? Is the "theology
of the death of God" inscribed in the line of tradition? The
legal death of God! That is unimaginable!
    And you can easily see that that is what we are dying of

---

1 Letter *E giunto*, of July 19, 1889, PIN 234-237.

at the present time: it is in the name of the religious liberty of Vatican II that the States still Catholic have been suppressed, that they have been laicized, that there has been erased from the constitutions of these States the first article, which proclaimed the submission of the State to God, its Author, or in which the State made a profession of the true religion.[1] The Freemasons did not want any more than that; now they have found the radical means: to compel the Church, by the voice of its Magisterium, to proclaim religious liberty, nothing more. But by this would be accomplished, by an inescapable conclusion, the laicization of the Catholic States.

You know well, it is a historical fact, it was published in the New York newspapers at that moment, that Cardinal Bea, on the eve of the Council, went to pay a visit to B'nai B'rith, the "sons of the alliance," a Masonic sect reserved for the Jews only, very influential in the Western one-world movement.[2] In his position as Secretary of the Secretariat for Christian Unity, just founded by John XXIII, he asked them, "Freemasons, what do you want?" They answered him, "Religious liberty. Proclaim religious liberty, and the enmity between Freemasonry and the Catholic Church will cease!" Well, they obtained it, this religious liberty; consequently the religious liberty of Vatican II is a Masonic victory! And this is corroborated by the fact that a few months ago President Alfonsin of Argentina, received officially at the White House in Washington, and by the B'nai B'rith in New York, was decorated by these Freemasons with the medal of religious liberty, because he has set up a regime of liberty of cults, of liberty of religion.[3]

So, we refuse the religious liberty of Vatican II, we reject it in the same terms in which the Popes of the nineteenth century rejected it, we base ourselves on their authority and nothing but their authority. What greater guarantee can we have of being in the truth than to be strong with the very force of tradition, of the constant teaching of Popes Pius VI, Pius VII, Gregory XVI, Pius IX,

---

1 Cf. below, Chapter XXXII, page 236-237.
2 Cf. H. le Caron, op. cit., p. 46.
3 *Journal de Genève*, Saturday, March 23, 1985.

Leo XIII, Benedict XV, etc., who all condemned religious liberty, as I will show you in our next chapter.

I will content myself with concluding this chapter by quoting for you again that passage from the Letter *E giunto* where Pope Leo XIII gives us once again proof of an admirable clearsightedness and force in his judgment on religious liberty (which he calls here liberty of cults):

> But it would be superfluous to insist on these reflections. On several occasions already, in official documents addressed to the Catholic world, We have shown how erroneous the doctrine is of those who, *using the seductive name of liberty of cult, proclaim the legal apostasy of society,* thus turning it away from its divine Author.

Religious liberty is the legal apostasy of society: remember this well. For this is what I answer to Rome every time they want to oblige me to accept all-inclusively the Council, and especially the Declaration on Religious Liberty. On December 7, 1965, I refused to put my signature at the bottom of this conciliar act; and twenty years later, my reasons for refusing this signature have only increased. One does not sign an apostasy!

Chapter X

Religious Liberty
Condemned by the Popes

> *"The civil liberty of all these cults
> propagates the pestilence of indifferentism."*
>
> Pius IX

I am going to collect in this chapter, at the risk of repeating myself, the texts of the main condemnations of religious liberty in the nineteenth century, in order that you may see clearly *what* has been condemned, and *why* the Popes have condemned it.

I
The Condemnation

Pius VI
Quod aliquantulum,
Letter of March 10, 1791
to the French Bishops of the National Assembly:

The necessary effect of the Constitution decreed by the assembly is to annihilate the Catholic religion and, with it, the obedience due to the kings. It is with this purpose that there is established, as a right of man in society, that absolute liberty which not only assures the right of not being disturbed about one's religious opinions, but grants besides that license to think, to speak, to write, and even to have printed with impunity in matters of religion everything that the most unregulated imagination can suggest; a scandalous right that nevertheless seems to the assembly to result from the natural equality and freedom of all men. But what could there be that is more senseless than to establish among men this equality and this unrestrained liberty which seems to stifle reason, the most precious gift that nature has given to man and the only one that distinguishes him from the animals?[1]

Pius VII
Post tam diuturnitas,
Apostolic Letter to the Bishop of Troyes, France,
Condemning the "Freedom of Cults and of Conscience,"
granted by the Constitution of 1814 (Louis XVIII):

A new source of pain with which Our heart is afflicted still more sharply and which, We acknowledge, causes us an extreme torment, dejection, and anguish, is the twenty-second article of the constitution. Not only is the freedom of forms of worship and of conscience permitted there, to use the very terms of the article; but there is promised support and protection to this liberty, and besides to the ministers of what are called the cults. There is to be sure no need of long discourses, addressing Ourselves to such a bishops as you, to make you recognize clearly with what a mortal wound the Catholic religion in France finds itself struck by this article. By the fact itself that the liberty of all the cults without distinction is established, truth is intermingled with error, and the holy and immaculate Spouse of Christ, the Church outside which there can be no salvation, is put into a class with the heretical sects and even with the Jewish perfidy. Moreover, by promising favor and support to the sects of the heretics and to their ministers one tolerates and favors not only their persons but also their errors. It is implicitly the disastrous and forever deplorable heresy that St. Augustine mentions in these terms: "It affirms that all the heretics are on the right path and speak the truth, an

---

1 PIN.I.

absurdity so monstrous that I cannot believe that any sect really professes it."[1]

Gregory XVI
Mirari vos,
Encyclical of August 15, 1832,
Condemning the Liberalism of Félicité de Lamennais:

From this poisoned source of Indifferentism is derived that false and absurd maxim or rather that delirium, that liberty of conscience must be procured and guaranteed for everyone. This is an error among the most contagious, to which the way is smoothed by this liberty of opinions, absolute and without restraint, which, for the ruin of the Church and the State, goes on spreading itself everywhere and which certain men, by an excess of impudence, do not fear to represent as advantageous to religion. "What death more fatal for souls than the freedom of error!" said St. Augustine.[2] By thus seeing removed from men all restraint capable of keeping them on the paths of truth, drawn along as they are, already to their loss by a natural inclination to evil, we say in truth that this shaft of the abyss is open, from which St. John saw smoke come up which obscured the sun, and locusts come out for the devastation of the earth.[3] From this, indeed, comes the lack of stability of minds; from this, the ever-growing corruption of the young people; from this, among the people, the contempt for the sacred laws, the most holy things and laws; from this, in a word, the most deadly scourge that can ravage the States; for experience attests it and the most remote antiquity teaches us this: in order to bring about the destruction of the richest, most powerful, most glorious, most flourishing States, all that was necessary was this liberty of opinion without restraint, this license for public discourses, this ardor for innovations.[4]

---

1 PIN. 19.
2 Commentary on Psalm 124.
3 Apocalypse 9:3.
4 PIN. 24; cf. Denzinger 1613-1614.

Pius IX
Quanta cura,
Encyclical of December 8, 1864
Reiterating the Condemnation of His Predecessor:

It is perfectly well known to you, Venerable Brethren, that today there are not lacking men who apply to civil society the impious and absurd principle of naturalism, as they call it: they dare to teach "that the perfection of the governments and civil progress demand absolutely that human society be established and governed without taking any more account of religion, as if it did not exist, or at least without making any difference between the different religions, between the true religions and the false ones." Furthermore, contrary to the teaching of Scripture, of the Church, and of the holy Fathers, they do not fear to affirm that "the best government is that in which there is not conceded to the authorities the duty of curbing the violators of the Catholic religion with the sanction of penalties, except when public tranquillity demands it."

As a consequence of this absolutely false idea of social government, they do not hesitate to favor that erroneous opinion, most fatal to the Catholic Church and to the salvation of souls, which Our Predecessor of happy memory, Gregory XVI, called a delirium,[1] namely, "that the liberty of conscience and of forms of worship is a right proper to every man; that it must be proclaimed in every well established State, and that the citizens have a right to full freedom to manifest their opinions loudly and publicly, whatever these may be, by word, by printing, or otherwise, without the ecclesiastical or civil authority's being able to limit it." Now, by supporting these foolhardy affirmations, they do not think, they do not consider that they are preaching "a freedom of perdition,"[2] and that "if it is always permitted to human opinions to enter into the conflict, there will never be lacking men who will dare to resist the truth and to put their confidence in the verbiage of human wisdom, an extremely harmful vanity that Christian faith and wisdom must carefully avoid, in accordance with the teaching of Our Lord Himself."[3]

---

1 Cf. above, *Mirari vos,* which Pius IX quotes very freely.
2 St. Augustine, Letter 105 (166).
3 St. Leo, Letter 164 (133); PIN. 39-40; cf. Denz. 1689-1690.

Pius IX
Syllabus:
A Collection of Condemned Modern Errors,
Extracted from *Acts of the Magisterium* of Pius IX,
published at the same time as *Quanta cura:*

77. In our time, it is no longer useful that the Catholic religion be considered as the only religion of the State, to the exclusion of all the other cults.

78. Therefore, it is with reason that, in some Catholic countries, the law has provided that the foreigners who go there enjoy the public exercise of their particular forms of worship there.

79. It is false that the civil liberty of all the cults and the full power left to all to manifest openly and publicly all their thoughts and all their opinions, throws the peoples more easily into corruption of morals and of the mind, and propagates the pestilence of Indifferentism.[1]

Leo XIII
Immortale Dei,
Encyclical of November 1, 1885
On the Christian Constitution of States:

...and from the moment when the people is supposed to be the source of all law and of all power, it follows that the State does not believe itself tied to any obligation towards God, does not officially profess any religion, and is not held to search out which is the sole true one among them all, or to prefer one to the others, or to favor one in the main; but that it should grant them all equality under the law, from the moment when the discipline of the republic suffers no detriment from this. Therefore everyone will be free to embrace the religion that he prefers, or not to follow any if none of them please him...

What follows has already been quoted in Chapter VIII,[2] and I refer the reader back to that.

What is Condemned?

What is common to all these pontifical condemnations

---

1 PIN. 53; cf. Denz. 1777-1779.
2 PIN. 143-146.

is religious liberty, designated under the name of *"freedom of conscience,"* or *"liberty of conscience and of forms of worship,"* namely: the right conceded to every man publicly to exercise the cult of the religion of his choice, without being disturbed by the civil power.

II
Motive for the Condemnation

You will have noticed in the preceding texts that the Popes are concerned to go back to the causes and to denounce the liberal origins of the right to religious liberty; it is essentially naturalistic and rationalistic Liberalism that is denounced, the one that pretends that human reason is the only arbitrator of good and evil (rationalism); that it belongs to each one to decide whether he should adore or not (indifferentism); finally, that the State is the origin of all law (state monism).

From this, certain modern theologians have felt able to infer three theses:

1. The Popes have condemned religious liberty not in itself but only because it seemed *"as if flowing from a naturalistic conception of man;"*[1] or, because it *"derived from the first premise of naturalistic rationalism,"*[2] or, from the two others: *"beyond the consequences* (religious liberty) *it is the principles that are alluded to here: the Church condemns rationalism, indifferentism, and state monism,"*[3] no more.

2. Faced with the concrete interpretations of the modern principles (struggle against the temporal power of the papacy, laicization of the Constitutions, plundering of the Church, etc.,), the Popes would have *"lacked the neces-*

---

1 Roger Aubert, *The Ecclesiastical Magisterium and Liberalism*, in *Tolerance and Human Community*, Casterman, 1951, p. 81.
2 John Courtney Murray, *Towards an Understanding of the Development of the Teaching of the Church on Religious Liberty*, in *Vatican II, Religious Liberty*, p. 112.
3 Jérôme Hâmer, O.P., *History of the Text of the Declaration*, in *Vatican II, Religious Liberty*, Cerf, Paris, 1967.

*sary serenity to judge the system of modern liberties in all objec-
tivity by seeking to take into account the true and the false"; "it
was inevitable that the first reflex of defense was an attitude of
total condemnation."*[1] It was difficult for these Popes to
*"recognize any value in the contents when the motivation was
hostile to religious values... thus for a long time they were not
friendly towards the ideal signified by the rights of man, because
they did not succeed in recognizing there the remote heritage of
the Gospel."*[2]

3. But it is possible today to rediscover the portion of
Christian truth contained in the principles of 1789 and thus
to reconcile the Church with the modern liberties, with
religious liberty in particular. Father Congar was the first
to trace the line to be followed in this regard:

> To reconcile the Church with a certain modern world
> could not be done by introducing as such into the Church
> the ideas of this modern world; this task implied a work
> in depth, by which the permanent principles of
> Catholicism take a new development by *assimilating,* after
> having *decanted* and if need be *purified* them, the worth-
> while contributions of this modern world.[3]

Roger Aubert made himself the faithful echo of this
view the following year; speaking of the collaborators of -
l'Avenir, Lamennais' Catholic-Liberal newspaper of the
nineteenth century, he says:

> They had not taken enough care to rethink the prin-
> ciples which, by means of the necessary discernments and
> *purifications,* would permit to be *assimilated* to Christianity
> the ideas of democracy and of liberty, which *born outside
> the Church,* had been developed in a spirit hostile to
> Christianity.[4]

Now, the work of purification and of assimilation of the

1 Roger Aubert, op. cit., p. 82.
2 International Theological Commission, *The Christians of Today Before the Dignity and
the Rights of the Human Person,* Pontifical Commission *Justice and Peace,* Vatican City,
1985, p. 44, quoted by *Documents épiscopat,* Bulletin of the Secretariat of the French
Episcopal Conference, October 1986, p. 15.
3 Yves Congar, O.P., *True and False Reform in the Church* (Unam Sanctam, 20), Cerf,
Paris, 1950, p. 345; quoted by Roger Aubert, op. cit. p. 102.
4 Roger Aubert, op. cit., pp. 81-82.

principles of 1789—Vatican II affirmed that this was its
primary objective:

> The Council intends above all to judge by this light (of
> the faith) the most prized values for our contemporaries
> (rights of man, liberty, tolerance) and to join them to their
> *divine source.* For these values, to the extent in which they
> proceed from the human character, which is a gift from
> God, are indeed *good;* but it is not rare that the corruption
> of the human heart turns them away from the required
> order: this is why they need to be *purified.*[1]

And this is indeed what the Council brought to reality.
Cardinal Ratzinger tells us:

> The problem in the 1960s was to *acquire* the best ex-
> pressed values of two centuries of "liberal" culture. They
> are in fact values which, even if they are *born outside the
> Church,* can find their place—*purified and corrected*—in its
> vision of the world. This is what has been done.[2]

*

I have wished to quote for you all these texts which
show the overwhelming consensus of all those theologians
who prepared, brought about, and carried out the Council.
Now, these affirmations, which go so far as literally to repeat themselves from one to the other, are only **an appalling imposture.** To state that the Popes did not see what
there is of true Christianity in the principles of 1789—this is
dramatic! Let us see a little closer:

1. To be sure, the Popes have condemned rationalism,
indifferentism of the individual, and state monism. But
they have not condemned only these! They have quite condemned the modern liberties *in themselves.* It is for what it
really means that religious liberty is condemned, and not
by reason of its historic motivations of the age; for, to take
only one example, the Liberalism of a Lamennais (condemned by Gregory XVI) is not the absolute and atheistic
Liberalism of the philosophers of the eighteenth century
(condemned by Leo XIII in *Immortale Dei*); and yet all those

---

1 *Gaudium et Spes*, II, #2.
2 *Conversation with Vittorio Messori*, in the monthly *Gesu*, November 1984, p. 72.

Liberals, whatever were their sometimes very diverse principles or their nuances, insisted on the same religious liberty. What is common to all the liberal philosophies is the claiming *of the right not to be disturbed by the civil authority in the public exercise of the religion of their choice;* their common denominator (as Cardinal Billot puts it) is the liberation from all restraint in religious matters. And the Popes have condemned this, as I am going to show you in a minute.

2. It is an impiety and an injustice towards the Popes to say to them, "You have wrapped up in the same condemnation the false principles of Liberalism and the good liberties that it proposes; you have committed an *historical error.*" It is not the Popes who have made a historical error or who were prisoners of historical circumstances; it is rather the theologians, who are imbued with a *historicist prejudice,* even if they deny it.[1] However, it suffices to read the historical exposés of Roger Aubert and John Courtney Murray on religious liberty to establish that they systematically relativize the statements of the Magisterium of the Popes of the nineteenth century, according to a principle that can be expressed thus: *"Every doctrinal pronouncement of the Magisterium is strictly relative to its historical context, in such a way that, if the context changes, the doctrine can change."* I do not need to tell you how much this relativism and this doctrinal evolutionism are opposed to the stability of the rock of Peter in the midst of human fluctuations, and permanently contrary to the immutable Truth which is Our Lord Jesus Christ. These theologians, in fact, are not theologians, or even good historians; for they have no idea of the truth or of a permanent doctrine of the Church, above all in social and political matters. They lose their way in their erudition and are prisoners of their own systems of interpretation; they are stuffed heads, but not good heads.

---

1 Fr. Murray, attempting to explain how the Magisterium could pass from condemning religious liberty in the nineteenth century to proclaiming it at Vatican II, declares at first: "This intelligibility is not accessible *a priori,* or simply by the play of the application of some *general theory of the development of doctrine. For the moment we have no general theory of this type."*

Pius XII was right to condemn their weathercock theology under the name of historicism:

> To that there is added a false historicism which, devoting itself to the bare events of human life, overthrows the foundations of all truth and all absolute law, in that which concerns as much the philosophy as the Christian dogmas themselves.[1]

3. As for reconciling the Church with the new liberties, this will be in actual fact the effort of Vatican II, in *Gaudium et spes* and in the Declaration on Religious Liberty. I will come back to this attempt, doomed to failure beforehand, to marry the Church to the Revolution.

*

For the moment, here are the true, immediate, and concrete motives for the condemnation of religious liberty by the Popes of the nineteenth century, motives that are *always valid*, as we can judge: it is absurd, impious, and leads the peoples to religious indifferentism. I take up again the very words of the Popes:

Absurd, religious liberty is this, because it grants the same rights to truth and to error, to the true religion and to the heretical sects. Now as Leo XIII says, "Right is a moral faculty; and, as we have said and as cannot be repeated too often, it would be absurd to believe that it belongs naturally and without distinction or discernment to the truth and to a lie, to good and to evil."[2]

Blasphemous, religious liberty is this also, because it "concedes to all religions equality under the law" and "puts the holy and immaculate Spouse of Christ on the level of the heretical sects and even of Jewish perfidy." Furthermore it implies "the religious indifferentism of the State," which is equivalent to being its "atheism": that which is the legal impiety of societies, the forced apostasy of the nations, the rejection of the social royalty of Our Lord Jesus

---

1 Encyclical *Humani generis*, of August 12, 1950; Pontifical Documents of Pius XII, XII, 303; cf. DS. 2306.
2 *Libertas*, PIN. 207.

Christ, the negation of the public law of the Church, its elimination from society or its subjugation to the State. Finally, it leads the peoples to religious indifference, as the *Syllabus* declares in condemning Proposition 77. This is evident: if now in these times, the Conciliar Church and the majority of Catholics are coming to see the ways of salvation in all religions, it is because this venom of indifferentism has been administered to them, in France and elsewhere, by almost two centuries of this diet of religious liberty.

Chapter XI

Freedom of the Press

"A deadly and abominable freedom, the true
oppression of the masses."

Leo XIII

If you continue reading the acts of the Popes, you can
take them one after the other and all of them have said
the same thing about the new liberties springing from
Liberalism: freedom of conscience and of forms of worship,
freedom of the press, freedom of education—these are
poisoned freedoms, false freedoms: because error is always
easier to spread than truth, evil easier to propagate than
good. It is easier to say to the people, "You can have
several wives," than "You can have only one for your
whole life." It is easier therefore to establish divorce, as if to
counterbalance marriage! Likewise, grant indifferently to
the true and the false the freedom to make their way
publicly, and most assuredly you will have favored error at
the expense of truth.

People like to say today that the truth makes its path
solely by its intrinsic power and that, to triumph, it does
not need the unseasonable and bothersome protection of
the State and its laws. The favoritism of the States towards
the truth is immediately accused of *injustice*, as if justice

consisted in holding an equal balance between the true and the false, virtue and vice. This is false: the first justice in regard to minds is to facilitate for them access to the truth and to forewarn them of error. That is also the first charity: *"veritatem facientes in caritate:"*[1] In charity, let us do what is true. The balancing among all opinions, the toleration of all kinds of behavior, moral or religious pluralism, are the mark of a society in full decomposition, which is the liberal society desired by Freemasonry. Now, it is against the establishment of such a society that the Popes of whom we speak have reacted without ceasing, affirming on the contrary that the State—the Catholic State primarily—does not have the right to permit such liberties, like religious liberty,[2] freedom of the press, and freedom of education.

Freedom of the Press

Leo XIII reminds the State of its duty to *moderate justly*, that is, to say, according to the requirements of the truth, the freedom of the press:

> And now, let us proceed with these considerations on the subject of the freedom to express by word or by the press everything that one wants to. Assuredly, if this liberty is not justly moderated, if it goes beyond limit and measure, such a liberty—it is hardly necessary to say it—is not a right; for a right is a moral faculty; and, as we have said and as it cannot be repeated too much, it would be absurd to believe that it belongs naturally, and without distinction or discernment, both to truth and to a lie, to good and to evil. The true and the good have the right to be propagated in the State with a prudent freedom, in order that a greater number profit from them. But deceitful doctrines, the most fatal pestilence of all for the mind, and the vices that corrupt the heart and morals, it is just for the public authority to practice solicitude in repressing them, so as to impede evil from spreading for the ruin of society. *The deviations of a licentious mind, which, for the ignorant multitude, easily become a real oppression, must in all justice be punished through the authority of the laws,* no less than criminal attempts of

---

1 Eph. 4:15.
2 See the preceding chapter.

violence committed against the weak. And this repression is the more necessary against these artifices of style and these subtleties of dialectic, especially when all this pleases the passions, and the unquestionably more numerous part of the population cannot in any way, or cannot without very great difficulty, stand on guard. Grant to everyone unlimited freedom to speak and to write, and nothing remains sacred and inviolable, nothing will be spared, not even those first truths, those great natural principles which should be considered a noble common patrimony for all humanity. Truth is thus little by little invaded by darkness; and the denomination of the most pernicious and the most diverse errors is seen to be established, something that often happens.[1]

Before Leo XIII Pope Pius IX, as we have seen, branded freedom of the press with infamy in the *Syllabus* (Proposition 79); and, still more, Gregory XVI in *Mirari vos:*

To that is connected freedom of the press, the most deadly liberty, an abominable liberty, for which we will never have enough abhorrence, and which certain men dare with so much turmoil and so much insistence to ask for and to spread everywhere. We tremble, venerable Brethren, when we consider with what monstrous doctrines, or rather with what prodigies of error we are overwhelmed; errors disseminated far and on all sides by an immense multitude of books, booklets, and other writings, small, it is true, in bulk, but huge in perversity, from which results the curse that covers the face of the earth and makes our tears flow. There are however men carried away by such an excess of impudence, who do not fear to uphold stubbornly, that the deluge of errors which follow from there is rather abundantly compensated by the publication of a few books printed to defend the truth of religion in the midst of this heap of iniquities.[2]

You see here unveiled by the pontiff the pseudo-principle of liberal "compensation," which pretends that it is necessary to compensate the truth with error, and conversely. This idea, we shall see, is the primary maxim of those who are called the Liberal Catholics, who do not support the pure and simple affirmation of the truth, but demand

---

1 Encyclical *Libertas*, PIN. 207.
2 PIN. 25.

that it be immediately counterbalanced with opposing opinions. And reciprocally, they judge that there is nothing to criticize in the free spreading of errors, provided that the truth has permission to make itself heard ever so little! This is the perpetual Utopia of the liberal, so-called Catholics, to which I will come back.

Chapter XII

Liberty in Education

*"Teaching should have as an object only
true things."*

Leo XIII, Pope

The third of the new liberties condemned by the Popes is
the liberty in education.

Be scandalized then, unsophisticated souls, liberal
minds who do not know yourselves, brain-washed by two
centuries of liberal culture! Yes, admit that you cannot get
over it, that you cannot understand it at all: the Popes condemn liberty in education. O surprise! O scandal! The
Pope—and what a Pope! Leo XIII, whom some call liberal,
condemns the sacrosanct freedom of instruction! But then
how shall we defend our Catholic schools, our free
schools? For the name of Catholic school has a musty smell
of sectarianism, a flavor of religious war, a far too confessional color, which is not good to show at a time when
everyone in our ranks is keeping his flag in his pocket.

I will have you wonder in passing at the soft and
sweetish liberal virtues, which surpass one another in
hypocrisy: foolishness, cowardice, and treachery join
hands here to sing in chorus, as in June 1984, in the streets
of Paris, the "Hymn of the Free School":

"Liberty, liberty! Thou art the only truth."

Which clearly means: we ask you only for liberty, in short... just a little bit of liberty for our schools; by means of which we have nothing to criticize in secular and obligatory freedom of education, in the liberty of the quasi-monopoly of the Marxist and Freudian school. Keep on calmly tearing out Jesus Christ, running down your country, staining our past, in the minds and hearts of eighty percent of the children; and we, for our part, to the twenty percent who remain, we will extol the merits of tolerance and of pluralism, we will denounce the errors of fanaticism and of superstition, in short, we will make people taste the charms of the only liberty.

*

I now leave to the Popes the care of showing us the falsity of this new liberty and the trap that it sets up for the true defense of Catholic instruction. And so first its *falsity.*

As regards what is called freedom of education, it does not have to be judged in any different way. It cannot be doubted that nothing but the truth must enter into souls, since it is in this that intelligent natures find their good, their end, their perfection: this is why education should have as its object only true things, and is meant for the ignorant and the learned, so that it can bring to the first the knowledge of truth, and to the second a strengthening of it. It is for this motive that the duty of whoever devotes himself to teaching is unquestionably to root out errors from the minds and to put up reliable protection against the encroachments of false opinions. It is thus obvious that the liberty which We are discussing, by arrogating to itself the right to teach everything according to its own fancy, is in flagrant contradiction with reason and that it was born to produce a complete upsetting of minds. The public power can grant such a license in society only by contempt for its duty. That is the more accurate as we consider what weight the professor's authority has for his hearers, and how rare it is that a disciple can judge for himself the truth of the master's teaching.

That is why this liberty, to remain honorable, also needs to be confined within determined limits; art and education must not with impunity have the power to become an instrument of corruption.[1]

Let us then remember the word of the Pope: the civil power cannot grant, in the so-called public schools, the liberty to teach Marx and Freud, or, still worse, the license to teach that all opinions and all doctrines have value, that none of them can claim the truth for itself alone, that all must be mutually tolerated. This is the worst of the corruptions of the mind: relativism.

*

And now here is what concerns the *pitfall* of freedom of education. For the Catholic, it consists in saying to the State, "We ask of you only liberty." Otherwise said: "the free school in the free State." Or again, "You certainly allow Marx and Freud in your secular school; grant freedom also to Jesus Christ in our free schools!" Now, this is a snare; it is to leave to the good pleasure of the State the care of determining the minimum of your Christian educational project tolerable in a secular society, for you to fall in there with docility yourselves. That would be an argument *ad hominem*—strictly speaking, acceptable—faced with a brutally persecuting regime, but facing a liberal Masonic power such as exists in the West, particularly in France, and in a country where the resources of Christianity are not exhausted, it is a cowardice and a *betrayal.* Catholics! Boldly show your fortitude! Openly manifest the rights of Jesus Christ over the minds redeemed by His Blood! Defend courageously the *full liberty* which the Church has to teach, by virtue of its divine mission! Insist too on the complete freedom of parents to give a Catholic education and instruction to their children, by virtue of their role as educators of their children. Such is the teaching of Pius XI in his Encyclical *Divini Illius,* of December 31, 1929, on education.

The function of civil authority that resides in the State is thus twofold: to protect the family and the individual

---

1 Leo XIII, *Libertas*, PIN. 209-210. See also the Letter *E giunto* of Leo XIII, already quoted, PIN. 240.

and let them progress, but without absorbing them or substituting for them.

In matters of education then, it is the right, or better said the duty, of the State to protect by its laws the previous right, defined above, that the family has of the Christian education of the child, and, as a consequence therefore to respect the supernatural right of the Church over this same education.

And further, in his Encyclical *Non abbiamo bisogno,* of June 29, 1931, against Fascism, which was strangling Catholic youth organizations, Pius XI has these very beautiful lines which are applied to the *full liberty* of education to which the Church has the right, as well as the souls themselves:

...The sacred and inviolable rights of souls and of the Church. It is a question of the right that souls have to procure for themselves the greatest spiritual good under the Magisterium and the educational work of the Church, the divinely established unique agent of that Magisterium and of that soul, in that supernatural order founded in the blood of God the Redeemer, necessary and obligatory for all, in order to participate in the divine Redemption. It is a question of the right of souls thus formed to communicate the treasures of the Redemption to other souls, by collaborating with the activity of the hierarchical apostolate. [Pius XI has in view Catholic Action.]

It is in consideration of this double right of souls that we were saying recently that we are happy and proud to fight the good fight for the freedom of consciences, not (as some, perhaps by inadvertence, have had Us say) for freedom of conscience, a way of speaking that is equivocal and too often used to mean the absolute independence of the conscience; an absurd thing in a soul created and redeemed by God...

It is a question moreover of the right, not less inviolable, of the Church to fulfill the imperative mandate that its divine Founder assigned to it, to bring to souls, to all souls, all the treasures of truth and of goods, doctrinal and practical, that He had Himself prepared for the world. *"Euntes docete omnes gentes... docentes eos servare omnia quaecumque mandavi vobis.* Go and teach all nations, teaching them to observe all things that I have entrusted to you." (Matt. 28:19-20).[1]

This doctrine applies particularly to the teaching given by Catholic schools.

I think that now you understand better the difference, the diametrical opposition, between the liberal *freedom of education*,[2] I would call it, and the *total freedom of instruction*[3] claimed by the Church, as one of its sacred rights.

*

What place does the doctrine of the Church leave to the State in teaching and education? The answer is simple: with the exception of certain schools preparatory to the public service, like the military schools for example, *the State is neither teacher nor educator*.[4] Its role is, according to the *principle of subsidiarity* applied above by Pius XI, to promote the foundation of free schools by parents and by the Church, and not to substitute itself for them. The State school, the principle of a "great national educational service," even if it is not secular and if the State does not claim a monopoly in education, is a principle contrary to the doctrine of the Church.

---

1 D.C. 574 (1931) col. 82; Pontifical teachings; *Education*, Desclée, 1960, no. 316.
2 Freedom to teach anything.
3 Freedom to teach the truth!
4 Parents are by nature the first educators of their children, and the Church has received from Our Lord the mission "to teach all nations." However, the State (the government) has not received such a mission, either from nature or from Christ! It has the duty to oversee and provide for the *common good*. It should not do by itself what can be done by others under it; it should not take over private enterprises (nationalizations) but rather be a just arbitrator between them. Similarly, it should not take over schools, but rather protect them and promote the good efforts of the parents and the church.

Chapter XIII

Is There a Public Law of the Church?

"The Church without the State is a soul without a body. The State without the Church is a body without a soul."

Leo XIII, *Libertas*

What is the status of the Church with regard to civil society? The answer to this question is the object of a special ecclesiastical science: the public law of the Church. You can consult the excellent treatises on the Church's public law by Cardinal Ottaviani and Silvio Romani, as well as the sources presented by Lo Grasso.[1]

I wish to show you how much Liberalism is opposed to the public law of the Church, how it destroys it, and thus how contrary Liberalism is to the faith, upon which rests entirely the public law of the Church.

---

1 See Bibliography.

The Principles of the Public Law of the Church

The principles of the public law of the Church are indeed truths of faith or deduced from the faith. They are:
1. *Independence of the Church.* The Church, which has as its purpose the supernatural salvation of souls, is a *perfect society*, supplied by its divine Founder with all the means to subsist by itself in a stable and independent fashion. The *Syllabus* condemns the following contrary proposition:

> The Church is not a true and perfect society fully free; it does not possess the proper and constant rights conferred on it by its divine founder, but it belongs to the civil power to define the rights of the Church as well as the limits within which it can exercise them.[1]

Such is indeed the state of subjection to which the Liberals want to reduce the Church in reference to the State! The *Syllabus* also radically condemns the plunderings of which the Church is periodically the victim on the part of the civil power, in its goods and its other rights. Never will the Church accept the *principle of common law;* never will it allow itself to be reduced to the simple common law of all legal associations in civil society, which must receive from the State both their approval and their limits. The Church therefore has the natural right to acquire, to possess, and to administer, freely and independently of the civil power, the temporal goods necessary to its mission (Code of Canon Law of 1917, canon 1495): churches, seminaries, chancery offices, monasteries, benefices (canons 1409-1410), and to be exempt from all civil taxes.[2] It has the right to run its schools and its hospitals, independent in themselves of all interference from the State. It has its own ecclesiastical tribunals to judge matters concerning the persons of clerics and the goods of the Church (canon 1552), to the exclusion of the civil tribunals in themselves (privilege of the forum). Clerics themselves are exempt from military service (privilege of exemption) (canon 121), etc...

On the whole, the Church claims sovereignty and independence by the very right of its mission: *"All power in*

---

1 Proposition 19, Denz. 1719.
2 Matt. 17:25

heaven and on earth has been given to me. Go then, teach all nations" (Matt. 28:19).
2. *Distinction between the Church and the State.* The State, which has the temporal common good as its direct goal, is also a perfect society, distinct from the Church and sovereign in its domain. This distinction is what Pius XII calls *the legitimate and healthy secularity of the State,*[1] which has nothing to do with the laicism that is a condemned error. Be careful then not to pass from one to the other. Leo XIII well expresses the necessary distinction between the two societies:

> God has divided the government of mankind between two powers: the ecclesiastical power and the civil power; the first one in charge of divine things, the second one charged with human things. Each of them is sovereign in its class; each is self-contained within limits perfectly determined and traced in conformity with its nature and to its special purpose. There is thus a sort of circumscribed sphere, in which each one exercises its action *jure proprio.*[2]

3. *Union between the Church and the State.* But distinction does not mean separation! How could the two powers ignore each other, since they are exercised over the same subjects and often also legislate on the same matters: marriage, family, school, etc.? It would be inconceivable that they could be opposed, when on the contrary their *unanimity of action* is required for the good of men. Leo XIII explains:

> The conflict, at this juncture, would be absurd, and would be openly repugnant to the infinite wisdom of the divine counsels; it is absolutely necessary then that there be a means, a process for making the causes of disputes and of fights disappear and for establishing accord in practice. And this accord, it is not without reason that it has been compared to the union that exists between body and soul, and that to greater advantage than to the two

---

1 Allocution to the inhabitants of the Marches, March 23, 1958, PIN. 1284.
2 Encyclical *Immortale Dei*, PIN. 136; cf. Denz. 1866.

married people; for the separation is particularly deadly
to the body since it deprives it of life.[1]

4. *Indirect jurisdiction of the Church over the temporal.* This
is to say that, in mixed questions, the Church, with regard
to the superiority of its end, will have precedence: "Thus,
everything which, in human things, is sacred by any claim,
everything that concerns the salvation of souls and the
worship of God, either by its nature, *or because of its purpose*, all that is in the province of the Church's authority."[2]
In other words, the rules of *union* and of harmony between
Church and State suppose an order, a hierarchy: that is to
say, an indirect jurisdiction of the Church over the temporal, an indirect right of intervention of the Church in the
temporal things which are normally in the jurisdiction of
the State. The Church intervenes there *"ratione peccati,"* by
reason of sin and of souls to save, to revive the expression
of Pope Boniface VIII.[3]

5. *Indirect subordination.* Conversely, the temporal is
directly subordinate to the spiritual: such is the fifth principle, a principle of faith, or at least of a theological certitude, which justifies the public law of the Church. Man is
indeed destined to eternal beatitude, and the goods of the
present life, temporal goods, are there to help him attain
this end: even if they are not proportioned to that, they are
indirectly ordered to it. The temporal common good itself,
which is the end of the State, is regulated to facilitate for
the citizens access to heavenly beatitude. Otherwise, it
would be only an apparent and illusory good.

6. *Ministerial function of the State vis-à-vis the Church.*
"Civil society," teaches Leo XIII, "must, by favoring public
prosperity, provide for the good of the citizens in a way
that not only does not place any obstacle, but assures all
the facilities possible for the pursuit and the acquisition of

---

1 Encyclical *Libertas*, PIN. 200. Yves de Chartres was already writing to the King,
   Robert the Pious, "As much as the body is worth if it is not ruled by the soul, so
   much is the temporal power worth if it is not modeled on ecclesiastical discipline."
2 *Immortale Dei*, PIN. 137.
3 Cf., Denz. 468, note.

that supreme and immutable good to which they aspire."[1]
St. Thomas says:

"The royal function [we would say the State] must procure the good life of the multitude according to what is necessary to help it obtain heavenly beatitude; that is to say that it must enjoin [in its order, which is the temporal] that which leads to this and, to the extent possible, prohibit what is contrary to it."[2]

The State therefore has vis-à-vis the Church a ministerial function, a role as servant: all in pursuing its end, the State must positively, although indirectly, help the Church attain its end, that is to say, saving souls!

This constant doctrine of the Church across the centuries deserves the note of *doctrina catholica*, and it requires all the bad faith of the Liberals to relegate it to the obscurantism of a bygone era.

According to them, it had value for "the sacral monarchies" of the Middle Ages, but no longer for the modern "constitutional democratic States."[3] This is truly nonsense, for our doctrine, deduced from Revelation and from the principles of natural order, proves as immutable and timeless as the nature of the common good and the divine constitution of the Church.

To support their deadly thesis of the separation of Church and State, the Liberals of yesterday and of today readily quote this sentence of Our Lord: "Render to Cæsar the things that are Cæsar's, and to God the things that are God's"[4]; they simply omit to say what Cæsar owes to God!

7. *Social reign of Our Lord Jesus Christ.* The last principle, which sums up from the top the public law of the Church, is a truth of faith: Jesus Christ, true God and true man, King of Kings, and Lord of Lords, must reign over societies no less than over individuals: the Redemption of souls is extended of necessity by the submission of States and of their laws to the sweet and light yoke of the law of Christ.

---

1 Ibid. PIN. 131.
2 *De regimine principum*, L 1, ch.XV.
3 Cf. John Courtney Murray, *Towards an Understanding of the Development of the Church's Doctrine on Religious Liberty*, pp. 128-129 (see bibliography).
4 Matt. 22:21

Not only, as Leo XIII says, must the State "have the holy and inviolable observances of religion respected, the duties of which unite man to God";[1] but civil legislation must be allowed to be impregnated with the law of God (Ten Commandments) and with the law of the Gospel, in such a manner as to be, in its domain, which is the temporal order, an **instrument of the work of Redemption** brought about by Our Lord Jesus Christ. That is, essentially, the realization of the social Reign of Our Lord Jesus Christ.

But just read the magnificent Encyclical of Pius XI, *Quas primas*, of December 11, 1925, on the social reign of Our Lord Jesus Christ! This doctrine is laid out there with an admirable clarity and authority! I still remember the moment when, as a young seminarian in Rome, I received with my colleagues that teaching of the Pope; with what joy, what enthusiasm our teachers commented on it to us! Re-read this sentence, which definitively crushes the laicism of the State:

> The States, in their turn, will learn from the annual celebration of this feast that the governors and the magistrates, as well as individuals, have the obligation to render to Christ a public worship and to obey His laws. The heads of civil society, for their part, will recall the Last Judgment, when Christ will accuse those who have expelled Him from public life, but also those who have scornfully set Him aside or ignored Him, and will have the most terrible vengeance from such outrages. For His royal dignity demands that the entire State be regulated by the commandments of God and Christian principles in the establishment of laws, in the administration of justice, in the intellectual and moral formation of youth, which must respect sound doctrine and the purity of morals.[2]

Henceforth, by its liturgy, the Church chants and proclaims the reign of Jesus Christ over civil laws. What a beautiful dogmatic proclamation, even if it is not yet *ex cathedra!*

It had to take all the frenzy of the enemies of Jesus

---

1 *Immortale Dei*, PIN. 131.
2 PIN. 569.

Christ to bring them to the point of tearing away his crown, when, in application of the Council of 1962, the innovators suppressed or truncated these three strophes of the hymn from the Vespers of the Feast of Christ the King:

Scelesta turba clamitat:
Regnare Christum nolumus;
Te nos ovantes omnium
Regem supremum dicimus.
(Stanza 2.)

The wicked mob screams out,
"We don't want Christ as king,"
While we, with shouts of joy, hail
Thee as the world's supreme King.

Te nationum præsides
Honore tollant publico,
Colant magistri, iudices,
Leges et artes exprimant.
(Stanza 6.)

May the rulers of the world
Publicly honor and extol Thee;
May the teachers and judges
reverence Thee.
May the laws express Thy order
and the arts reflect Thy beauty.

Submissa regum fulgeant
Tibi dicata insignia:
Mitique sceptro patriam
Domosque subde civium.
(Stanza 7.)

May kings find renown
In their submission and dedication
to Thee.
Bring under Thy gentle rule
Our country and our homes.

Chapter XIV

How They Have Uncrowned Jesus Christ

> *At the last judgment, Christ will accuse those who have expelled Him from public life and will have the most terrible vengeance from such an outrage.*
>
> Pius XI

At the risk of repeating myself, I come back to the social kingship of Our Lord Jesus Christ, that *dogma of the Catholic faith*, which no one can put in doubt without being a heretic: yes, exactly: a heretic!

Do They Still Have the Faith?

Make a judgment then on the dying faith of the Apostolic Nuncio in Bern, Bishop Marchioni, with whom I had the following conversation on March 31, 1976, in Bern:

–Archbishop Lefebvre: "Some dangerous things can easily be seen... In the declaration on religious liberty, there are some things contrary to what the Popes have taught: it is decided that there can no longer be Catholic States!"

–The Nuncio: "But of course, that is evident!"

–Archbishop Lefebvre: "Do you think that that is going to do the Church any good, this suppression of the Catholic States?"

–The Nuncio: "Ah, but you understand, if we do that, we will get a greater religious freedom with the Soviets!"

–Archbishop Lefebvre: "But the social Reign of Our Lord Jesus Christ, what are you doing about that?"

–The Nuncio: "You know, that is impossible now; perhaps in the distant future?... Right now, this Reign is in individuals; we have to open ourselves up to the masses."

–Archbishop Lefebvre: "But the encyclical *Quas Primas*, what do you do with that?"

–The Nuncio: "Oh... the Pope would not write that any more, now!"

–Archbishop Lefebvre: "Did you know that in Colombia it was the Holy See that asked for the suppression of the Christian constitution of the State?"

–The Nuncio: "Yes, and here also."

–Archbishop Lefebvre: "In the Valais?"

–The Nuncio: "Yes, in the Valais. And now, you see, I am invited to all the meetings!"

–Archbishop Lefebvre: "Then you approve the letter that Bishop Adam [Bishop of Sion, in the Valais] wrote to the faithful of his diocese to explain to them why they should vote for the law of separation of Church and State?"

–The Nuncio: "You see, the social kingship of Our Lord, it is very difficult now..."

You see, he no longer believes in it: it is an "impossible" or "very difficult" dogma, "which would not be written now any more"! And how many people think like this today! How many are incapable of understanding that the Redemption of Our Lord Jesus Christ must be brought about with the help of civil society, and that the State therefore must become, within the limits of the temporal order, the instrument of the application of the work of the Redemption. They answer you, "Oh, those are two different things; you are mixing politics and religion!"

And yet, all has been created for Our Lord Jesus Christ, and therefore for the accomplishment of the work of the Redemption: everything, including civil society, which, I have told you, is itself a creature of the Good Lord! Civil society is not a pure creation of the will of men; it results above all from the social nature of man, from the fact that God has created men so that they will live in society; it is written into nature by the creator. Therefore civil society itself, no less than individuals, must render homage to God, its author and its end, and *serve the redeeming design of Jesus Christ.*

*

In September 1977 I gave a conference in Rome at the residence of Princess Palaviccini, and I read there a document from Cardinal Colombo, archbishop of Milan, saying that the State should not have a religion, that it should be *"without ideology."* Well, far from contradicting me, the cardinal responded to my attack in *L'Avvenire d'Italia* by repeating the same thing, saying it again with still more force throughout his article, so much so that it was entitled *"Io Stato non puo essere altro que laico"*: the State cannot be anything but secular, therefore without religion! A cardinal said that! What idea does he have of the Redemption of Our Lord Jesus Christ? That is unheard of! Look at how much Liberalism has penetrated the Church. If he had said that twenty years before, it would have had the effect of a bomb in Rome; everyone would have protested; Pope Pius XII would have contradicted it and taken measures. But now, that is normal, that seems normal. So it is essential for us to have the conviction of this truth of faith: everything, including civil society, has been devised to serve, directly or indirectly, the redeeming plan of Our Lord Jesus Christ.

Condemnation of the Separation of Church and State

I stipulate first that the Popes have condemned the separation of Church and State only in so far as it is a doctrine and in its application to the nations that have a *Catholic majority.* Obviously the possible *tolerance* of other cults in a city that is otherwise Catholic is not condemned, nor, with greater reason, the *fact* of the plurality of cults that exists in numerous foreign countries which do not belong to what was called in times past Christendom.

This being specified, I affirm with the Popes that it is an impiety and an error close to heresy to pretend that the State should be separated from the Church, and the Church from the State. The spirit of faith of a Saint Pius X, his profound theology, his pastoral zeal, rise up with vigor against the laicizing enterprise of the separation of Church and State in France. Here is what he declares in his Encyclical *Vehementer nos*, of February 11, 1906, that I invite you to meditate on:

> That the State must be separated from the Church is an absolutely false thesis, a very pernicious error.
>
> Based indeed on this principle that the State must not recognize any religious cult, it is first of all very seriously injurious to God; for the Creator of man is also the Founder of human societies; and he keeps them in existence as he sustains us there. We therefore owe him not only a private worship, but a public and social worship in order to honor him.
>
> Moreover, this thesis is the very clear negation of the supernatural order. It indeed limits the action of the State to the sole pursuit of public prosperity during this life, which is only the proximate reason for public societies; and it is not concerned in any way, as being foreign to it, with their last reason for existence, which is the eternal beatitude offered to man when this very short life will have come to an end. And since the present order of things, which unfolds in time, finds itself subordinated to the acquisition of that supreme and absolute good, not only must the civil power not place an obstacle in front of this acquisition, but it must besides help us in this.
>
> This thesis likewise upsets the order very wisely established by God in the world, an order that demands a harmonious concord between the two societies. These two societies, religious society and civil society, have indeed the same subjects, although each of them exercises its authority over them in its own sphere. It inevitably results from this that there will be many matters of which the knowledge and judgement will be in the province of one and of the other. Now, when the accord between State and Church comes to disappear, from these common

matters the seeds of disputes will easily swarm; they will become very sharp on both sides; thus the notion of truth will be clouded from this and souls will be filled with a great anxiety.

Finally, this thesis inflicts grave damage onto civil society itself; for it cannot prosper or last a long time when place is not given there to religion, which is for man a supreme rule and sovereign mistress for the inviolable protection of his rights and his duties.

Remarkable Continuity of this Doctrine

And the holy Pope then relies on the teaching of his predecessor, Leo XIII, from whom he quotes the following passage, showing by the *continuity* of the doctrine the authority with which it is vested:

Therefore, the Roman pontiffs have not ceased, according to the circumstances and the times, refuting and condemning the doctrine of separation of Church and State. Our illustrious Predecessor Leo XIII, particularly, several times and magnificently exposed what should be, according to Catholic doctrine, the relations between the two societies.

There follows the passage from *Immortale Dei* that I have quoted to you in the preceding chapter, and again this quotation:

Human societies cannot, without becoming criminal, conduct themselves as if God did not exist, or refuse to be concerned with religion as if it were a foreign thing to them or something that could not serve them in any way... As for the Church, which has God himself as its originator, to exclude it from the active life of the nation, from the laws, from the education of youth, from domestic society, is to commit a great and pernicious error.[1]

We have only to reread once more that passage of *Immortale Dei* to ascertain that Leo XIII in his turn affirms that he is only taking up again the doctrine of his predecessors:

These doctrines, which human reason rejects, and which have a very considerable influence on the running of public things, the Roman Pontiffs, Our predecessors, in

---

1 Leo XIII, *Immortale Dei*, cf. PIN. 149.

full consciousness of what the Apostolic Charge demanded of them, have never suffered them to be expressed with impunity. So that, in his Letter-Encyclical *Mirari vos*, of August 15, 1832, Gregory XVI, on the subject of the separation of Church and State, expresses himself in these terms: "We cannot expect for the Church and the State the best results from the tendencies of those who pretend to separate the Church from the State and to disrupt the mutual harmony between the priesthood and the empire. Indeed the instigators of an unrestrained liberty dread this harmony, which has always been so favorable and beneficial to religious and civil interests."

In the same manner, Pius IX, each time that the occasion presented itself, condemned the false opinions that were most in vogue; and afterwards he had a collection made of them,[1] in order that, in such a deluge of errors, Catholics might have a sure direction.[2]

I conclude that such a doctrine, which teaches the union that must exist between the Church and the State and condemns the opposed error of their separation, takes on, by its perfect continuity with four successive Popes from 1832 to 1906, and from the solemn declaration that Saint Pius X made on this at the consistory of February 21, 1906, a maximum authority, and beyond a doubt even the guarantee of infallibility.

*

How then does a nuncio Marchioni or a Cardinal Colombo arrive at denying this doctrine, which is derived from the faith and is probably infallible? How an ecumenical council managed to put it aside, in the museum of archaic curiosities, this is what I will explain to you soon by telling you about the penetration of Liberalism into the Church owing to a movement of pernicious thought, which is *liberal Catholicism*.

---

1 The *Syllabus*, in which condemned proposition number 55 is stated thus: "The Church must be separated from the State, and the State from the Church."
2 *Immortale Dei*, PIN. 151.

Part II

Liberal Catholicism

Chapter XV

The Great Betrayal

To reconcile the Church with the Revolution, such is the concern of the Liberals called Catholics.

Unknown

To the Catholic doctrine of the social Kingship of Our Lord Jesus Christ and the union between Church and State, the Liberals, claiming to be Catholics, object that it is doubtlessly true, but inapplicable, even in the Catholic countries:

–In theory, one can accept *the thesis* proposed by the Popes and the theologians.

–In practice, one must yield to circumstances and place himself resolutely into *the hypothesis*: to promote religious pluralism and the liberty of forms of worship:

> The liberal Catholics have not ceased responding that they have a will for orthodoxy equal to that of the most intransigent and a sole concern for the interests of the Church; the conciliation that they have sought is not theoretical, abstract, but practical.[1]

---

1 DTC. Tome IX, col. 509, article *Catholic Liberalism.*

This is the famous distinction between the thesis (doctrine) and the hypothesis (practice in given circumstances). This distinction, I ask you to observe, is susceptible of a correct interpretation: the application of principles must take the circumstances into consideration, and this is done by circumspection, which is a part of the virtue of *prudence*. Thus, the presence in a Catholic nation of large Moslem, Jewish, and Protestant minorities can prompt a *tolerance* of these cults in a city otherwise Catholic by a State that continues to recognize the true religion, because it believes in the social Reign of Our Lord Jesus Christ!

But be careful! For the liberal Catholics, that is not the question! According to them, in practice, the principles, which are nevertheless by definition rules of action, must not be applied or advocated because they are inapplicable, they say. This is obviously false: must we renounce the preaching and the application of the commandments of God, "Thou shalt have only one God," "Thou shalt not kill," "Thou shalt not commit adultery," because people want no more of this? Because modern mentality tends to the liberation from all moral rules? Is it necessary to renounce the social Kingship of Jesus Christ in a country under the pretext that Mohammed or Buddha wants a place there? In short, *they refuse to believe in the practical efficacy of the truth.* They think that they can still affirm Catholic principles in theory, and act always contrary to these principles: this is the intrinsic incoherence of the so-called liberal Catholics.

Here is what Cardinal Billot, S.J., says of this:

> The Liberalism of the "liberal Catholics" escapes all classification and has only one sole distinctive and characteristic note, that of *perfect and absolute incoherence.*[1]

And the Cardinal remarks that the title of "liberal Catholic" is itself a contradiction in terms, an incoherence, since "Catholic" supposes a subjection to the human and divine order of things, while "liberal" means precisely emancipation from this order, a revolt against Our Lord Jesus Christ.

---

1 Father Le Floch, *Cardinal Billot, Light of Theology*, p. 57.

To finish, here is how Cardinal Billot judges the famous distinction between thesis and hypothesis of the Liberals, claiming to be Catholics:

> From the fact that the concrete order of things differs from the ideal conditions of theory, it follows that concrete things will never have the perfection of the ideal; but there follows nothing more.

Thus, from the fact of the existence of dissident minorities in a Catholic nation, it follows that religious unanimity will never be perfectly realized, perhaps, that the social reign of Jesus Christ will never have the perfection that the principles set forth; but it does not follow that this Reign is to be warded off in practice and that religious pluralism should become the rule!

You see then already that there is in liberal Catholicism (a term that I use with repugnance, because it is a blasphemy) a *betrayal* of the principles that refuse to be admitted, a practical apostasy of the faith in the social Kingship of Our Lord Jesus Christ. Deservedly can it be said, *"Liberalism is a sin,"*[1] in speaking of Catholic Liberalism.

There is also—I will come back to this in the following chapter—an *intellectual confusion* at the bottom of this error, a mania of kept-up confusions, a refusal to define anything: such as this confusion between *tolerance* and *tolerantism*: tolerance is a Catholic principle and is, under certain circumstances, a duty of *charity* and of political *prudence* towards the minorities. Tolerantism is, on the contrary, a liberal error which wants to grant to all dissidents indiscriminately and under all circumstances, and in *justice*, the same rights as the ones enjoyed by those who are in the truth, moral or religious. Now, as can be observed in other realms, to make of charity a justice is to upset the social order; it is to kill justice and charity.

---

1 Dom Felix Sarda y Salvany.

Chapter XVI

The Liberal Catholic Mentality

> *"There are tyrannical weaknesses, evil deficiencies, and conquered ones deserving of being so."*
>
> Charles Maurras

A Sickness of the Mind

More than a confusion, liberal Catholicism is a *"sickness of the mind"*;[1] the mind does not manage to repose simply in the truth. The mind does not dare to affirm anything, without the counter-affirmation immediately presenting itself to it, which it feels obliged to pose as well. Pope Paul VI was the type itself of this divided mind, of this double-faced being—this could be read even physically on his face—perpetually tossed about between contradictory things and enlivened by a pendulum movement oscillating regularly between tradition and novelty: an intellectual schizophrenia, will some people say?

---

1 Father A. Roussel, *Liberalism and Catholicism*, p. 16.

I believe that Father Clerissac has most profoundly perceived the nature of this sickness. It is a *"lack of integrity of
the mind,"* he writes,[1] of a mind that does not have *"enough
confidence in the truth"*:

> This lack of integrity of the mind, in the ages of
> Liberalism, is explained on the psychological side by two
> manifest traits: Liberals are receptive and feverish; recep-
> tive, because they too easily assume the states of mind of
> their contemporaries; feverish, because out of fear of of-
> fending these varied states of mind, they are in a con-
> tinual apologetic uneasiness. They seem to suffer them-
> selves from the doubts that they are fighting; they do not
> have enough confidence in the truth; they want to justify
> too much, demonstrate too much, adapt too much, or
> even excuse too much.

To Put Oneself into Harmony with the World

To excuse too much! How well that is said: they want
to excuse everything from the Church's past: the Crusades,
the Inquisition, etc... To justify and demonstrate, it is very
timidly that they do this, especially if it is a question of the
rights of Jesus Christ. But to adapt—to that, for sure, they
devote themselves, it is their principle:

> They set out from a practical principle and from a fact
> that they judge to be undeniable: this principle is that the
> Church would not know how to be understood in the
> concrete sphere where it must accomplish its divine mis-
> sion, without *putting itself into harmony with it.*[2]

It is thus that, later on, the Modernists will want to
adapt the preaching of the Gospel to the false critical
science and to the false immanentist philosophy of the age,
*"striving to render Christian truth accessible to minds trained to
refuse the supernatural."*[3] Therefore, according to them, in
order to convert those who do not believe in the supernatural, an abstraction must be made of the revelation of
Our Lord, of grace, of miracles—if you are dealing with

1 Humbert Clerissac, O.P., *The Mystery of the Church*, ch. VII.
2 DTC, Tome IX, col. 509.
3 Jacques Marteaux, *Catholics in Anxiety*, passim.

atheists, do not speak to them of God, but put yourself onto their level, at their pitch; go into their system! By this means you are going to become a Marxist-Christian: it will be they who will convert you!

It is the same reasoning that the Mission of France[1] held and that numerous priests hold still today with regard to the apostolate in the working world: if we want to convert them, we have to toil with the workers, not appear as priests, have their preoccupations, know their demands; and we will thus succeed in being the leaven in the dough. By this means there are priests who have been converted and have become union agitators! It will be said, "Yes, but, you understand, we had to be totally assimilated to this sphere, not offend it, not give it the impression that we want to evangelize it or force the truth onto it!" What an error! Those people who do not believe any more thirst for the truth, they are hungry for the bread of truth that these misled priests no longer want to break for them!

It is this false reasoning again that has been given to the missionaries: but no, do not preach Jesus Christ right away to these poor natives who above all are dying of hunger! First give them something to eat, then tools, next teach them to work, instruct them in the alphabet, in hygiene... and contraception, why not? But do not speak to them of God: their stomachs are empty! But I will say this: it is precisely because they are poor and deprived of the goods of the earth that they are extraordinarily open to the Kingdom of Heaven, to "Seek first the kingdom of heaven," to the Good Lord, who loves them and has suffered for them, so that they can take part, by their miseries, in His redeeming sufferings. If on the contrary you pretend to place yourself onto their level, you will only wind up making them cry out about injustice and inflaming hatred in them. But if you bring God to them, you lift them up, you raise them, you genuinely enrich them.

To Be Reconciled with the Principles of 1789

In politics, liberal Catholics see in the principles of 1789

---

1 The Mission of France was the "experiment" of the worker-priests in the 1950's.

Christian truths, doubtless a little bit dissolute; but, once purified, the modern ideals are on the whole assimilable by the Church: liberty, equality, fraternity, democracy (ideology), and pluralism. This is the error that Pius IX condemns in the *Syllabus*: "The Roman Pontiff can and should be reconciled and come to terms with progress, Liberalism, and modern civilization."[1]

The Catholic Liberal declares, "What do you want? One cannot indefinitely be against the ideas of his time, row without ceasing against the current, appear backward or reactionary." The antagonism between the Church and the secular liberal spirit, without God, is no longer desired. They want to reconcile what is irreconcilable, make peace between the Church and the Revolution, between Our Lord Jesus Christ and the Prince of this world. We cannot imagine an enterprise more blasphemous, and more dissolving of the Christian spirit, of the good fight for the faith, of the spirit of the crusade, that is to say, of the zeal to conquer the world for Jesus Christ.

From Faint-heartedness to Apostasy

In all this so-called Catholic Liberalism, there is a lack of faith, or more precisely a *lack of the spirit of faith*, which is a spirit of totality: to submit all to Jesus Christ, to restore all, "to sum up everything in Christ," as Saint Paul says (Eph. 1:20). They dare not to insist on the totality of the rights of the Church; they are resigned without a struggle; they accommodate themselves even quite well to laicism; they finally arrive at approving of it. Dom Delatte and Cardinal Billot well characterize this tendency to apostasy:

> A wide furrow henceforth divided [with Falloux and Montalembert on the liberal side of France in the nineteenth century] the Catholics into two groups: those who had as their first concern the Church's liberty of action and the upholding of its rights in a society still Christian; and those who firstly endeavored to determine the measure of Christianity that modern society could tolerate, in order then to invite the Church to reduce it-

---

1 Condemned proposition no. 80; Denz. 1780.

self to that.[1]

All of liberal Catholicism, says Cardinal Billot, is self-contained in a maintained ambiguity, "the confusion between tolerance and approval":

> The question between the Liberals and us is not to know whether, being given the malice of the world, it is necessary to *tolerate* with patience what is not in our power, and to work at the same time to avoid greater evils and to bring about all the good that remains possible; but the question is precisely whether it is fitting *to approve* [the new state of things], to celebrate the principles that are the foundation of this order of things, to *promote* them by word, by doctrine, by works, as the so-called liberal Catholics do.[2]

It is thus that a Montalembert with his slogan *"Free Church in a free State"*[3] will make himself the champion of the separation between Church and State, refusing to admit that this mutual liberty will lead inevitably to the situation of an enslaved Church in a despoiling State. It is thus as well that a de Broglie would write a liberal history of the Church in which the excesses of the Christian Cæsars prevail over the benefit of the Christian Constitutions. And thus also a Jacques Piou will make himself the herald of the rallying of French Catholics to the republic: not so much to the state of fact of the republican regime, as to the democratic and liberal ideology. Here is, quoted by Jacques Ploncard d'Assac,[4] the canticle of the *Popular Liberal Action* of Piou in the 1900s:

> We are for liberal action,
> We want to live in freedom
> Yes, or no, at will.
> Liberty is our glory.
> Let us cry out: "Long live Liberty!"
> We want to believe or not to believe.
>
> Let us acclaim liberal action,

---

1 *Life of Dom Guéranger*, Tome II, p. 11.
2 *Cardinal Billot, Light of Theology*, pp.58-59.
3 Speech at Malines, August 20, 1863.
4 *The Occupied Church*, D.P.F. 1975, p. 136.

Liberal, liberal,
That the law be equal for all,
Be equal.
Long live the liberal action of Piou.

The liberal Catholics of 1984 did no better when they struck up their canticle of the free school in the streets of Paris:
"Liberty, liberty, thou art the only truth!"
What a plague, these liberal Catholics! They put their faith into their pocket and adopt the maxims of the age. What incalculable harm they have caused the Church by their lack of faith and their apostasy.

I will conclude with a page from Dom Guéranger, full of that spirit of faith of which I have spoken to you:

Today more than ever society needs doctrines that are strong and consistent with one another. In the midst of the general dissolution of ideas, only an affirmation, a firm, well-founded, uncompromising affirmation, will be able to make itself accepted. Transactions become more and more fruitless, and each one of them carries away a shred of the truth. Show yourselves, therefore, to be such as you are in reality, convinced Catholics. *There is a grace attached to the full and entire confession of the faith.* This confession, the Apostle tells us, is the salvation of those who make it; and experience demonstrates that it is also the salvation of those who hear it.[1]

---

1 *The Christian Sense of History*, Nouvelle Aurore, Paris, 1977; pp. 31-32.

Chapter XVII

The Popes
and Liberal Catholicism

"Catholic Liberalism is a veritable plague."

Pius IX

Father Roussel collected in his book[1] a whole series of declarations from Pope Pius IX condemning the Catholic Liberals' attempt to blend the Church and the Revolution. Here are some of them, which it is good for us to ponder.

What afflicts your country and prevents it from meriting the blessings of God is the mixture of principles. I will say the word, and I will not keep it secret; what I fear is not all those wretches from the Paris Commune... What I fear is this unhappy politics, this Catholic Liberalism which is a veritable scourge... This seesaw game which would destroy Religion. Without doubt one must practice charity, do what is possible to bring back those who have lost their way; it is not, however, necessary for that to share their opinions...[2]

---

1 *Liberalism and Catholicism*, 1926.
2 To the pilgrims of Nevers, June, 1871.

*

Therefore, venerable Brother [the bishop of Quimper], notify the members of the Catholic Association that, on the numerous occasions when We have reproved the partisans of liberal opinions, We have not had in view those who hate the Church and whom it would be useless to name; but rather those whom We have just indicated, who, preserving and supporting the hidden virus of the liberal principles that they have absorbed with milk, under the pretext that it is not contaminated with an evident malice and is not, according to them, detrimental to Religion, easily infect the minds, and thus propagate the seeds of those revolutions from which the world has been shaking for a long time.[1]

*

Nevertheless, and although the children of the world are more clever than the children of light, their ruses [of the enemies of the Church] would doubtless have less success if a great number among those who carry the name of Catholic did not extend to them a friendly hand. Yes, alas! There are those who seem to want to walk in agreement with our enemies, and do their best to establish an alliance between the light and the darkness, an accord between justice and iniquity, by means of those doctrines that are called "liberal-Catholic," which, resting on the most pernicious principles, flatter the secular power when it invades spiritual things and impel minds to respect, or at least to tolerance, of the most iniquitous laws, absolutely as if it were not written that no one can serve two masters. Now these are assuredly more dangerous and more deadly than declared enemies. Both because they further their efforts without being noticed, perhaps without suspecting it; ...and because, living on the edge of formally condemned opinions, they give themselves a certain appearance of integrity and of irreproachable doctrine, thus alluring the imprudent lovers of conciliation and deceiving the honest people, who would revolt against a declared error. In this way they divide the minds, tear up unity, and weaken the forces

---

1 Brief to a Catholic Circle in Quimper, 1873.

that must be reunited in order to turn them all together against the enemy...[1]

We can do nothing but approve of your having undertaken to defend and to explain the decisions of our *Syllabus*, especially those which condemn the so-called Catholic Liberalism, which, counting a great number of adherents among upright men themselves, and seeming to deviate less from the truth, is more dangerous for the others; more easily deceives those who do not keep themselves on their guard; and, destroying the Catholic spirit imperceptibly and in a hidden manner, diminishes the forces of the Catholics and increases those of the enemy.[2]

*

Can Catholic Liberals dare, after such condemnations, to refuse the epithet of traitors, of turncoats, of dangerous enemies of the Church?

To finish with Catholic Liberalism considered in general, here is the judgement of an authorized witness: Emile Keller, French deputy in 1865, in his book *The Syllabus of Pius IX—Pius IX and the Principles of 1789*:

What is then this transaction which has been pursued for long years and which is formulated today in a manner more and more urgent? What place do they want to give to the Church in an edifice from which it was first to be excluded? Liberals and governors accept it willingly as an auxiliary. But their full independence, their sovereignty without limit, and their entire liberty of action are reserved outside it and its authority. They give up to it the realm of consciences, provided that on its side it leave politics to them and recognize the social efficacy of the modern ideas known by the name of principles of 1789. Captured by this seductive snare, many generous spirits do not understand that these principles, so moderate, can be rejected. Some go away from the Church, imagining, absurdly, that it really demands the sacrifice of progress and of liberty. Certain others, on the contrary, not daring to deny the virtue of the modern formulas, make laborious efforts to persuade the Church to accept, like

---

1 Brief to the Catholic Circle in Milan, 1873.
2 Brief to the editors of a Catholic newspaper in Rodez, December, 1876.

them, the reconciliation that is offered to it. By dint of good will, they believe it proven to them that, some nuances aside, the principles of 1789 are pure Christian principles, that it would be artful to take possession of them and to bring them gradually and smoothly to be recognized and blessed by the Holy See.[1]

That is it! That is exactly what took place at the time of Vatican II: the Liberals succeeded in having the principles of 1789 blessed by the Pope and by the Council. I will attempt to show this to you later.

---

1 Op. cit., p. 13.

Chapter XVIII

The Myth of Liberty by Itself:

From Lamennais to Sangnier

"They do not fear to make blasphemous reconciliations between the Gospel and the Revolution."

Saint Pius X

Catholic Liberalism, scarcely established, is going to rise up to the assault on the Church under the *flag of progress*. Let me call forth some names from this progressive Liberalism.

I

Lamennais (1782-1854)

Félicité de Lamennais, a priest who will be rebellious against the Church and unfaithful to his priesthood, founds his Liberalism on the myth of the *progress of humanity*, which is manifested by the growing aspirations of the peoples for liberty. This movement, he says, *"has its indestructible principle in the first and fundamental law by vir-*

tue of which humanity tends to disengage itself progressively from the ties of infancy, to the extent that, the intelligence being emancipated by Christianity's growing and developing itself, the peoples attain, so to speak, the age of man."[1] In the Middle Ages, humanity in its infancy needs the Church's guardianship; today, having become adults, the peoples should liberate themselves from that guardianship by separating the Church from the State. As for the Church, it must adapt itself to this new order of things which it has created itself: *"a new social order, founded on an immense development of freedom, which Catholicism has rendered necessary by developing itself in souls the true notion and the sentiment of the right."*[2] The prospectus drawn up to present the program of the newspaper *l'Avenir* presents the perfectly liberal outcome of Lamennais's theory:

> All the friends of religion must understand that it needs only one lone thing: liberty.

This was to want to reduce the Church to the common right of all religious associations or confessions before the law. Pope Gregory XVI could not fail to condemn this error, and he did so in the Encyclical *Mirari vos* of August 15, 1832, condemning:

> ... those who wish to separate the Church from the State and to break the mutual harmony of the empire and the priesthood. [For, he explains,] what is certain is that this harmony, which was always so favorable and so healthful for the interests of religion and for those of the civil authority, is dreaded by the partisans of an unbridled liberty.[3]

In it he condemns as well:

---

1 *Complete Works*, Tome X, pp. 317-318, quoted by DTC, Tome VIII, col. 2489.
2 *Right* .(in Latin) means here, and in many other places in this book, what one is entitled to. The Church has always taught justice (*iustitia*, from *ius*, in Latin, which is an outward movement of the soul "to give to others what we owe them" (St. Thomas). But preaching to respect the rights of our neighbor by giving them what we owe them is an attitude of mind very different from the modern liberal attitude of claiming from our neighbors what they owe us! The first attitude is giving of self, the second is self-centered. There is no need of virtue for the second one! The whole modern confusion about "social justice" is a confusion of these two attitudes. (Note of Editor of The Angelus Press.)
3 Cf. Denz. 1615.

This absurd maxim, or rather this delirium, that freedom of conscience must be assured and guaranteed to anyone, whoever he may be.[1]

And, to be sure, the Church could not put up with the revolutionary and liberal principle of freedom for all, of the same freedom recognized for all religious opinions without discrimination! As for the myth of the progressive emancipation of humanity, the Catholic faith gives this its true name: apostasy of the nations.

II

Marc Sangnier and "The Sillon"

Despite the condemnations of the Popes, progressive Liberalism continues its penetration into the Church. Father Emmanuel Barbier wrote a small book entitled *The Progress of Catholic Liberalism in France under the Pontificate of Pope Leo XIII.* (This work keeps all its value in spite of the prudential condemnation which affected it then.) He has a chapter that treats of *"progressive Catholicism,"* of which the author says this: "The expression 'progressive Catholicism' is that which Mr. Fogazzaro has an affection for in his novel *Il Santo* to indicate the ensemble of reforms that he asks of the Church in its doctrine, its interior life, and its discipline. There is almost an identity of leaning between the movement that we have studied in France and that of which Mr. Fogazzaro is right now the spokesman most listened to in Italy."

This is to tell you that Modernism and liberal Catholicism are closely related behaviors and have related tactics, if it is known that Fogazzaro exposed shamelessly the plan to penetrate the Church through Modernism.[2]

*

It was in 1894 that Marc Sangnier founded his magazine *Le Sillon*, which would become a youth movement dreaming of reconciling the Church with the prin-

---

1 PIN, 24; cf. Denz. 1613.
2 Cf. Ploncard d'Assac, *The Occupied Church*, ch. XV: *A Secret Society within the Church?*

ciples of 1789, socialism, and universal democracy on the
basis of the advances in human consciousness. The
penetration of his ideas in the seminaries and the more and
more indifferentist evolution of the movement impelled
Saint Pius X to write his Letter *Notre Charge Apostolique*, of
August 25, 1910, which condemns the dream of the reform
of society cherished by the leaders of the *Sillon*:

> It is their dream to change its natural and traditional
> bases and to promise a future city built on other prin-
> ciples, which they venture to proclaim as more produc-
> tive, more beneficial, than the principles on which repose
> the present Christian city...

> The *Sillon* has the noble concern for human dignity.
> But it understands this dignity in the manner of certain
> philosophers whom the Church is far from praising. The
> first ingredient in this dignity is liberty, understood in
> the sense that, except in matters of religion, every man is
> autonomous. From this fundamental principle, it draws
> the following conclusions: Today the people are in guar-
> dianship under an authority distinct from themselves,
> and they must free themselves from it: political emancipa-
> tion... A political and social organization founded on this
> double basis, liberty and equality, to which fraternity will
> soon come to join itself. That is what they call Democracy.

After having denounced, after Leo XIII, the false slogan
of liberty-equality, Saint Pius X makes out the sources of
the progressive Liberalism of the *Sillon*:

> Finally, at the basis of all the falsifications of the fun-
> damental social ideas, the *Sillon* sets out a false concept of
> human dignity. According to it, man will be truly man,
> worthy of the name, only on the day when he has ac-
> quired a conscience enlightened, strong, independent,
> autonomous, able to do without a master, obeying only
> itself, capable of assuming and carrying the most serious
> responsibilities without forfeit. These are the grand
> words with which the sentiment of human pride is ex-
> alted...

> Well! Mistrust towards the Church, their mother, is in-
> spired in your Catholic youth; they are taught that for
> nineteen centuries it has not yet succeeded in the world
> in establishing society on its true bases; that it has not
> understood the social ideas of authority and of liberty, of

equality, of brotherhood, and of human dignity... The breath of the Revolution has passed this way... We do not have to demonstrate that the advent of universal democracy is of no consequence to the action of the Church in the world...

Saint Pius X then denounces the indifferentism of the *Sillon*, which takes after that of Vatican II like a brother:[1]

> What must be thought of this respect for all the errors and of the strange invitation, made by a Catholic to all the dissidents, to strengthen their convictions by study and to make of them ever more abundant sources of new powers? What must be thought of an association in which all religions and even free thought[2] can be loudly manifested as they like?

And the holy Pope goes to the bottom of the thing:

> The Sillon... henceforth constitutes only a miserable tributary of the great organized movement of apostasy, in all the countries, for the establishment of a universal Church which will have neither dogmas, nor hierarchy, nor order for the mind, nor restraint for the passions... We know only too well the murky dens where these pernicious doctrines are worked out... The leaders of the Sillon have not been able to defend themselves from this: the exaltation of their sentiments... has carried them away towards a *new Gospel*..., their ideal being connected with that of the Revolution, they do not fear to make blasphemous reconciliations between the Gospel and the Revolution...

Finally the holy pontiff concludes by restoring the truth on the genuine social order:

> ...The Church, which has never betrayed the happiness of the peoples by dangerous alliances, does not have to escape the past... It is enough for it to recover, with the cooperation of the true workers of social restoration, the

---

1 Cf. *Dignitatis humanæ*, no. 4.
2 *Free thought* is only a ramification of Freemasonry.

organisms broken by the Revolution[1] and to adapt them, in the same Christian spirit which inspired them, to the new surroundings created by the *material evolution* of contemporary society:[2] for the *true friends of the people are neither revolutionaries nor innovators, but traditionalists.*

We can see thus in what energetic and precise terms Pope Saint Pius X condemns progressive Liberalism and defines the truly Catholic attitude. It is my greatest consolation to be able to testify for myself that I am faithful to the doctrine of this canonized Pope. The passages that I have quoted for you clarify in a unique way the conciliar doctrines in this matter, which I am soon going to dwell on.

---

1 Saint Pius X is indicating here the professional corporations, agents of social harmony, all of them opposed to the trade-unionism that is the agent of the class struggle.

2 Evolution concerns a material and technical progress, but man and society remain subject to the same laws. Vatican II, in *Gaudium et spes*, will ignore this distinction and will founder anew in the progressivism of the *Sillon*.

Chapter XIX

The Mirage of Pluralism:

From Jacques Maritain to Yves Congar

It is under the banner of progress that so-called Catholic Liberalism has arisen to the assault on the Church, just as I showed you in our previous topic. There was nothing lacking to it except to put on *the mantle of philosophy* in order to penetrate with all security the Church, which up to then had anathematized it! A few names too will illustrate this liberal penetration into the Church up to the eve of Vatican II.

Jacques Maritain (1882–1973)

One is not mistaken in calling Jacques Maritain the father of the religious liberty of Vatican II. For his part,

Paul VI had nourished himself with the political and social theses of the liberal Maritain since 1926; and he acknowledged him as his teacher. Saint Pius X assuredly had been better inspired in choosing as a teacher Cardinal Pie,[1] from whom he borrowed the central passage of his inaugural encyclical, *E supremi apostolatus* and his motto, "To restore all things in Christ."

Alas, Maritain's motto, which would become that of Paul VI, was rather, "To set up all things in man!" In recognition of his old master, on December 8, 1965, the day of the closing of the Council, Paul VI confided to him the text of one of the final *messages* of the Council to the world. Now, here is what one of those texts declared, the *message to the governors*, read by Cardinal Lienart:

> In your earthly and temporal city, he mysteriously builds his spiritual and eternal city, his Church. And what does it ask of you, this Church, after almost two thousand years of vicissitudes of all sorts in its relations with you, the powers of the earth; what does it ask of you today? It has told you, in one of the major texts of this Council: *It asks of you only liberty*. The liberty to believe and to preach its faith, the freedom to love its God and to serve him, the freedom to live and to bring to men its message of life. Do not fear it: it is in the image of its Master, whose mysterious action does not encroach on your prerogatives but heals everything human of its fatal decrepit state, transfigures it, fills it with hope, with truth, and with beauty.[2]

He thus canonizes the maritainian thesis of the *"vitally Christian society,"* according to which, in a progressive and necessary movement, the Church, renouncing the protection of the secular sword, emancipates itself from the bothersome guardianship of the Catholic heads of State,

---

1 A priest from the diocese of Poitiers and a religious, recounts Father Theotime de Saint Just, were received one day by Saint Pius X. "Oh! the diocese of Cardinal Pie!" the Pope said to them, raising his hands. "I have close by the works of your Cardinal, and now for many years I have read a few pages from them almost every day." Saying this, he took one of the volumes and put it into the hands of his visitors. From the thinness of the binding, they could confirm that it had to have belonged to the parish priest of Salzano or to the spiritual director of the seminary of Treviso a long time before getting into the Vatican.

2 Pontifical Documents of Paul VI, Ed, Saint Augustin, Saint-Maurice, 1965, p. 685.

and, contenting itself henceforth with liberty alone, reduces itself now to being no more than the evangelical yeast hidden in the dough or the sign of salvation for humanity. This "emancipation" of the Church is accompanied, Maritain acknowledges, by a reciprocal emancipation of the temporal from the spiritual, of civil society from the Church, by a laicization of public life, which, in certain respects, a "loss." But this loss is largely compensated for by the *progress* that liberty makes from it; and by the religious pluralism set up legally in civil society. Every spiritual family would enjoy its own juridical status and equitable liberty.[1] There is thus, throughout human history, a law that is revealed, a "*double law of the degradation and of the upsweeping of the energy of history*": the law of the emergence of the consciousness of the person and of liberty, and the correlative law of the degradation of the quantity of the temporal means put at the service of the Church and of its triumphalism:

> While the wearing away of time and the passivity of matter naturally dissipate and degrade the things of this world and the energy of history, the creative forces which are the property of the spirit and of liberty... increase more and more the quality of this energy. The life of human societies advances and progresses thus at the expense of many losses.[2]

You will recognize the famous "*creative energy*" of Bergson and the not less famous "*emergence of consciousness*" of Teilhard de Chardin. This whole beautiful world— Bergson, Teilhard, Maritain—has dominated and corrupted Catholic thought for decades.

But, you will object to Maritain, what becomes of the social kingship of Our Lord, in your "vitally Christian society," if the State no longer recognizes Jesus Christ and his Church? Listen closely to the philosopher's answer: Christianity (or the social kingship of Jesus Christ) is capable of several successive historical realizations, essentially diverse but analogically one; medieval Christianity of

---

1 Cf. *Integral Humanism*, ch. V, pp. 180-181.
2 *The Rights of Man and the Natural Law*, p. 34.

the "sacral" and "theocratic" type (what ambiguities in those terms!), characterized by the abundance of temporal means at the service of unity in the faith, must be succeeded today by a *"new Christianity"* characterized, as we have seen, by the reciprocal emancipation of the temporal and the spiritual, and by the religious and cultural pluralism of the city.

What skill, in the usage made of the philosophical theory of analogy, very simply to deny the social kingship of Our Lord Jesus Christ! Now, that Christianity can be realized in different manners in the monarchy of Saint Louis and in the republic of Garcia Moreno, that is obvious; but that the maritainian society, the pluralist "vitally Christian" city, will still be Christendom and realize the social kingship of Jesus Christ, this is what I deny absolutely: *Quanta cura, Immortale Dei,* and *Quas primas* assure me, on the contrary, that Jesus Christ does not have thirty-six ways of reigning over a society; he reigns by "informing," by modeling the civil laws according to his divine law. It is one thing to uphold a society in which there is in fact a *plurality* of religions, as in Lebanon for example, and to do what one can so that Jesus Christ will still be "the pole"; it is something else to advocate *pluralism* in a city that still has a large Catholic majority and to want—this is the last straw—to baptize this system with the name of Christianity. No! The "new Christianity" imagined by Jacques Maritain is only a dying Christianity which has apostasized and rejected its King.

*

Jacques Maritain, in actual fact, was dazzled by the civilization of the openly pluralist type in the United States, in the midst of which the Catholic Church, reveling in the system of mere liberty, saw a remarkable soaring in the number of its members and in its institutions. But is this a sufficient argument in favor of the principle of pluralism? Let us ask the Popes for the answer.

Leo XIII, in the Encyclical *Longinqua oceani,* of January 6, 1895, praises the progress of the Church in the United States. Here is his judgment on it. He writes to the

American bishops:

> With you, thanks to the good constitution of the State, the Church not being constricted by the ties of any law, being defended against violence by common law and the fairness of judgments, has obtained the guaranteed liberty to live and to act without obstacle. All these observations are true; however, we have to beware of an error: that one does not go on from there to conclude that the best situation for the Church is that which it has in America, or indeed that it is always permitted and useful to separate and to disunite the principles of civil affairs and those of sacred things as in America.
>
> Indeed, if the Catholic religion is honored among you, if it is thriving, if it is even growing, this has to be attributed entirely to the divine fruitfulness enjoyed by the Church, which, when no one is opposed to it, when nothing places an obstacle in its way, spreads out by itself and gains ground; yet *it would produce still many more fruits if it enjoyed, not only freedom, but the favor of the laws too and the protection of the public authorities.*[1]

More recently, Pius XII notes like Leo XIII that religious pluralism can be a sufficient favorable condition for the development of the Church; and he even emphasizes that there is in our time a tendency to pluralism:

> [The Church] knows also that for some time events have been developing rather in the other direction, that is to say, towards the multiplicity of religious confessions and of conceptions of life within the one same national community, where the Catholics constitute a more or less strong minority.
>
> It can be interesting and even surprising for History to encounter in the United States of America an example, among others, of the manner in which the Church succeeds in blooming out in the most dissimilar situations.[2]

But the great Pope indeed kept himself from concluding that it was necessary to put one's shoulder to the wheel in the direction of the "wind of History" and to promote from now on the principle of pluralism! On the contrary, he

---

1 *Apostolic Letters of Leo XIII*, Bonne Presse, Tome IV, pp. 162-165.
2 Discourse at the Tenth International Congress of Historical Sciences, September 7th, 1955. *Pontifical Documents of Pius XII, Tome XVII, p. 294.*

reaffirms the Catholic doctrine:

> The historian should not forget that, though the
> Church and the State knew hours and years of struggle,
> there were, from Constantine the Great down to the con-
> temporary and even recent era, tranquil periods, often
> prolonged, during which they collaborated with full un-
> derstanding in the education of the same persons. The
> Church does not hide that in principle it considers this
> collaboration as normal, and that it regards as an ideal the
> unity of the people in the true religion and the unanimity
> of action between itself and the State.[1]

Let us firmly hold on to this doctrine and beware the
mirage of pluralism. If the wind of History seems to be blow-
ing right now in this direction, it is assuredly not the
Breathing of the divine Spirit, but indeed rather, across two
centuries of the work of undermining Christianity, the gla-
cial wind of Liberalism and of the Revolution![2]

*

Yves Congar and Others

Father Congar is not one of my friends. A *periti* at the
Council, he was, with Karl Rahner, the principal author of
the errors that I have since not ceased combatting. He
wrote, among others, a little book entitled *Archbishop
Lefebvre and the Crisis in the Church.* Now you are going to
see Father Congar, following Maritain, initiate us into the
hidden things of the evolution of the historical context and
of the wind of History. He says:

> It cannot be denied that such a text [the conciliar dec-
> laration on religious liberty] says materially anything but
> what the *Syllabus* of 1864 said, and even practically the
> contrary of propositions 15, 77, and 79 of that document.
> The *Syllabus* also defended a temporal power which,
> taking note of a new situation, the papacy renounced in
> 1929. The historico-social context in which the Church is
> called to live and to speak was no longer the same, and
> we had learned of the results. Already in the nineteenth

---

1 Loc. cit.
2 Cf. *Archbishop Lefebvre and the Holy Office*, pp. 54-55.

century, "Catholics had understood that the Church
would find a better support for its liberty in the asserted
conviction of the faithful than in the favor of the princes."[1]

Unfortunately for Father Congar, these "Catholics" are
none other than the liberal Catholics condemned by the
Popes; and the teaching of the *Syllabus*, far from being de-
pendent on fleeting historical circumstances, constitutes a
mass of truths logically deduced from revelation and as *immutable* as the faith! But our adversary carries on and insists:

> The Church of Vatican II, by the declaration on
> religious liberty, by *Gaudium et spes*—The Church in the
> modern world: significant title!—has been clearly
> situated in the pluralist world of today, and without ab-
> juring the greatness it has had, has cut the chains that
> had kept it on the shores of the Middle Ages. One cannot
> remain fixed on one moment of history![2]

There it is! The sense of history pushes on to pluralism.
Let us allow the bark of Peter to go in that direction, and
let us abandon the social Kingship of Jesus Christ on the
remote shores of a past time. You will find these same theories in Father John Courtney Murray, S.J., another conciliar expert, who dares to write, with a pompous gravity
equalled only by its self-conceit, that the doctrine of Leo
XIII on the union between Church and State is strictly *relative* to the historical context in which it is expressed:

> Leo XIII was strongly influenced by the historical no-
> tion of personal political power exercised in a paternalis-
> tic fashion over society as over a large family.[3]

---

1 Op. cit., pp. 51-52.
2 Loc. cit.
3 *Towards an Understanding of the Development of the Church's Doctrine on Religious
Liberty*, in *Vatican II, Religious Liberty*, p. 128.

And so, the trick is played: the monarchy has been succeeded everywhere by the regime of *"the democratic and social constitutional State,"* which, as our theologian assures
us, and Bishop De Smedt will repeat at the Council, *"is not a
competent authority to be able to pass a judgement of truth or of
falsity in religious matters."*[1] Let us allow Father Murray to
proceed:

> His proper work is marked by a strong *historical con-
> sciousness.* He knew the times in which he was living, and
> wrote for them with an admirable *historical and concrete
> realism...*[2] For Leo XIII, the structure known by the name
> of Catholic confessional State... was never more than a
> *hypothesis.*[3]

What ruinous doctrinal relativism! With such principles, all truth can be relativized by making an appeal to
the historical consciousness of a transient moment! Was
Pius XI, writing *Quas primas*, a prisoner of historical points
of view? And Saint Paul as well, when he affirms of Jesus
Christ: "He must reign"? (I Cor.15: 25.)

*

I think that you have grasped, with Maritain, Yves
Congar, and associates, the perversity of historical
doctrinal relativism. We are dealing with people who have
no idea of the truth, no concept of what can be an immutable truth. It is laughable to report that these same
liberal relativists, who were the real authors of Vatican II,
are coming now to dogmatize that Council that they
however declared to be pastoral, and to want to impose the
conciliar novelties onto us as definitive and untouchable
doctrines! And they get angry if I dare say to them: "Oh,
you say that *Quas primas*, the Pope would no longer write

---

1 *Relatio de reemendatione schematis emendati,* May 28, 1965, document 4SC, pp. 48-49. A
   more cynical declaration of the official atheism of the State and of the denial of the
   social Kingship of Jesus Christ cannot be imagined, and this from the lips of an
   official reporter from the editing commission on the conciliar declaration on
   religious liberty!
2 One would think that he was reading Jacques Maritain: his "sundry historical
   heavens" and his "concrete historic ideal" (cf. *Integral Humanism,* pp. 152-153) make
   us wonder which has influenced the other!
3 Op. cit., p. 134.

that today! Well, I say to you: It is your council that would no longer be written today; it is already overtaken. You cling to it because it is your work; but I hold on to Tradition, because it is the work of the Holy Ghost!"

Chapter XX

The Direction of History

I have tried to show you in the preceding chapters how the liberal Catholics such as Lamennais, Maritain, and Yves Congar have a not very Catholic view of the *sense of history*. Let us try to go deeply into their point of view and to judge it by the light of faith.

Sense or Nonsense?

For the Catholics called liberal, history has a *sense*, that is to say, a direction. This direction is immanent, it is from here below, it is liberty. Humanity is urged on by an immanent breathing in the direction of a growing consciousness of the dignity of the human person, setting out in the direction of an always more extensive freedom from all constraint. Vatican II will become the echo of this theory by saying, following Maritain:

> The dignity of the human person is, in our time, the object of an ever more live consciousness; always more numerous are those who claim for man the possibility of acting by virtue of his own options and with all free responsibility.[1]

---

1 Declaration on Religious Liberty, preamble.

That it is desirable that man determine his own way freely towards the good, no one will dispute; but that our age, and that the direction of History in general, are marked by a growing consciousness of human dignity and freedom, that is what is very questionable! Only Jesus Christ, by conferring onto the baptized the dignity of children of God, shows men in what consists their true dignity, the *freedom of the children of God* of which Saint Paul speaks.[1] To the extent that the nations have submitted themselves to Our Lord Jesus Christ, human dignity and a healthy freedom indeed have been seen to develop. But since the apostasy of the nations set up by Liberalism, we have no alternative but to report on the contrary that, Jesus Christ no longer reigning, "the truths diminishing among the sons of men,"[2] human dignity is more and more despised and crushed and liberty reduced to a slogan empty of content.

Has there ever been seen, in any era of history, so colossal and radical an enterprise of slavery as the Communist technique of the slavery of the masses?[3] If Our Lord invites us to "discern the signs of the times,"[4] then all the voluntary blindness of the Liberals and an absolute order of silence has been required in order that an ecumenical council, called together precisely to discern the signs of our time,[5] *fall silent* on the most manifest sign of the times, which is Communism! This silence suffices by itself to cover this Council with shame and with reprobation in the eyes of all History, and to show the ridiculousness of the allegation from the preamble of *Dignitatis humanæ* that I have quoted to you.

Therefore, if History has a *direction*, it is to be sure not the immanent and necessary pushing of humanity towards dignity and liberty, which the Liberals invent *"ad excusan-*

1 Romans 8:21.
2 Ps. 11:2
3 Read Jean Madiran, *The Old Age of the World*, DMM, Jarze, 1975.
4 Mt. 16:4.
5 Cf. Vatican II, *Gaudium et Spes*, n.4, #1, 11 #1.

das excusationes suas,"[1]

Jesus Christ, Center of History

Then, what is the true *direction* of history? Is there even a direction to history?

History is all ordered to a person, who is the *center* of history, and who is Our Lord Jesus Christ, because, as Saint Paul reveals it:

In Him all things have been established in heaven and on earth, things visible and invisible, the thrones, the dominions, the principalities, the powers, all has been created by Him and in Him, and He Himself is before all, and all things have in Him their consistency. He is the head of the body which is the Church, He who is the principle... in order that in all things he hold the first place. For God has willed that all the fullness abide in Him; He has willed to reconcile through Him all things with Himself, those which are on the earth and those which are in the heavens, by making peace by the blood of His cross."[2]

Jesus Christ is therefore the pole of History. History has only one sole law: *"He must reign;"*[3] if He reigns, true progress and prosperity also reign, which are goods more spiritual than material! If He does not reign, it is decadence, decay, slavery in all its forms, the reign of the Evil One. This is what Holy Scripture promises besides: *"The nation and the kingdom that will not serve Thee shall perish, those nations will be entirely destroyed."*[4] Books have been written that are otherwise excellent on the philosophy of history, but I admit to you my surprise and my impatience in reporting that this absolute capital principle is omitted in these or not put into the place it deserves. Now it is *the* principle of the philosophy of History; and, what is more, it is a truth of faith, a veritable dogma revealed and a hundred times verified by the facts!

---

1 Ps. 140, v. 4: " incline not my heart to evil words; to make excuses in sins." excuse their Liberalism, to cover with the specious mask of progress the biting north wind that Liberalism has made to blow for two centuries over Christianity.
2 Col. 1:17-21.
3 I Cor. 15:25.
4 Isaias 60:12.

This is then the response to the question posed: what is the direction of History? Well, history has no direction, no *immanent* direction. There is no direction to history, there is a *goal* of history, a transcendant *goal;* it is the *"recapitulation of all things in Christ,"* it is the submission of the whole temporal order to His redemptive work, it is the mastery of the Church militant over the temporal city, which prepares the eternal reign of the Church triumphant in heaven. Therefore, faith affirms to us, and the facts show it, History has one first pole: the Incarnation, the Cross, Pentecost; it has had its full blossoming in the Catholic city, whether this is the empire of Charlemagne, or the republic of Garcia Moreno. And it will have its appointed time, it will attain its final pole, when the number of the elect is complete, after the time of the great *apostasy* (II Thess. 2:3); are we not living this now?

A Liberal Objection against the Catholic City

You have indeed understood, I think, from what I have said, that in History there is no immanent law of the progress of human liberty, or any immanent law of the emancipation of the temporal city in regard to Our Lord Jesus Christ.

But, the Liberals say, like Prince Albert of Broglie in his book *The Church and the Roman Empire in the Fourth Century*, the government that you advocate, with the union between Church and State, which was that of the Christian Cæsars, Romans or Germans, has always led to the subjection of the Church by the Empire, to a bothersome dependence of the spiritual power vis-à-vis the temporal sword. The alliance of the throne and the altar has never been, says the author, "either durable, or sincere, or effective."[1] The freedom and mutual independence of the two powers therefore is of no value.

I leave to Cardinal Pie the care of responding to these liberal accusations; he does not hesitate to qualify these foolhardy affirmations as "revolutionary banalities":

> If several princes, still neophytes and too little disac-

---

1 Op. cit., Tome IV, p. 424, quoted by Father Théotime de Saint Just, p. 55.

customed to the absolutist aspects of pagan Cæsarism, have changed their legitimate protection since the beginning into oppression; if they have (ordinarily in the interest of heresy and at the request of heretical bishops) proceeded with a rigor that is not according to the spirit of Christianity, there have been found in the Church men of faith and men of courage, such as our Hilarys and our Martins, such as the Athanasiuses and the Ambroses, to call them back to the spirit of Christian gentleness, to repudiate the apostolate of the sword, to declare that religious conviction is never imposed by violence, finally to proclaim eloquently that the Christianity that had propagated itself in spite of the persecution of the princes could still do without their favor and did not have to give itself in vassalage to any tyranny. We know and we have weighed each one of the words of these noble athletes of the faith and of the freedom of the Church their mother. But, while protesting against the excesses and the abuses, while reprimanding the reversions that are ill-timed and unintelligent, sometimes even challenging to the principle and to the rules of priestly immunity, never has any of these Catholic doctors doubted that it was the duty of the nations and of their heads to make a public profession of Christian truth; to conform to this their acts and their institutions; and even to forbid by laws, whether preventive or repressive, according to the dispositions of the times and the minds, the injuries that assumed a character of obvious impiety and brought trouble and disorder to the bosom of civil and religious society.[1]

That the system of "liberty alone" means progress over the realm of the union between the two powers is an error that I have already underscored and that this text of Cardinal Pie well illustrates. The Church has never taught that the direction of History and progress consisted in the ineluctable tendency to reciprocal emancipation of the temporal in relation to the spiritual. The sense of History of the Jacques Maritains and the Yves Congars is only a misinterpretation. This emancipation that they describe as progress is only, in point of fact, a ruinous and blasphemous divorce between the city and Jesus Christ. And all the impudence of *Dignitatis humanæ* was needed to

---

1 Third synodal instruction on the principal errors of the present time, *Works* V, 178.

canonize this divorce, and this—the supreme imposture—
in the name of revealed truth!

"Our society," declared John Paul II, on the occasion of
the conclusion of the new concordat between the Church
and Italy, *"our society is characterized by religious pluralism";*
and he drew the consequence from this: the separation of
Church and State is postulated by this evolution. But at no
time has John Paul II passed judgement on this change,
either in order to deplore the laicization of society, or to say
simply that the Church was resigning itself to a situation of
fact. No! His declaration, like that of Cardinal Casaroli, was
made by praising the separation of Church and State as
being the ideal system, the outcome of a normal and
providential historical process in which there is nothing to
criticize! In other words: "Long live the apostasy of the nations—in this is progress!" Or again: "We must not be pes-
simists! Down with the prophets of misfortune! Jesus
Christ no longer reigns? What is the difference? All is
going well! The Church is, in any case, on the march
towards the accomplishment of its history. And then, after
all, Christ is coming, alleluia!" This smug optimism amidst
so many ruins already piled up, this peculiarly half-witted
eschatologism, are they not the fruits of the Spirit of error
and of aberration? All that seems to me absolutely diabolical.

Part III

The Liberal Conspiracy of Satan Against the Church and the Papacy

Chapter XXI

The Conspiracy of the Alta Vendita of the Carbonari

So now we have arrived, in our brief historical outline of Catholic Liberalism, at the eve of Vatican II. But before analyzing the victory won at the Council by Liberalism, I would like to go back a little to show you how the penetration of Liberalism into all the hierarchy and even into the papacy itself, unthinkable two centuries ago, was nonetheless conceived, foretold, and organized as early as the beginning of the last century by Freemasonry. It will be sufficient to produce the documents that prove the existence of this plot against the Church, of this *"supreme attempt"* against the papacy.

*

The secret papers of the *Alta Vendita* of the Carbonari that fell into the hands of Pope Gregory XVI embrace a period that goes from 1820 to 1846. They were published at the request of Pope Pius IX by Cretineau-Joly in his work *The Roman Church and Revolution.*[1] And with the brief of approbation of February 25, 1861, which he addressed to the author, Pius IX guaranteed the authenticity of these documents; but he did not allow anyone to divulge the true names of the members of the *Alta Vendita* implicated in this correspondence. These letters are absolutely bewildering; and, if the Popes have asked that they be published, it is so that the faithful will know the conspiracy hatched against the Church by the secret societies, that they will know its plan and be guarded against its possible fulfillment. I will say no more about this now; but you will tremble as you read these lines. I am not inventing anything; I am only reading, without making any secret that they are taking place today! Without hiding the fact that the most audacious of their projects are even surpassed by the present-day reality! So let us read! I will emphasize only what should strike us the most.

*

The Pope, whoever he is, will never come to the secret societies: it is up to the secret societies to take the first step towards the Church, with the aim of conquering both of them.

The task that we are going to undertake is not the work of a day, or of a month, or of a year; it may last several years, perhaps a century; but in our ranks the soldier dies and the struggle goes on.

We do not intend to win the Popes to our cause, to make of them neophytes of our principles, propagators of our ideas. That would be a ridiculous dream; and if events turn out in some way, if Cardinals or prelates, for example, of their own free will or by surprise, should enter into a part of our secrets, this is not at all an incentive for desiring their elevation to the see of Peter. That elevation would ruin us. Ambition alone would have led them to apostasy; the requirements of power would force

---

1 2nd volume, original edition, 1859; reprinted by Circle of the French Renaissance, Paris, 1976; Mgr. Delassus produced these documents again in his work *The Anti-Christian Conspiracy*, DDB, 1910, Tome III, pp. 1035-1092.

them to sacrifice us. What we must ask for, what we should look for and wait for, as the Jews wait for the Messiah, is *a Pope according to our needs...*

With that we shall march more securely towards the assault on the Church than with the pamphlets of our brethren in France and even the gold of England. Do you want to know the reason for this? It is that with this, in order to shatter the high rock on which God has built his Church, we no longer need Hannibalian vinegar, or need gunpowder, or even need our arms. We have the little finger of the successor of Peter engaged in the plot; and this little finger is as good, for this crusade, as all the Urban IIs and all the Saint Bernards in Christendom.

We have no doubt that we will arrive at this supreme end of our efforts. But when? But how? The unknown is not yet revealed. Nevertheless, as nothing should turn us aside from the plan drawn up, and on the contrary everything should tend to this, as if as early as tomorrow success were going to crown the work that is barely sketched, we wish, in this instruction, which will remain secret for the mere initiates, to give to the officials in charge of the supreme Vente some advice that they should instill in all the brethren, in the form of instruction or of a memorandum...

Now then, to assure ourselves a Pope of the required dimensions, it is a question first of *shaping for him, for this Pope, a generation worthy of the reign we are dreaming of.* Leave old people and those of a mature age aside; go to the youth, and, if it is possible, even to the children... You will contrive for yourselves, at little cost, a reputation as good Catholics and as pure patriots.

This reputation will put access to our doctrines into the midst of the young clergy, as well as deeply into the monasteries. In a few years, by the force of things, this young clergy will have overrun all the functions; they will govern, they will administer, they will judge, they will form the sovereign's council, they will be called to choose the Pontiff who should reign. *And this Pontiff, like most of his contemporaries, will be necessarily more or less imbued with the* Italian and *humanitarian principles* that we are going to begin to put into circulation. It is a small grain of black mustard that we are entrusting to the ground; but the sunshine of justice will develop it up to the highest power, and you will see one day what a rich harvest this small seed will produce.

In the path that we are laying out for our brethren, there are found great obstacles to conquer, difficulties of more than one kind to master. They will triumph over them by experience and by clearsightedness; but the goal is so splendid that it is important to put all the sails to the wind in order to reach it. You want to revolutionize Italy, look for the Pope whose portrait we have just drawn. You wish to establish the reign of the chosen ones on the throne of the prostitute of Babylon, *let the Clergy march under your standard, always believing that they are marching under the banner of the apostolic Keys.* You intend to make the last vestige of the tyrants and the oppressors disappear; lay your snares like Simon Bar-Jona; lay them in the sacristies, the seminaries, and the monasteries rather than at the bottom of the sea: and if you do not hurry, we promise you a catch more miraculous than his. The fisher of fish became the fisher of men; you will bring friends around the apostolic Chair. You will have preached *a revolution in tiara and in cope, marching with the cross and the banner,* a revolution that will need to be only a little bit urged on to set fire to the four corners of the world.[1]

Here is another excerpt from a letter of "Nubius" to "Volpe," of April 3, 1824:

Our shoulders have been laden with a heavy burden, dear Volpe. We have to bring about the immoral education of the Church, and arrive, by small, well graded, although rather poorly defined, means, at the *triumph of the revolutionary idea by a Pope.* In this scheme, which has always seemed to me to be of a superhuman reckoning, we are still groping our way as we walk...[2]

"Superhuman reckoning," says Nubius; he means a diabolical reckoning! For this is to calculate the subversion of the Church by its head himself, which Mgr. Delassus[3] calls *the supreme attempt,* because nothing more subversive for the Church can be imagined than a Pope won over to the liberal ideas, than a Pope using the power of the keys

1 Permanent instruction of 1820, op. cit., pp. 82-90.
2 Op. cit., p. 129.
3 *The Problem of the Present Hour,* DDB., 1904, Tome I, p. 195.

of Saint Peter in the service of the counter-Church! Now, is this not what we are living right now, since Vatican II, since the new Canon Law? With this false ecumenism and this false religious liberty promulgated at Vatican II and applied by the Popes with a cold perseverance in spite of all the ruins that these have been producing for more than twenty years!

Without the infallibility of the magisterium of the Church's having been involved, perhaps even without any heresies properly so called having been maintained, we are seeing the systematic *autodemolition* of the Church. "Autodemolition" is a word of Paul VI, who implicitly exposed the true culprit: for who can "autodemolish" the Church, if not he who has the mission of maintaining it on the rock? And what acid is there more effective for dissolving this rock, than the liberal spirit penetrating the successor of Peter himself!

This plan is of a diabolical inspiration and a diabolical fulfillment! But it is not only the enemies of the Church who have revealed it. It is also the Popes who have very explicitly unmasked it and foretold it. This is what we shall see in a later chapter.

Chapter XXII

The Popes Unmask the Conspiracy of the Sect

The conspiracy of the liberal sect against the Church consisted, as I have shown you in the preceding chapter, in rising up to the assault on the Church by using its hierarchy, in perverting it up to the highest degree.

But the Popes, with the clear vision of their responsibility and the enlightenment with which God was able to endow them, clearly saw and denounced this program.

Leo XIII (1878-1903) saw this *subversio capitis* in advance, this subversion of the head; and he described it in black and white, in all its crudity, by composing the **small exorcism** against Satan and the fallen angels. Here is the passage in question, which figures in the original version but was suppressed in the subsequent versions by I do not know which successor of Leo XIII, who perhaps found this text impracticable, unthinkable, unpronounceable. And yet, a hundred years from its composition, this text seems to us now on the contrary to be of a burning truthfulness:

> Behold, very cunning enemies have filled the Church, Spouse of the immaculate Lamb, with bitterness; have watered it with absinthe; they have cast ungodly hands

onto all that is desirable in it. Where the See of the
blessed Peter and the Chair of Truth were established like
a light for the nations, there they have set the throne of
abomination of their impiety; in order that, once the
shepherd is struck down, they may be able to disperse the
flock.

How is this possible? you will say. I do not know at all,
I admit it; but there it is, more and more, day after day. It
causes us a keen anxiety, poses a painful question: which
Popes therefore are the ones who allow the autodemolition? Who puts their hands into it? Saint Paul was
already saying for his time, "The mystery of iniquity is already at work."[1] What would he say now?

*

Next it is Saint Pius X's (1903-1914) turn to tell the anguish that binds him in the face of the progress brought
about by the sect even in the interior of the Church. In his
inaugural encyclical *E supremi apostolatus*, of October 4,
1903, he expresses his fear that the time of apostasy that
the Church was entering may be the time of the Anti-
Christ—this must be understood as *Anti-Christ*, counterfeit
of Christ, usurper of Christ. Here is the text:

We experienced a sort of terror in considering the
deadly conditions of humanity at the present hour. Can
anyone not be aware of the sickness so deep and so
serious which, at this moment much more than in the
past, torments human society and which, growing worse
from day to day and eating away at it right down to the
core, is carrying it away to its ruin? Venerable Brethren,
you know this illness; in regard to God, it is surrender
and apostasy. And, beyond any doubt, there is nothing
which leads more surely to ruin, according to this word
of the prophet: *Behold, those who go away from Thee shall
perish.*[2]

And the holy Pontiff continues further:

---

1 II Thessalonians 2:7.
2 Psalm 72:27.

In our time, it is only too true that the nations have trembled and the peoples have contemplated insane projects against[1] their Creator. And this cry of his enemies has become all but common: Withdraw from us.[2] From this come the habits of life, as much private as public, where no account is taken of his sovereignty. Much more, there is no effort or artifice that is not put to work in order entirely to abolish the memory and even the idea of Him.

He who thinks these things over has the right to fear that such a perversion of minds is the beginning of the evils announced for the end of time, and perhaps their establishing of contact with the earth, and that truly *the son of perdition* of whom the Apostle speaks[3] may have already made his arrival in our midst. So great is the boldness and so great is the frenzy with which they throw themselves everywhere into the attack on religion, they batter the dogmas of the faith, they strain with an obstinate exertion to annihilate every relation of man with the Divinity! In return—and there you have, in the words of the same Apostle, the proper nature of the Antichrist—man, with a temerity beyond words, has usurped the place of the Creator by raising himself up *above everything that bears the name of God.* It is to such a point that, powerless to extinguish the notion of God completely in himself, he nevertheless shakes off the yoke of his majesty and dedicates to himself the visible world as a kind of temple, where he pretends to receive the adorations of his fellow creatures. *He sits in the temple of God, where he shows himself as if he were God himself.*[4]

Then Saint Pius X concludes by recalling that God triumphs in the end over his enemies, but that this certitude of faith "does not excuse us, insofar as it depends on us, from hastening the divine work," that is to say, the triumph of Christ the King.

Saint Pius X again, in his encyclical *Pascendi*, of September 8, 1907, on the Modernist errors, denounces with clear-

---

1 Psalm 2:1.
2 Job 21:14.
3 II Thess. 2:3.
4 II Thess. 2:2.

sightedness the infiltration of the Church by the Modernist sect, an infiltration already in progress, which was, as I have told you,[1] the ally of the liberal sect in the plan to demolish the Catholic Church. Here are the passages of this document most salient to my purpose:

What particularly requires Us to speak without delay is that the agents of error are not to be sought for today among our declared enemies. They are hiding—and it is a cause for very sharp apprehension and anguish—in the very midst and in the heart of the Church, enemies so much the more fearsome as they are less openly enemies. We are speaking, Venerable Brethren, of a great number of lay Catholics and, what is still more to be deplored, of priests, who, under pretense of love for the Church, absolutely short on solid philosophy and theology, impregnated on the contrary right down to the marrow with a venom of error derived from the adversaries of the Catholic faith, set themselves up, with contempt for all modesty, as renovators of the Church. In closed phalanxes, with audacity, they begin the assault on everything that there is of the most sacred in the work of Jesus Christ, without respecting His very person, which they reduce, with a sacrilegious temerity, even to a pure and simple humanity.

Those men may be astonished that We rank them among the enemies of the Church. No one will have just reason to be surprised at this who, putting aside their intentions, of which the judgement is reserved to God, will indeed attempt to examine their doctrines, and their system of word and action. Enemies of the Church, to be sure they are this; and to say that it does not have any worse ones is not to stray from the truth. It is not from outside, indeed, as has been already noted, it is from within that they contrive its ruin. The danger lies today almost in the very veins and bowels of the Church: their blows are so much more certain as they know the Church more intimately. Add to this that it is not to the branches or to the shoots that they have put the axe, but to the very root, that is to say, to the faith and to its deepest fibers. Then, once this root of immortal life is severed,

---

1 It is under the flag of progress, of evolution, that the Liberals have risen to the assault on the Church. Cf. Chapter XVIII.

they set themselves the task of making the virus circulate throughout the tree, in such a way that no part of the Catholic faith remains protected from their hand, and that there is no part that they do not strive with great care to corrupt.[1]

Saint Pius X next unveils the tactics of the Modernists:

And while they are pursuing their pernicious scheme by a thousand paths, nothing is so insidious or so false as their tactics: blending in themselves the rationalist and the Catholic, they do it with such a refinement of cunning that they easily deceive minds that are not well informed. Consumed moreover with audacity, they are not put back by any kind of consequences, but rather endure them boldly and obstinately. Along with this, something very fitting for bringing in changes, a whole life of activity, a singular diligence and ardor in all kinds of study, morals usually commendable for their severity.... You are not unaware, Venerable Brethren, of the sterility of Our efforts; one moment they bow their heads, just to lift them again immediately even more prideful....[2]

And in the way of a tactic of the Modernists (thus they are called commonly and with good reason), a really very insidious tactic, they never expose their doctrines methodically and in their entirety; but they break them up as it were and disperse them here and there, a fact which leads to their being judged as changeable and undecided, when their ideas, on the contrary, are perfectly settled and consistent. It is important here, and above all, to present these same doctrines from one single viewpoint, and to show the logical connection that binds them to one another.[3]

To stay inside the Church in order to make it evolve—such is the keynote of the Modernists' policy:

They follow their path; reprimanded and censured, they go forward, always covering up, under the false-tongued exterior of compliance, a boldness without limit. They hypocritically bow their heads, while, with all their thoughts, with all their energy, more boldly than ever before, they pursue the plan laid out.

---

1 *Pascendi*, nn. 2-3.
2 Ibid., n. 3.
3 Ibid., n. 4.

This is their intention and their tactics: both because they hold that authority must be stirred up, not destroyed, and because it is important for them to remain in the midst of the Church in order to be at work there and alter the common consciousness little by little: acknowledging thus, but without being aware of it, that the common consciousness is therefore not with them, and that it is against every right of which they claim to be the interpreters.[1]

*

Pascendi stopped the audacity of the Modernists for a time, but before long the methodical and progressive occupation of the Church and of the hierarchy by the Modernist and liberal sect took root again more than ever before. The liberal theological intelligentsia would before long hold the higher places in the specialized reviews, the congresses, the great printing houses, the centers of pastoral liturgy, perverting the Catholic hierarchy from top to bottom, scorning the latest condemnations of Pope Pius XII in *Humani Generis*. The Church and the papacy would soon be ripe for the *"Etats Généraux,"*[2] for a liberal surprise attack such as took place in 1789 in France, on the occasion of an ecumenical council, foretold and awaited for a long time by the sect, as we shall see in the following chapter.

---

1 Ibid., n. 37.
2 This assembly marked the beginning of the French Revolution.

Chapter XXIII

The Subversion of the Church brought about by a Council

The details of the enterprise of subverting the Church and the papacy planned by the Masonic sect were seen more than a century ago by a great *illuminé*, Canon Roca. Bishop Rudolf Graber in his book *Athanasius* quotes the works of this Roca (1830-1893), a priest in 1858, honorary Canon in 1869. Excommunicated afterwards, he preached revolution and announced the coming of the synarchy. In his writings he often speaks of a *"newly illuminated Church,"* which would be, he declares, influenced by the socialism of Jesus and of His Apostles. He predicts, "The new Church, which will probably no longer be able to keep anything of the teaching and of the primitive form of the ancient Church, will nonetheless receive the blessing and the canonical jurisdiction from Rome." Roca also proclaims the liturgical reform: "Divine worship such as the liturgy, the ceremonial, the ritual, such as the prescriptions of the Roman Church regulate them, will undergo a transformation *following an ecumenical council*... which will give it back the respectable simplicity of the apostolic golden age, in accordance with the new conditions of consciousness and of modern civilization."

Roca specifies the fruits of this council: "One thing will stand out which will astound the world and which will throw the world onto its knees before its Redeemer. This thing will be the demonstration of the perfect accord between the ideals of modern civilization and the ideals of Christ and his Gospel. This will be the consecration of the New Social Order and the solemn baptism of modern civilization."

In other words, all the *values* of the so-called *liberal culture* will be recognized and canonized following the council in question.

Then you have what Roca writes about the Pope: "A sacrifice is being prepared, which will introduce a solemn penance.... The papacy will fall; it will die under the sacred knife that *the Fathers of the last council* will forge. The pontifical Cæsar is the consummated host for the sacrifice." (It must be admitted that all that is in a fair way to happen as Roca says, unless Our Lord prevents it!) Roca finally designates the new priests who will appear, with the name of "progressives"; he speaks of the suppression of the cassock, of the marriage of priests... so many prophecies!

Observe how Roca indeed saw the determining role of a final ecumenical council in the subversion of the Church!

*

But it is not only the enemies of the Church who have put their finger on the confusion that an ecumenical council would bring which met at a time when the liberal ideas had already well penetrated the Church.

At the secret consistory of May 23, 1923, relates Father Dulac,[1] Pius XI questioned the Cardinals of the Curia on the timeliness of summoning an ecumenical council. There were about thirty there: Merry del Val, De Lai, Gasparri, Boggiani, Billot. Billot was saying, "The existence of

---

1 Raymond Dulac, *Episcopal Collegiality at the Second Council of the Vatican*, Paris, Cèdre, 1979, pp. 9-10.

profound differences in the midst of the episcopacy itself cannot be concealed.... [They] run the risk of giving place to discussions that will be prolonged indefinitely." Boggiani recalled the Modernist theories, from which, he said, a part of the clergy and of the bishops are not exempt. "This mentality can incline certain Fathers to present motions, to introduce methods incompatible with Catholic traditions."

Billot is still more precise. He expresses his fear of seeing the council "maneuvered" by "the worst enemies of the Church, the Modernists, who are already getting ready, as certain indications show, to bring forth *the revolution* in the Church, *a new 1789.*"

When John XXIII revived the idea, already cherished before him by Pius XI,[1] to summon an ecumenical council, Father Caprile relates,[2] "He read the documents in the course of some walks in the Vatican gardens...." That is all. But his decision was made. On several occasions he affirmed that he had made it under a sudden inspiration of the Holy Ghost:[3]

> Obeying an *interior voice* that we consider as having come directly from *a higher impulse*, We have judged the moment to be opportune to offer to the Catholic Church and to all the human family a new ecumenical council.[4]

This "inspiration from the Most High," this "divine solicitation," as he still called it, he received on January 25, 1959, while he was preparing to celebrate a ceremony at Saint Paul's Outside the Walls in Rome; and he unburdened himself about it immediately after the ceremony to the eighteen Cardinals present. But was this inspiration truly divine? That seems doubtful; its origin seems to me something else altogether.

---

1 Op. cit., p. 10; Brother Michael of the Holy Trinity, *The Whole Truth on Fatima, the Third Secret*, pp. 182-199.
2 In his history of Vatican II; cf. Dulac, op. cit., p. 11.
3 Cf. *John XXIII and Vatican II Under the Fires of the Luciferian Pentecost*, in *The Social Reign of Mary*, Fatima, January-February 1985, pp. 2-3.
4 Bull *Humanæ salutis*.

In any case, a consideration of an old friend of Cardinal Roncalli, the future John XXIII, is enlightening on this subject. At the news of the death of Pius XII, the old Dom Lambert Beauduin, a friend of Roncalli's, confided to Father Bouyer: "If they elect Roncalli, everything would be saved; he would be capable of calling a council and of consecrating ecumenism."[1] As Father Bonneterre shows, Dom Lambert Beauduin knew Cardinal Roncalli well; he *knew* from 1958 that Roncalli, once having become Pope, would bring ecumenism to reality—and do this, if at all possible, by means of a council. Now he who speaks of ecumenism speaks of religious liberty and Liberalism. The "revolution in tiara and cope" was not an improvisation. I will attempt in the next conference to let you relive the unfolding of this at the time of the Second Vatican Council.

---

1 L. Bouyer, *Dom Lambert Beauduin, a Man of the Church*, Casterman, 1964, pp. 180-181, quoted by Father Didier Bonneterre in *The Liturgical Movement*, Ed. Fideliter, 1980, p. 119.

Part IV

A Revolution
in Tiara And Cope

Chapter XXIV

The Robber Council of Vatican II

It is advantageous to find a precedent to the Second Vatican Council, at least in regard to the methods that were used in it by the active liberal minority which quickly became the majority. In this respect the general Council of Ephesus (449) is to be mentioned, under the title that Pope Saint Leo I afterwards gave it: the *"robber council of Ephesus."* It was presided over by an ambitious and unscrupulous bishop : *Dioscorus*, who, through the help of his monks and of imperial soldiers, exerted an unheard-of pressure on the Fathers of the council. The presidency that the papal legates claimed was refused them; the pontifical letters were not read. This council, which was not ecumenical for that reason, ended by declaring orthodox the heretic *Eutyches*, who upheld the error of monophysitism (one sole nature in Christ).

Vatican II was likewise a *robber council*, except for this difference, that the Popes (John XXIII, then Paul VI), although present, did not oppose the surprise attack of the liberals with resistance, or at least very little, and even favored their enterprises. How was this possible? Proclaiming this council to be *"pastoral"* and not dogmatic, putting the stress on *aggiornamento* and *ecumenism*, these Popes at the outset deprived the council and themselves of the intervention of the charism of infallibility which would have protected them from all error.

In the present conference, I will relate for you *three* of the maneuvers of the liberal clique at Vatican II.

Attack on the Conciliar Commissions

The *Pélerin Magazine* of November 22, 1985, reported some very instructive secrets told by Cardinal Liénart to a journalist, Claude Beaufort, in 1972, on the first general session of the Council. I will read to you *in extenso* that article entitled *"Cardinal Liénart: 'The Council, the Apotheosis of My Life.'"* I will content myself with bringing my observations to this.[1]

October 13, 1962: the council Vatican II holds its first working session. The order of the day foresees that the Assembly designates the members of the specialized Commissions called to help it in its task. But the 2300 Fathers gathered in the immense nave of Saint Peter's hardly know one another. Can they, right away, elect competent teams? The Curia evades the difficulty: along with the balloting forms are distributed the lists of the former preparatory commissions established by itself. The invitation to renew the same teams is clear....

What would be more normal than to reelect to the conciliar commissions those who for three years had prepared irreproachable texts in the midst of the preparatory commissions? But obviously this proposal could not be to the liking of the innovators

On entering the basilica, Cardinal Liénart was informed of this very ambiguous procedure by Cardinal Lefebvre, Archbishop of Bourges. Both of them know the great diffidence of the pre-conciliar commissions, their cast of mind very Roman and not very much harmonized to the sensibility of the universal Church. They dread

---

1 *Le Figaro* of December 9, 1976, published extracts of a "Journal of the Council" drawn up by Cardinal Liénart. Michel Martin comments on these excerpts in his article "L'ardoise refilée," in N. 165 of the *Courier of Rome* (January 1977).

that the same causes will produce the same effects. The bishop of Lille sits on the Board of presidency for the Council. This position, his interlocutor judges, permits him to intervene, to thwart the workings, to insist on the lapse of time necessary in order that the episcopal conferences may be able to propose representative candidacies.

The Liberals thus dread the "Roman" theologians and schemas. In order to obtain commissions of a liberal—let us use this word—sensibility, new lists must be prepared which will include members of the world-wide liberal *mafia*: a little organization and at the beginning immediate intervention will attain the goal.

Helped by Bishop Garrone, Cardinal Lefebvre prepared a text in Latin. He slipped it to Cardinal Liénart.

Here you have a text already completely prepared by Cardinal Lefebvre, Archbishop of Bourges.[1] There has therefore not been any improvisation, but premeditation, let us say, preparation, organization, between cardinals of liberal sentiment.

Ten years later, this one [Cardinal Liénart] recalled his state of mind on that day in the following terms:

I was cornered. Either, convinced that this was not reasonable, I would say nothing and fail in my duty; or indeed I would speak out. We could not resign from our function, which was to elect. So, I took my paper. I leaned over towards Cardinal Tisserant, who was beside me and who was presiding, and said to him, "Eminence, I cannot vote. This is not reasonable, we do not know one another. I ask you for the floor."

He answered me, "That is impossible. The order of the day does not foresee any debate. We have assembled simply to vote. I cannot give you the floor."

I said to him, "Then I am going to take it." I got up and, trembling, read my paper. I immediately realized that my intervention met the anxiety of all those who were there. They applauded. Then Cardinal Frings, who was a little farther away, got up and said the same thing. The applause got louder. Cardinal Tisserant offered to ad-

---

1 Not to be confused with his cousin Archbishop Marcel Lefebvre!

journ the session and to give a report to the Holy Father.
All this had lasted scarcely twenty minutes. The Fathers
left the basilica, thus sounding the alarm for the jour-
nalists. They put together some fictional stories: "The
French bishops in revolt at the Council," etc. This was not
a revolt, it was a discreet consideration. By my rank and
by circumstances, I was obliged to speak; otherwise I
would be giving up. For inwardly this would have been a
resignation.

Leaving the conciliar *aula*, a Dutch bishop straightfor-
wardly expressed his thought and that of the liberal
bishops, French and German, by throwing out at a priest
among his friends who was some distance away, "Our first
victory!"[1]

IDOC, or the Poisoning

One of the liberal clique's most effective means of pressure on the Council was IDOC,[2] the Institute of Documentation, at the service of the productions of the liberal intelligentsia, which flooded the conciliar Fathers with in-
numerable texts. IDOC itself declared that it had distributed, up to the end of the third conciliar session, more
than four million sheets! The organization and the productions of IDOC went back to the Dutch episcopal conference; the financing was assured in part by Father
Werenfried (alas) and by Cardinal Cushing, archbishop of
Boston in the United States. The huge secretariat was located on the Via dell'Amina in Rome.

On our side, the conservative bishops, we had certainly
tried to counterbalance this influence, thanks to Cardinal
Larraona, who placed his secretariat at our disposal. We
had typewriters and copiers and a few people, three or
four. We were very busy, but this was insignificant in comparison with the organization of IDOC! Some Brazilians,
members of the T.F.P., helped us with an unheard-of devotion, working at night to copy the studies that had been
written up by five or six bishops, that is to say, the direct-

---

1 Cf. Ralph Wiltgen, "The European Alliance," *The Rhine Flows into The Tiber*, pp.
  16-17.
2 International Documentation of the Council.

ing committee of the *Cœtus Internationalis Patrum*, which I had founded with Bishop Carli, Bishop of Segni, and Bishop de Proença Sigaud, Archbishop of Diamantina in Brazil. Two hundred and fifty bishops were affiliated with our organization.[1] It was with Father V. A. Berto, my personal theologian; with the above-mentioned bishops; and with others like Bishop de Castro Mayer and some Spanish bishops that we drew up these texts, which were copied at night. And early in the morning, these few Brazilian friends left by car to distribute our sheets in the hotels, in the letter-boxes of the conciliar Fathers, as IDOC was doing with an organization twenty times larger than ours.

IDOC, and many other organizations and meetings of liberals, are the illustration of the fact that there was a *conspiracy* in this council, a plot prepared in advance, from years before. They knew what had to be done, how to do it, who was going to do it. And unfortunately this plot succeeded; the great majority of the council was poisoned by the power of the liberal propaganda.

Craftiness of the Writers of the Conciliar Schemas

It is certain that with the 250 conciliar fathers of the *Coetus* we tried with all the means put at our disposal to keep the liberal errors from being expressed in the texts of the Council. This meant that we were able all the same to *limit the damage*, to change these inexact or tendentious assertions, to add that sentence to rectify a tendentious proposition, an ambiguous expression.

But I have to admit that we did not succeed in purifying the Council of the liberal and modernist spirit that impregnated most of the schemas. Their drafters indeed were precisely the experts and the Fathers tainted with this spirit. Now, what can you do when a document is in all its parts drawn up with a false meaning? It is practically impossible to expurgate it of that meaning. It would have to be completely recomposed in order to be given a Catholic spirit.

What we were able to do was, by the *modi* that we introduced, to have interpolated clauses added to the

---

1 Cf. Wiltgen, op. cit., p. 147.

schemas; and this is quite obvious: it suffices to compare the first schema on religious liberty with the fifth one that was written—for this document was five times rejected and five times brought back for discussion—in order to see that we succeeded just the same in reducing the subjectivism that tainted the first drafts. Likewise for *Gaudium et spes*, the paragraphs can easily be seen which were added at our request and which are there, I would say, like pieces brought back onto an old coat. It does not *stick* well together. The logic of the early drafting is no longer there. The additions made to lessen or to counterbalance the liberal assertions remain there like foreign bodies.

It was not only we, the conservatives, who had such paragraphs added; Pope Paul VI himself, you know, had a *preliminary explanatory note* added to the Constitution on the Church, *Lumen gentium*, in order to rectify the false notion of collegiality which is insinuated in the text at n. 22.[1]

But the annoying thing is that the Liberals themselves practiced this system in the text of the schemas: assertion of an error or an ambiguity or a dangerous orientation, then immediately after or before, an assertion in the opposite direction, intended to tranquillize the conservative conciliar fathers.

Thus in the Constitution on the Liturgy, *Sacrosanctum concilium*, by writing at n. 36 #2: "A more extensive role can be granted to the vernacular language," and by entrusting to the episcopal assemblies the care of deciding whether the vernacular language will be adopted or not (cf. n. 36 #3), the drafters of the text opened the door to the suppression of Latin in the liturgy. In order to soften this intention, they took care to write at first, at n. 36 #1: "The use of the Latin language, except for particular law, will be kept in the Latin rites." Reassured by this assertion, the Fathers swallowed the two others without a problem.

Likewise, in the declaration on religious liberty, *Dignitatis humanæ*, of which the last schema was rejected by numerous Fathers, Paul VI himself had a paragraph added which said in substance: "This declaration contains noth-

---

1 Cf. Wiltgen, op. cit., pp. 224 sq.

ing that is contrary to tradition."[1] But everything that is inside is contrary to tradition! Thus someone will say, "Just read it! It is written, 'There is nothing contrary to tradition!'"— well, yes, it is written. But that does not stop everything from being contrary to tradition! And that sentence was added at the last minute by the Pope in order to force the hand of those—in particular the Spanish bishops—who were opposed to this schema. And indeed this maneuver unfortunately succeeded; and instead of 250 "no's" there were only seventy-four—because of a little sentence: "There is nothing contrary to tradition"! Well, let us be logical! They changed nothing in the text! It is easy after the fact to stick on a tag, a label of innocence! Unbelievable behavior!

Let us stop at this point on the robbery aspect, and go on now to *the spirit of the Council.*

---

1 *Dignitatis humanæ*, n.1, in fine; cf. Chapter XXVII.

Chapter XXV

The Spirit of the Council

What ambiguities and heterodox orientations could have been avoided if Vatican II had been a dogmatic council and not a so-called *pastoral* one!

Now, when we examine the successive drafts of the conciliar documents, we perceive the *orientations* that they express. Let me take up some of these.

The Priesthood of the Faithful

To be sure, *Lumen gentium* distinguishes between the common priesthood of the faithful and the ministerial priesthood of the priests (n. 10). Good. But then the text comprises long pages that speak of the priesthood in general, confusing the two, or making of the priesthood of the priests one function among others of the common priesthood (n. 11).

Exaltation of the Conscience Above the Law

Likewise, it is well said that man must submit himself to the *law* of God (*Dignitatis humanæ* n. 2). But then the liberty of man is exalted, the personal conscience (n. 3); it comes to the point of upholding the objection of conscience (ibid. n. 3) in a manner so general that it is false: "Man must not be

compelled to act against his conscience." Now, this is true
only of a true conscience or of an invincibly erroneous conscience! The result is a tendency to put conscience above
the law, subjectivity above the objective order of things,
whereas it is quite evident that conscience is created to
conform itself to the law.

Liberal Definition of Liberty

In like manner, at all times, particularly in the declaration on religious liberty, it is repeated that there must be no
compulsion, no coercion (*Gaudium et spes* n. 47; *Dignitatis
humanæ*, nn. 1, 2, 3, 10). Liberty is defined as the absence of
constraint. Now it is indeed obvious that there is no society
without the physical coercion of penalties or the moral
coercion of the fear of the penalties which the laws include!
Otherwise you have anarchy. And Our Lord Jesus Christ is
to be sure not the last one to resort to constraint: what
moral coercion is stronger than that in this sentence, "He
who does not believe will be condemned" (Mk 16:16)? The
thought of hell is heavy on consciences. This is a good, and
it is a coercion. Therefore, there are very certainly some
good and salutary coercions!

Confusions and Incoherences

Furthermore, there is no distinction in *Dignitatis
humanæ* among the religious acts exempt from coercion on
the part of the State; we would have to distinguish the internal and external, the private and public acts, and not to
attribute to them all the same liberty (cf. n. 2)!

In a Catholic country, one is well entitled to prevent the
false forms of worship from being publicly displayed, to
limit their propaganda!

If the State truly does not have the right to intervene in
religious matters, then parents no longer have the right to
pass on to their children, and to impose upon them, a
religion either! It results in the absurd if liberty in religious
matters is generalized without any distinction!

Tendency towards Religious Indifferentism

If one asserts that every religion is a path towards God, or that the State is not qualified to pass judgment on the truth of such or such a religion, he is saying nonsense that borders on the heresy that is called *indifferentism*: indifferentism of the individual or indifferentism of the State vis-à-vis the true religion.

Now, that the Council exhibits this indifferentism or a tendency in this direction is undeniable. By exalting the individual conscience, the spiritual values, and the value for salvation of the other religions (*Nostra ætate*, n. 2; *Unitatis redintegratio*, n. 3; *Dignitatis humanæ*, n. 4), it supports individual indifferentism. By uttering unheard-of absurdities, as Bishop De Smedt did about the incompetence of the State to judge of religious truth and to recognize definitively the true God, they propagate the indifferentism of the State, the atheism of the State.

The fruits of this spirit and of these pernicious doctrines are there: no longer does anyone among Catholics still maintain that in Catholic countries the State must recognize the true religion, assist it by its laws, and in the same way prevent the false religions from propagating themselves! No longer does anyone!

Now if, for example, Colombia in 1966 was a country still 95 percent Catholic, this is thanks to the State, which by its constitution prevented the propagation of the Protestant sects: an invaluable help to the Catholic Church! By protecting the faith of the citizens, these laws and these heads of State will have contributed to leading to heaven millions of individuals, who will have eternal life thanks to these laws, and would not have had it without this!—but now in Colombia it is ended! This fundamental law has been suppressed at the request of the Vatican, in application of the religious liberty of Vatican II! Thus right now the sects are multiplying rapidly; and these poor simple people are disarmed in the face of the propaganda of Protestant sects spoiled with money and with means, who come and come again unceasingly to indoctrinate the illiterate. I am not making it up. And this indeed, is it not a true oppression of consciences, something Protestant and

Masonic? That is where the so-called religious liberty of the Council ends up!

Tendency towards Naturalism

Read Chapter V of *Gaudium et spes* on international relations, international organizations, peace, and war: you will find there practically no reference to Our Lord Jesus Christ. Can the world be organized without Our Lord Jesus Christ? Have peace without the *Princeps pacis*? This is impossible! Now, the world is plunged into war and subversion, particularly because it is plunged into sin. First of all, therefore, it must be given the grace of Jesus Christ; it must be converted to Our Lord. He is the only solution to the problem of peace in the world. Without Him, one is speaking into a void.

It was Bishop Hauptmann, Rector of the Catholic Institute of Paris, who presided over the commission that drew up this text. This commission met with Protestants, in Switzerland, having as its objective that this chapter could please and have an effect on international society. How do you expect all that to be supernatural, truly marked with the sign of Our Lord Jesus Christ?

I will limit my enumeration of things to these. I do not say that everything is bad in this council, that there are not some fine texts to meditate on. But I assert, with the evidence in my hands, that there are some documents that are dangerous and even erroneous, which show *liberal tendencies*, modernist tendencies, which afterwards inspired the reforms that are now bringing the Church down to the ground.

Chapter XXVI

Searching and Dialogue, Death of the Missionary Spirit

The liberal Catholic spirit, as we have seen, does not have enough confidence in the truth. The conciliar spirit loses the hope of ever attaining the truth: beyond a doubt the truth exists, but it is the object of an indefinite pursuit.

That means, as we shall see, that society cannot be organized on the truth, on the Truth which is Jesus Christ. In all this the key-word is "searching"—or again orientation, tendency towards the truth, appeal to the truth, advancing towards the truth. The conciliar and post-conciliar jargon abounds in this vocabulary of movement and of "dynamics."

The Vatican II Council indeed canonized searching in its Declaration on Religious Liberty: *"The truth must be sought according to the manner proper to the human person and to his social nature, namely, by means of a free investigation...."* The Council puts searching into the first place, ahead of instruction and education! Reality, however, is otherwise: children get strong religious convictions by a solid education; and once they are acquired, anchored in the minds, and expressed in religious worship, why search any more? Moreover, "unrestricted research" has very rarely led to religious and philosophical truth. The great Aristotle is not immune from errors. The philosophy of open investigation results in Hegel. And what is there to say of the supernatural truths? Speaking about the pagans, here is what Saint Paul writes: *"How will they believe, if no one preaches to them? And how will anyone preach to them, if missionaries are not sent?"* [1] It is not the search that the Church must proclaim, but the need for the mission: *"Go, teach all nations"* (Mt. 28:19); such is the only order given by Our Lord. How many souls will be able to find the truth, remain in the truth, without the help of the magisterium of the Church? This free searching is a total unreality, at bottom, a radical naturalism.

And in practice, what is it that distinguishes a free searcher from a free thinker?

The Values of the Other Religions

The Council took pleasure in exalting the salvific values, or the values—period—of the other religions. Speaking of the non-Catholic Christian religions, Vatican II teaches that *"Although we believe them to be victims of deficiencies, they are not in any way devoid of meaning and of value in the mystery of salvation."* [2] This is a heresy! The only means of salvation is the Catholic Church. Insofar as they are separated from the unity of the true faith, the Protestant communions cannot be used by the Holy Ghost. He can act only directly on the souls or make use of the means (for example, baptism) which, in themselves, do not bear any indication of separation.

One can be saved *in* Protestantism, but not *by* Protestantism! In heaven there are no Protestants, there are only Catholics!

With regard to the non-Christian religions, this is what the Council declares:

---

1 Romans 10:15.
2 Decree on Ecumenism, *Unitatis redintegratio*, n. 3.

The Catholic Church does not reject anything of what is true and holy in these religions. It considers with *respect* these ways of acting and of living, these rules and these doctrines, which, although they differ on many points from what It itself holds and proposes, nevertheless bring a ray of the Truth that enlightens all men.[1]

What? I should respect the polygamy and the immorality of Islam? Or the idolatry of Hinduism? To be sure, these religions can keep some sound elements, signs of natural religion, natural occasions for salvation; even preserve some remainders of the primitive revelation (God, the fall, a salvation), hidden supernatural values which the grace of God could use in order to kindle in some people the flame of a dawning faith. But none of these values belongs in its own right to these false religions. Their attributes are their aberration far from the truth, the deficiency of faith, the absence of grace, superstition, even idolatry. In these people, these false cults are only "vanity and affliction of spirit," if not even forms of worship rendered to the demons! The wholesome elements that can subsist still belong by right to the sole true religion, that of the Catholic Church; and it is this one alone that can act through them.

Religious Syncretism

To speak, therefore, of the values for salvation of the other religions, I repeat, is a heresy! And "to respect their ways of acting and their doctrines" is a way of talking which scandalizes true Christians. Go speak to our African Catholics about respecting the animist rites! If a Christian were caught while participating in such rites, he would be suspect of apostasy and excluded from the mission for a year. When you reflect, John Paul II made such an animistic gesture in Togo![2] Likewise at Madras, February 5, 1986, a sugar cane was brought into his presence woven in the form of a cross, which signifies *the Hindu offering to the carnal god*; then, during the offertory procession, there were

---

1 Declaration on the Non-Christian Religions, *Nostra ætate*, n. 2.
2 *Osservatore Romano*, August 11, 1985, p. 5.

brought to the altar some *coconuts*, a typical offering of the
Hindu religion to its idols; and finally a woman put the
sacred ashes onto John Paul II by running her hand across
his forehead.[1] The scandal of the true Indian Catholics was
at its height. To these people, confronted daily in all the
corners of the streets with the idolatrous temples and the
mythological beliefs of the Buddhists and the Hindus, it is
not necessary to go and speak of *"recognizing, preserving,
and helping to advance the spiritual, moral, and socio-cultural
values which are found in these religions"!*[2]

If, in the first centuries, the Church was able to baptize
pagan temples or consecrate the days of the pagan fes-
tivities, it is because its prudence avoided upsetting respectable customs and because its wisdom knew how to
discern the elements of natural piety that were not to be
suppressed from the idolatrous hodgepodge of which it
had cleansed the minds of the new converts. And
throughout the history of the missions, the Church has not
lacked this spirit of intelligent mercy. Is not the Church's
"note" of catholicity precisely its capacity to reunite in a
sublime unity of faith the peoples of all times, of all races,
and of all localities, without suppressing their legitimate
diversities? It can be said that the discernment was made a
long time ago, in regard to all religions, and that there is no
more to do! Thereupon Vatican II comes to ask of us a new
respect, a new discernment, a new assimilation, and a new
construction. And in what terms! And in what concrete ap-
plications! This is called "inculturation." No, that is not the
wisdom of the Church!

The spirit of the Church has led it to inscribe in its liturgy some timely words, intended for our time, under Pope
Pius XII, a little before the Council: read the offertory
prayer from the Mass of the Sovereign Pontiffs, extracted
from the divine calling of the prophet Jeremias:[3]

---

1 It is a question not of the *"Tilac"* that John Paul II received on February 2nd at Delhi
   (cf. *Fideliter*, n. 51, p. 3), but of the sacred ashes or *"Vibhuti"* (cf. *Indian Express*,
   February 6th, 1986).
2 Vatican II, *Nostra ætate*, n. 2.
3 Jer. 1:10.

> Behold I have put my words into thy mouth, behold I
> have established thee over the nations and over the
> kingdoms, to root up and to destroy, to build and to
> plant.

For my part, I never attempted to convert the hut of an
animist priest into a chapel. When a sorcerer died (often by
poison!), we immediately burned his hut, to the great joy of
the children! In the sight of all tradition, the order given by
John Paul II in *Redemptor hominis:* "Never destruction, but
taking into account of values, and a new construction" is
nothing less than the utopia of an armchair theologian. Indeed, clear-headed or not, this is an explicit urging on to
religious syncretism.

Dialogue

Dialogue is not a discovery of the council. Paul VI in *Ecclesiam suam*[1] is its author: dialogue with the world,
dialogue with the other religions. But it must be admitted
that the council singularly aggravated the liberal tendency.
Thus:

> The truth must be sought... by means... of exchange
> and dialogue, by which some set forth to the others the
> truth that they have found or think that they have found,
> in order to help each other reciprocally in the search for
> truth.[2]

Hence, in the same way as the unbeliever, the believer
should always be searching! Saint Paul, however, really
pinned down the false doctors "who are always learning,
without ever arriving at the knowledge of the truth"![3] For
his part, the unbeliever could provide the believer with the
elements of truth that are lacking to him! The Holy Office,
in its instruction of December 20, 1949, on ecumenism,
nevertheless dispelled this error and, speaking of the
return of the separated Christians to the Catholic Church,
said: *"We will, however, avoid speaking on this point in such a
manner that, in coming back to the Church, they delude themsel-*

---

1 August 6, 1964.
2 *Dignitatis humanæ* n. 3.
3 II Tim. 3:7.

ves that they are providing it with an essential element that it would have been lacking up to now.[1] What contact with non-Catholics can supply us with is from human experience, but not doctrinal elements!

Furthermore, the Council considerably altered the attitude of the Church towards other religions, the non-Christian ones in particular. In a conversation that I had on September 13, 1975, with the secretary of Bishop Nestor Adam, then bishop of Sion, this secretary came to agree with me: yes, something has changed in the missionary orientation of the Church. But he added: "And it was necessary that this change take place." He said to me, "For example, now, in those who are not Christians, or in those who are separated from the Church, we look at what there is of good, the *positive*, in them. We try to discern, in the values that they have, the seeds of their salvation."

Of course, every error has its true, positive aspects; there is no error in the pure state, just as absolute evil does not exist. Evil is the corruption of a good, error is the corruption of the truth, in a subject that nonetheless keeps its nature, certain natural qualities, and certain truths. But there is a very great danger in basing oneself on the residue of truth that error preserves. What would we think of a doctor who, called to the bedside of a sick person, would declare, "Oh, but this sick person still has something; it is not as bad as that!" In regard to the sickness, there would be no use in saying to this doctor, "But then, look at the sickness, can't you see that he is sick? He has to be taken care of, or he is going to die!" He will reply to you, "Oh, after all, he is not as bad as all that. Besides, my method is to pay no attention to the disease that is in my patients—that is negative—but to the remainder of health that is in them."

In such a case, I will say, let us leave the sick to die of their lovely death! The result is that, by dint of our saying to non-Catholics or non-Christians, "After all, you have an upright conscience, you have some means of salvation,"

---

1 Instruction *"de motione œcumenica."*

they wind up by believing that they are not sick. And then how to convert them after that? Now, this spirit has never been that of the Church. On the contrary, the missionary spirit has always been openly to show to the sick their wounds, so as to heal them, to bring them the remedies that they need. To stand before non-Christians, without telling them that they need the Christian religion, that they cannot be saved except through Our Lord Jesus Christ, is an inhuman cruelty. In the beginning of a private conversation, to make a *captatio benevolentiæ* by praising whatever is honorable in their religion, this is indeed legitimate. But to raise that up to being a doctrinal principle, this is an error, it is to deceive souls! The "salvific values of other religions" is a heresy! To make of this a basis for the missionary apostolate is to wish to keep souls in error! This "dialogue" is anti-missionary to the highest degree! Our Lord sent his Apostles not to dialogue, but to preach! Now, as it is this spirit of liberal dialogue that has been inculcated since the Council in the priests and the missionaries, we can understand why the conciliar Church has completely lost the missionary zeal, the very spirit of the Church!

*

But that is enough about free searching and dialogue; let us go on from there to the outcome of these conciliar discoveries, namely, religious liberty. We will discuss it in its historical, then its individual, and, finally, its social aspects.

Chapter XXVII

Vatican II in the Light of Tradition

Religious liberty... does not involve any prejudice to traditional Catholic doctrine....

Moreover, speaking of this religious liberty, the holy Council intends to develop the doctrine of the most recent Sovereign Pontiffs on the inviolable rights of the human person....[1]

It is this preamble, which is supposed to be reassuring, that immediately precedes the conciliar declaration on religious liberty. It is presented thus as being written down in the line of tradition. But what is it in reality? The question arises about the fact that, as we have seen, the Popes of the nineteenth century condemned, under the name of liberty of conscience and of forms of worship, a religious liberty which resembles, like a sister, that of Vatican II.

---

1 *Dignitatis humanæ*, n. 1.

I

Quanta Cura and Vatican II

Propositions condemned by Pius IX in *Quanta cura*.	Propositions asserted by Vatican II in *Dignitatis humanæ*.
(A) "The best condition of society is that in which there is not conceded to the authorities the duty to repress the violators of the Catholic religion by legal penalties, except when the public peace demands this."	(AA) "In religious matters, let no one be impeded from acting according to his conscience, in private or in public, alone or associated with others, within just limits."
(B) "Liberty of conscience and of forms of worship is a right proper to every man."	(BB) "The person has a right to religious liberty. This liberty consists in what... follows:" =(AA)
(C) "Which must be proclaimed and guaranteed in every correctly established society."[1]	(CC) "This right of the human person to religious liberty must be recognized in the juridical order of society, in such a manner that it constitutes a civil right."[2]

The parallel is striking. The analysis of this[3] brings us to conclude that the doctrines are contradictory. Father Congar himself admits that *Dignitatis humanæ* is contrary to the *Syllabus* of the same Pius IX:

---

1 PIN. 40, Denz. 1689-1690.
2 *Dignitatis humanæ*, n. 2.
3 Cf. Michel Martin, *"Courrier de Rome,"* n. 157, and the special issue of November, 1985; Father Bernard Lucien, Appendix on the opposition between Vatican II and the Encyclical *Quanta Cura*, in *Letter to a Few Bishops*, Société Saint Thomas d'Aquin, Paris, 1983.

It cannot be denied that the affirmation of religious liberty by Vatican II says materially something other than what the *Syllabus* of 1864 said, and even just about the opposite of propositions 16, 17, and 19 of this document.[1]

*

Vatican II is materially contrary to Pius IX, but not *formally*. That is what the supporters of the conciliar text pretend. They are specific, as I have besides already told you:[2] the condemnation of religious liberty in the nineteenth century is a historical error; the Popes condemned it, but in fact they intended only to condemn *the indifferentism* which was then inspiring it: "Man is free to have the religion that pleases him; therefore he has a right to religious liberty." In other words, the Popes struck too hard, blindly, without discernment, through fear of that absolute Liberalism which furthermore was threatening the temporal pontifical power. Father Congar takes up this explanation and quotes his sources:

> Father John Courtney Murray, who belonged to the intellectual and religious elite of the elite, has shown that, materially saying quite the opposite from the *Syllabus*—this latter is from 1864 and it is, as Roger Aubert has proven, conditioned by precise historical circumstances—the Declaration [of the council on religious liberty] was the consequence of the battle by which, in the face of Jacobinism and the totalitarianisms, the Popes more and more strongly led the fight for the dignity and the liberty of the human person made to the image of God.[3]

On the contrary, we have seen that Roger Aubert and John Courtney Murray are themselves prisoners of the historicist prejudice which makes them erroneously relativize the doctrine of the Popes of the nineteenth century![4]

---

1 Yves Congar, O.P., quoted by Father Georges de Nantes, CRC, no. 113, p. 3 –For the *Syllabus* see our Chapter X. Cardinal Ratzinger, for his part, sees in the conciliar text *Gaudium et spes* a *"counter-Syllabus,"* "to the extent that it represents an attempt at an official reconciliation of the Church with the world such as it has become since 1789," since the rights of man (*The Principles of Catholic Theology*, Tequi, Paris, 1985, p. 427.)
2 Chapter X.
3 Yves Congar, DC. 1704, 789.
4 Cf. Chapter X.

In reality, the Popes have condemned religious liberty in itself, as a freedom that is absurd, ungodly, and leading the peoples to religious indifference. This condemnation remains; and, with the authority of the constant ordinary magisterium of the Church (if not of the extraordinary magisterium, with *Quanta Cura*), it weighs on the conciliar declaration.

II

Religious Liberty, a Fundamental Right?

Is religious liberty written down, as Father Congar assures us above (and *Dignitatis humanæ* in its preamble), in the line of the *fundamental rights* of the human person defined by the recent Popes in the face of Jacobinism and the totalitarianisms of the twentieth century?[1] Let us first read a few statements of the "fundamental right of the cult of God":

> Man, insofar as [he is] a person, possesses rights that he holds from God and that must remain, with regard to the community, beyond any injury that would tend to negate them, to abolish them, or to neglect them.[2]

> ...The believer has an *inalienable right to profess his faith* and to revive it as it needs to be revived. Laws which stifle or make difficult the profession and the practice of this faith are in contradiction with natural law.[3]

> To promote respect for, and the practical exercise of, the fundamental rights of the person, namely: the right to maintain and to develop the corporeal, intellectual, and moral life, in particular the right to a religious formation and education: the *right to the private and public worship of God*, including charitable religious action....[4]

Objectively, the "worship of God" in question can be only the true cult of the true God; for, when we speak of

---

1 Cf. Ph. I. André-Vincent, O.P., *Religious Liberty, a Fundamental Right*, Paris, Téqui, 1976; cf. *Archbishop Lefebvre and the Holy Office, Itinéraires*, no. 233, pp. 68-81.

2 PIN. 677.

3 Pius XI, Encyclical "*Mit brennender Sorge*" of March 14, 1937; DC. 837-838, p. 915.

4 Pius XII, Radio message, December 24, 1942.

an *objective right* (the concrete object of the right: such a cult), it can be a question only of something that is true and morally good. Pius XII teaches:

> What does not correspond to the truth and to the moral law does not objectively have any right to existence, or to propaganda, or to action.[1]

This is moreover the obvious sense of the text of Pius XI: "believers" and "faith" refer to the followers of the true religion, under the circumstances the German Catholics persecuted by Nazism.

But what, finally, did and always do the totalitarian and atheistic regimes attack, if not the foundation itself of all religious right? The antireligious action of the Soviet communist regime aims at ridiculing and suppressing all religious worship, whether it be Catholic, Orthodox, or Moslem. What they want to abolish is the right, implanted in the subject, and corresponding to the duty of this person to honor God, leaving out of account its concrete practice in such or such a cult, Catholic, Orthodox, etc. Such a right is called a *subjective right*, because it concerns the subject and not the object. For example, I have the subjective right to render worship to God; but it does not follow from that that I have the objective right to exercise the Buddhist cult!

In the light of this completely classical and elementary distinction, you will understand that, in the face of militant atheism, the Popes of this century, especially Pius XII, have insisted precisely on the subjective right to the worship of God, a right that is totally fundamental; and it is this meaning that must therefore be given to the expression "fundamental right to the worship of God." This has not kept these Popes from claiming besides, when it was necessary, explicitly and concretely, the subjective and objective right of Catholic "souls."[2]

The perspective of Vatican II is completely different. The Council, as I am going to show you, defined a right not only subjective but objective to religious liberty, an entirely concrete right, that every man would have, to be respected

---

1 Pius XII, allocution *Ci riesce* to jurists, December 6, 1953; PIN. 3041.
2 Cf. Pius XI, Encyclical *Non Abbiamo*, of June 29, 1931.

in the *exercise of his form of worship, whatever it may be.* No! The religious liberty of Vatican II is situated at the antipodes of the fundamental rights defined by Pius XI and Pius XII!

Chapter XXVIII

The Religious Liberty of Vatican II

According to Vatican II, the human person would have the right, in the name of his dignity, not to be impeded from exercising his religious worship, whatever it might be, in private or in public, unless this troubles the public tranquillity and morality.[1] You will acknowledge that the public morality of the "pluralist" State promoted by the Council is not by nature going to cramp this liberty a great deal, any more than the advanced rotting of liberal society would limit the right to the liberty of "partnership," if it were proclaimed in an indistinct way by the couples who are living together unwed, and the married couples, in the name of their human dignity!

Thus you, Moslems, pray undisturbed in the very midst of our Christian streets; build your mosques and your minarets beside the steeples of our churches. The Church of Vatican II assures you that no one should hinder you from this, and the same for you Buddhists, Hindus...

---

1 Cf. Declaration on Religious Liberty, *Dignitatis humanæ*, n. 2.

In return for this, we Catholics will ask you for religious freedom in your countries, in the name of the liberty that we grant you in ours. We will also be able to defend our religious rights in the face of the communist regimes, in the name of a principle declared by so dignified a religious assembly, and already recognized by the U.N. and Freemasonry. This is moreover the consideration that Pope John Paul II made to me on the occasion of the audience that he granted to me on November 18, 1978: "You know," he said to me, "religious liberty has been very useful for us in Poland, against communism!" I wanted to respond to him, "Very useful, perhaps, as an argument *ad hominem*, since the communist regimes have the freedom of worship inscribed in their Constitutions,[1] but not as a doctrinal principle of the Catholic Church!"

I

Religious Liberty and Truth

This is, at all events, what Father Garrigou-Lagrange answered in advance:

> We can... make of the liberty of worship an argument *ad hominem* against those who, while proclaiming the liberty of worship, persecute the Church (secular and socializing States) or impede its worship directly or indirectly (communist States, Islamic ones, etc.). This argument *ad hominem* is fair, and the Church does not disdain it, using it to defend effectively the right of its own liberty. But it does not follow that the freedom of cults, considered in itself, is maintainable for Catholics as a *principle*, because it is in itself absurd and impious: indeed, truth and error cannot have the same rights.[2]

I like to repeat this: only truth has rights; error has no rights. This is the teaching of the Church. Leo XIII writes:

> A right is a moral faculty; and, as we have said and as it cannot be repeated too often, it would be absurd to believe that it belongs, naturally and without distinction

---

1 Alongside the right of anti-religious propaganda!
2 Cf. Réginald Garrigou-Lagrange, O.P., *De Revelatione*, Tome II, p. 451, 8th objection (Ferrari and Gabalda, editors, 1921).

or discernment, to the truth and to the untruth, to the good and to the bad. The truth, the good have the right to be propagated in the State with a prudent liberty, in order that a greater number profit from them; but the untrue doctrines, the most fatal pestilence of all for the mind... it is just that the public authority use its solicitude to repress them, in order to prevent the evil from spreading out for the ruin of society.[1]

It is clear, in light of this, that the doctrines and the cults of the erroneous religions have of themselves no right to be allowed to express themselves and propagate themselves freely. In order to evade this tautology, it was objected at the Council that truth and error properly speaking have no rights: it is persons who have rights, who are "subjects of rights." From there, they tried to dodge the problem by posing it on a purely subjective level, and by hoping thus to be able to leave the truth out of account! But this attempt had to be in vain, as I am now going to show you, by placing myself into the very problematic of the Council.

Put onto the subjective level of the "subject of rights," religious liberty is the same right granted to *those who adhere* to religious truth and to *those who are* in error. Is such a right conceivable? Upon what does the Council base it?

The Rights of Conscience?

At the start of the Council, some people wanted to found religious liberty on the *rights of conscience*: "Religious liberty would be fruitless if men could not make the imperatives of their conscience pass over into exterior and public acts," proclaimed Bishop De Smedt in his introductory speech (*Documentation catholique*, January 5, 1964, col. 74-75). The argument was the following: everyone has the duty to follow his conscience, because this is for everyone the immediate rule of action. Now this holds not only for a true conscience, but also for an invincibly erroneous conscience, in particular that of numerous followers of the false religions. Thus these people have the duty to follow

---

1 Encyclical *Libertas*, PIN. 207.

their conscience, and therefore they must be left free to follow it and to carry on their worship.

The foolishness of this reasoning was quickly discovered, and they had to resign themselves to making fire with other kindling. Indeed invincible error, that is, inculpable error certainly excuses from all moral fault; but it does *not* make the action *good;*[1] and consequently it *does not give any rights* to its perpetrator! A right can be based only on the objective norm of the law, and in the first place on the divine law, which regulates in particular the manner in which God wants to be honored by men.

The Dignity of the Human Person?

Since conscience did not furnish a sufficiently objective foundation, they thought they could find one in the dignity of the human person. *"The Council of the Vatican declares... that the right to religious liberty has its basis in the very dignity of the human person."*[2] This dignity consists in the fact that man, gifted with intelligence and free will, is ordained by his nature itself to know God, which he cannot do if he is not left free.[3] The argument is this: *man is free; therefore he must be left free.* Or again: man is endowed with free will; therefore he has the right to freedom of action. You recognize the absurd principle of all Liberalism, as Cardinal Billot calls it. It is a sophism: free will is located in the domain of BEING; moral liberty and the liberty of action stem from the realm of ACTING. It is one thing what a man is by his nature, and it is something else what he becomes (good or bad, in the truth or in error) by his acts! The *radical* human dignity is indeed that of an intelligent nature, capable therefore of personal choice; but his *final* dignity consists in adhering "in act" to the true and to the good. It is this final dignity which merits for each one the moral liberty (faculty of acting) and the liberty of action (faculty of not being impeded from acting). But to the extent in which man adheres to error or attaches himself to

---

1 St. Thomas, Ia IIæ, 19, 6 and ad. 1.
2 *Dignitatis humanæ* n. 2.
3 Ibid.

evil, he loses his final dignity or does not attain it; and nothing more can be founded on it! This is what Leo XIII magnificently taught in two texts hidden from view by Vatican II. Speaking of the false modern liberties, Leo XIII writes in *Immortale Dei*:

> If the intelligence adheres to false ideas, if the will chooses evil and attaches itself to it, neither the one nor the other reaches its perfection. Both of them fall short of their inborn dignity and become corrupt. It is therefore not permitted to bring to light and to expose to the eyes of men that which is contrary to virtue and to truth, and even less still to place this license under the tutelage of the protection of the laws.[1]

And in *Libertas* the same pope specifies what true religious liberty consists in and upon what it must be founded:

> Another liberty that is also very loudly proclaimed is that which is named liberty of conscience. If it is understood by this that everyone can indifferently, at his pleasure, render worship to God or not, the arguments which have been given above suffice to refute this.[2] But it can be understood also in the sense that *man has in the State the right to follow, according to the consciousness of his duty, the will of God, and to fulfill His precepts*[3] *without anyone's being able to impede him from this. This liberty, the true liberty worthy of the children of God, which so gloriously protects the dignity of the human person,* is above all violence and all oppression. It has always been the object of the wishes of the Church and of its particular affection.[4]

There you have true dignity, true religious liberty; false dignity, false religious liberty!

Religious Liberty, a Universal Right to Tolerance?

Father Ph. André-Vincent, who was very much interested in this question, wrote to me one day to put me on my guard: be careful, he said to me, the Council is claiming for the followers of the false religions not the *"affirmative"*

---

1 PIN. 149.
2 It is a question of the religious indifferentism of the individual.
3 It is obviously a question, speaking concretely, of the precepts of the true religion!
4 PIN. 215.

right to *practice* their cult, but only the *"negative"* right *not to be impeded* in the exercise, public or private, of their worship. In short, Vatican II would have done nothing but to generalize the classic doctrine of tolerance.

Indeed, when a Catholic State, for the sake of the civil peace, for the cooperation of all in the common good, or in a general way to avoid a greater evil or to procure a greater good, judges that it should *tolerate* the practice of this or that false worship, it can either "close its eyes" on this worship by a tolerance in actual fact by not taking any coercive measures in opposition to it, or even concede to its followers the *civil right not to be disturbed* in the exercise of their worship. In this latter case, it is a question of a purely negative right. The Popes, furthermore, do not fail to emphasize that civil tolerance does not grant any "affirmative" right to the dissidents, any *right to practice* their worship; for such an affirmative right can be based only on the truth of the worship that is considered:

> If the circumstances require it, deviations from the rule can be tolerated, when they have been introduced with a view to avoiding greater evils, without however elevating them to the dignity of a right, seeing that there cannot be any right against the eternal laws of justice.[1]

> While conceding *rights* only to what is true and honorable, the Church is nevertheless not opposed to the tolerance that the public authorities believe that they should make use of with regard to certain things contrary to truth and justice, with a view to a greater evil to be avoided or a greater good to obtain or preserve.[2]

> No State, no community of States, whatever may be their religious character, can give a positive mandate or a positive[3] authorization to teach or to do what would be contrary to religious truth or to moral good...

> An essentially different question is this: in a community of States, can one, at least in determined circumstances, establish the norm that the free exercise of a belief or of a religious practice in effect in a member-State

---

1 Pius IX, Letter *Dum civilis societas*, of February 1st, 1875, to Mr. Charles Perrin.
2 Leo XIII, *Libertas*, PIN. 219.
3 Or, let us say, *affirmative*.

not be impeded throughout all the territory of the community by means of coercive laws or ordinances of the State?[1] (And the pope answers affirmatively: yes, "in certain circumstances" such a norm can be established).

Father Baucher sums up this doctrine in an excellent manner: he writes, "In decreeing tolerance, the legislator is supposed to intend to create, for the profit of the dissidents, not the right or the moral faculty to practice their worship, but only the right not to be disturbed in the exercise of this worship. Without ever having the right to act wrongly, one can have the right not to be prevented from acting wrongly, when a just law prohibits this hindrance for sufficient motives."[2]

But he justly adds: the *civil right to tolerance* is one thing, when this is guaranteed by the law with a view to the common good of such or such a nation, under the determined circumstances; the *pretended natural and inviolable right* to tolerance for all the adherents of all the religions is something else, when it is by principle, and therefore in every circumstance!

The civil right to tolerance, indeed, even if the circumstances that justify it seem to be multiplying nowadays, remains nonetheless strictly relative to these circumstances. Leo XIII writes:

> The toleration of evil belonging to the principles of political prudence must be rigorously encircled within the limits required by its reason for being, that is to say, by the public welfare. This is why, if it is harmful to the public welfare, or if it is for the State the cause of a greater evil, the consequence is that it is not permitted to make use of it; for, under these conditions, the reason for being is absent.[3]

Thus, it would have been very difficult at Vatican II, relying on the acts of the previous magisterium, to proclaim a natural and universal right to tolerance. Furthermore, they carefully avoided the word "tolerance,"

---

1 Pius XII, allocution *Ci riesce* to Italian jurists, of December 6, 1953.
2 DTC, Tome IX, col. 701, article *Liberté*.
3 *Libertas*, PIN. 221.

which seemed much too negative; for what is tolerated is always an evil. Now, they wanted to put forward the positive values of all religions.[1]

Religious Liberty, a Natural Right to Immunity?

Without invoking tolerance, the Council thus defined a simple natural right to immunity: the right not to be disturbed in the practice of one's worship, whatever it may be.

The craftiness, or at least the artful step, was obvious: not being able to define a right *to the exercise* of every form of worship, since such a right does not exist for the erroneous cults, they strained their ingenuity to formulate a natural right *to immunity alone*, which would hold for the adherents of all the cults. Thus all the "religious groups" (a modest term concealing the Babel of religions) would naturally revel in the *immunity from all restraint* in their "public worship of the supreme Divinity" (what divinity is this, for heaven's sake?). And they would profit also from the "right not to be prevented from teaching and from manifesting their faith (what faith?) publicly, by word of mouth and in writing."[2]

Can a greater confusion be imagined? All the followers of all the religions, the true one as well as the false ones, boiled down to absolutely the same base of equality, would enjoy one same natural right, under the pretext that this is only a "right to immunity." Is this conceivable?

It is, rather, evident that of themselves, by the mere claim of their erroneous religion, the followers of this religion do not possess any natural right to immunity. Let me illustrate this truth through a concrete example. If the longing ever took hold of you to impede the public prayer of a group of Moslems on a street, or even to disturb their worship in a mosque, you would possibly sin against charity and assuredly against prudence; but you would not

---

1 I have said what should be thought of these values in Chapter XXVI. I will not come back to that here.
2 *Dignitatis humanæ,* 4.

cause *any injustice* to these believers. They would not be wronged in any of the goods to which they have a right, or in any of their rights to these goods:[1] in any of their *goods*, for their true good is not to carry on their false worship without obstacles, but to be able one day to exercise the true worship; in any of their *rights*, because they have a right precisely to practise the "worship of God in private and in public"[2] and not to be impeded from this. But the cult of Allah is not the worship of God! Indeed, God Himself has revealed the worship by which He wants to be honored exclusively, which is the worship of the Catholic religion.[3]

If, therefore, in natural justice, one does not do any wrong to these believers in any way by disturbing or preventing their worship, the reason is that they do not have *any natural right not to be disturbed* in the exercise of it.

*

It will be objected that I am "negative," that I know not how not to consider the positive values of the erroneous forms of worship. I have responded to this allegation by speaking to you above about "searching."[4] It will be retorted to me then that the basic orientation of the souls of the followers of the false cults remains upright and that it should be respected, and likewise the cult in which it is involved should be respected. I could not be opposed to the cult without shattering these souls, without breaking their orientation towards God. Thus, because of its religious error, the soul in question indeed does not have the right to practice its worship; but from the fact that it is not-withstanding, I would say, "connected with God," from that claim, it would have a right to immunity in the exer-

---

1 This distinction is brought about by Pius XII on the subject of the organic taking of parts done on the bodies of the deceased. Cf. Discourse to specialists in eye surgery, May 14, 1956.
2 Pius XII, Christmas radio message, December 24th, 1941. PIN. 804.
3 This explanation, as brief as it is, avoids for me the necessity of using the rather complicated terms, objective and subjective right, concrete and abstract right.
4 Cf. Chapter XXIV.

cise of its worship. Every man would have thus a *natural right to civil immunity* in religious matters.

Let us admit for the moment this alleged naturally direct orientation of every soul towards God in the practice of its worship. It is not at all obvious that the duty of respecting its worship for that reason is a duty of natural justice. It seems to me, rather, that it is a question of a pure *duty of charity!* If this is the way it is, this duty of charity does not grant to the adherents of the false cults any natural right to immunity, but prompts the civil authorities to grant them a civil right to immunity. Now the Council proclaims for every man, without proving anything, precisely a *natural right to civil immunity.* It appears to me that, on the contrary, the practice of the false cults cannot exceed the status of a simple *civil right to immunity,*[1] which is a completely different thing!

Let us carefully distinguish on the one hand the virtue of *justice*, which, by assigning their duties to some, gives to others the corresponding right, that is to say, the power to demand, and, on the other hand, the virtue of *charity*, which indeed imposes duties onto some, without however assigning any right to the others.

A Natural Orientation of Every Man towards God?

The Council[2] invokes, beyond the fundamental dignity of the human person, his natural quest for the divine: each man, in the exercise of his religion, whatever it may be, would be in fact oriented towards the true God, even in an unconscious search for the true God, "rooted in God," if you will; and by this claim he would have a natural right to be respected in the practice of his worship.

If a Buddhist, therefore, burns sticks of incense before the idol of Buddha, according to Catholic theology, he commits an act of idolatry; but in light of the new doctrine uncovered by Vatican II, he expresses "the supreme effort of a man to search for God."[3] This religious act therefore has a

---

1 Which the government may or may not grant, according to a judgment of prudence.
2 *Dignitatis humanæ* 2-3.
3 John Paul II, discourse to the general audience, October 22, 1986.

right to be respected, this man has a right not to be impeded from performing it, he has a right to religious liberty.

First, there is an obvious contradiction in affirming that all men devoted to the false cults are *of themselves, naturally,* turned towards God. An erroneous cult, of itself, can only turn souls away from God, because it puts them onto a path which of itself does not lead to God.

It can be admitted that, in the false religions, certain souls can be oriented towards God; but this is because they do not attach themselves to the errors of their religion! It is not *through* their religion that these souls turn towards God, but *in spite of* it! Therefore, the respect that is owed to these souls would not imply that respect is owed to their religion.

In any case, the identity and the number of such souls, which God deigns to turn towards Him by His grace, remains perfectly hidden and unknown. It is certainly not a great number. A priest who came from a country of mixed religions informed me one day of his experience of those who live in the heretical sects; he told me of his surprise to ascertain how very stubborn these persons usually are in their errors and how little disposed to examine the remarks that a Catholic may make to them, how little docile to the Spirit of Truth.

The identity of the souls truly oriented towards God in the other religions thus remains the secret of God and escapes human judgment. It is therefore impossible to found any natural or civil right on this. That would be to make the juridical order of society rest upon purely hazardous, even arbitrary suppositions. That would be to base the social order definitively upon the subjectivity of each one and to build a house on sand.

I will add this: I have been sufficiently in contact with the religions of Africa (animism, Islam), but it can be said as much of the religion of India (Hinduism), in order to be able to affirm that the lamentable consequences of original sin are verified among their followers, in particular the blindness of the intellect and their superstitious fear. In this respect, to uphold, as Vatican II does, a naturally direct orientation of all men towards God, is totally unrealistic and a pure naturalistic heresy! May God deliver us from subjectivistic and naturalistic errors! They are the unmistakable mark of the Liberalism which inspired the religious liberty of Vatican II. But they can lead only to social chaos, to the Babel of religions!

Evangelical Mildness

Divine revelation, the Council assures us, "shows in what respect Christ held the liberty of man to be in the accomplishment of his duty of believing in the word of God."[1] Jesus, "meek and humble of heart," gives an order, "let the cockle grow up until the harvest"; "he does not break the crumpled reed and does not put out the smoking wick."[2]

Here is the response. When the Lord gives the order to let the cockle sprout, he does not grant it a right not to be uprooted; but he gives this advice to the harvesters "in order not to root up at the same time the good grain." This is a counsel of *prudence*: it is better sometimes not to scandalize the faithful by the spectacle of the repression of unbelievers;[3] at times it is better to avoid a civil war that nontolerance would instigate. Likewise, if Jesus does not break the crumpled reed and makes of this a pastoral rule for his apostles, it is by *charity* towards those who are led astray, in order not to turn them farther away from the truth, which could happen if coercive means were used against their cults. It is clear that there is from time to time a duty of prudence and of charity, on the part of the Church and of Catholic States, towards the followers of false cults; but such a duty does not of itself confer on others any right! By not distinguishing the virtue of justice (the one that assigns rights) from the virtue of prudence and from that of charity (which of themselves confer only duties), Vatican II

---

1 *Dignitatis humanæ*, 9.
2 Ibidem, 11; cf. Mt. 13:29, Isaias 42:3.
3 Note from Editor of Angelus Press: St. Paul said that God reserves for Himself the punishment of the wicked: "Revenge is mine, I will repay, saith the Lord." The duty to punish the wicked is difficult to exercise with virtue. Though the civil authorities have received from God this duty (Rom. 13:4), it is oftentimes prudent for them to apply it only in the cases of manifest wickedness.

sinks into error. To make justice out of charity is to pervert the social and political order of the city.

And even if, by an impossibility, one should consider that Our Lord all the same gives to the cockle a right "not to be uprooted," this right would remain quite *relative* to the particular reasons that motivate it. It would never be a natural and inviolable right! Saint Augustine writes, "Where we do not have to be afraid to uproot the good grain at the same time, let not the strictness of discipline go to sleep";[1] let not the practice of the false cults be tolerated! And Saint John Chrysostom himself, so little a supporter of the suppression of dissidents, does not, however, exclude the repression of their forms of worship. He says, "Who knows, moreover, whether a certain part of this cockle would not be changed into good grain? If therefore you rooted it up at present, you would hurt the next harvest, by rooting out those who can change and become better. He [the Lord] does not forbid us, assuredly, to repress the heretics, to make them be quiet, to refuse them freedom of speech, to disperse their assemblies, to repudiate their oaths; what He prohibits is to spill their blood and to put them to death."[2] The authority of these two Fathers of the Church seems to me sufficient to refute the improper interpretation that the Council gives of evangelical mildness. Our Lord doubtless did not preach draconian behavior, but this is no reason to disguise him as an apostle of liberal religious toleration!

The Liberty of the Act of Faith

Finally there is invoked the *liberty of the act of faith.*[3] There we have a double argument, of which here is the first part: To impose, for religious reasons, limits onto the practice of a dissident cult would be indirectly to compel its adherents to embrace the Catholic faith. Now the act of

---

1 *Contra epist. Parmeniani*, 3,2; quoted by Saint Thomas, *Catena aurea*, in Matthæum XIII, 29-30.
2 *Homily 46 on Saint Matthew*, quoted by Saint Thomas, loc. cit. The question of putting heretics to death is of no importance to our purpose here.
3 *Dignitatis humanæ*, 10.

faith must be exempt from all compulsion: "Let no one be compelled to embrace the Catholic faith against his will."[1]

I answer, with sound moral theology, that such a constraint is legitimate, according to the rules of the *voluntarium indirectum*, the indirectly voluntary act or effect. It has indeed for its direct object to limit the dissident cult, which is a good,[2] and for its only *indirect* and remote effect to urge certain non-Catholics on to be converted, with the risk that some may become Catholics more through fear or social expediency than from conviction: something which is not desirable in itself, but can be permitted when there is a proportionate reason.

The second argument is much more essential and demands some expansion. It rests on the *liberal idea of the act of faith*. According to Catholic doctrine,[3] faith is a consent, a submission of the intelligence to *the authority of God* who reveals, under the impulse of the *free* will, itself moved by grace. On the one hand, the act of faith must be free, that is to say, must avoid all external restraint which would have as its object, or its direct effect, to extort it against the subject's will.[4] On the other hand, the act of faith being a submission to divine authority, no power and no third person has the right to thwart the beneficial ascendancy of the First Truth, which has an inalienable right to illuminate the intelligence of the believer. It follows from this that the believer has a right to religious liberty: no one has the right to compel him, and no one has the right to prevent him from embracing the divine revelation or from prudently performing the corresponding external cultic acts.

---

1 Canon Law of 1917, canon 1351.
2 It is a good for the Catholic religion, and even for the temporal common good, when it is based on the religious unanimity of the citizens.
3 Vatican I, Dogmatic constitution *Dei Filius*, Denz. 1789, 1810; Saint Thomas IIa IIæ, q. 2, a9; q4, a2.
4 Cf. above.

Now, forgetful of the objective, quite divine and supernatural character of the act of divine faith, the Liberals, and following them the Modernists, make of the faith the expression of the *subjective conviction* of the subject[1] at the termination of his personal search[2] in order to try to respond to the great questions that the universe makes him ask.[3] The fact of the external divine revelation, its being proposed by the Church, gives a place to the creative inventiveness of the subject; or at least the latter should do its best to go and meet the former.[4] If this is the way it is, divine faith is reduced to the rank of the religious convictions of the non-Christians, who fancy themselves to have a divine faith, whereas they have only a human persuasion: their motive for adhering to their creed not being the revealing divine authority, but the free judgment of their mind. Now, there you have their basic inconsistency. The Liberals claim that they keep in this act of very human persuasion the marks of inviolability and of exemption from all constraint, which belong only to the act of divine faith! They assure us that by the acts of their religious convictions, the followers of the other religions are put into relation with God and that, from then on, this relation must be removed from all constraint that would be attempted on it. "All the *religious faiths* are respectable and untouchable," they say.

But these last allegations are manifestly false. For, through their religious convictions, the adherents of the other religions do nothing but cling to the imaginations of their own mind, human productions that have in themselves nothing of the divine, either in their cause, or in their object, or in the motive for adhering to them.

That does not mean that there is no truth in their convictions, or that they cannot be keeping some traces of the primitive or subsequent revelation. But the presence of

---

1 Cf. St. Pius X, Encyclical *Pascendi*, n. 8; Denz. 2075.
2 Cf. Vatican II, *Dignitatis humanæ*, n. 3.
3 Cf. Vatican II, *Nostra ætate*, n. 2.
4 Father Pierre-Reginald Cren, O.P., shamelessly opposes his personalist conception of revelation to the Catholic notion of the faith: "Revelation: dialogue between the divine liberty and human liberty"; he gives this title in his article dedicated to the freedom of the act of faith (*Lumière et Vie*, n. 69, *Religious liberty*, p. 39).

these *semina Verbi* is not sufficient by itself to make of their convictions an act of divine faith! This is true more especially as this supernatural act, if God wanted to stir it up by his grace, would in most cases be impeded by the presence of the multiple errors and superstitions to which these men continue to adhere.

In face of the subjectivism and the naturalism of the Liberals, we must reaffirm today the objective and supernatural character of the divine faith which is the Christian and Catholic faith. It alone has an absolute and inviolable right to respect and to religious liberty.

II

Vatican II and the Catholic City

Let us make the point. The conciliar declaration on religious liberty turns out, to begin with, to be contrary to the constant magisterium of the Church.[1] Moreover, it is not located along the line of the fundamental rights defined by the recent Popes.[2] Furthermore, we have just seen that it does not rest on any foundation, rational or revealed. Finally it is important to examine whether it is in accord with the Catholic principles which regulate the relations of the temporal city with religion.

Limits of Religious Liberty

Vatican II stipulates first of all that religious liberty must be confined within "just limits,"[3] "according to the juridical rules... consistent with the objective moral order, which are required in order effectively to safeguard the rights of all... the authentic public peace... as well as the protection due to public morality."[4] That is all very reasonable, but leaves aside the *essential question*, which is this: does not the State have the duty, and therefore the right, *to safeguard the religious unity of the citizens* in the true

---

1 Chapter XXVII, first part.
2 Ibid, second part.
3 *Dignitatis humanæ*, 1.
4 Ibid, 7.

religion and to protect the Catholic souls against scandal and the propagation of religious error and, *for these reasons only,* to limit the practice of the false cults, even to prohibit them if need be?

Such is nonetheless the doctrine of the Church, set out with vigor by Pope Pius IX in *Quanta cura,* in which the Pontiff condemns the opinion of those who, "contrary to the doctrine of Scripture, of the Church, and of the holy Fathers, do not fear to affirm that 'the best government is that in which the office of repressing the violators of the Catholic religion by the sanction of penalties is not conceded to the government, except when the public peace demands it.'"[1] The obvious meaning of the expression "violators of the Catholic religion" is: those who publicly practice a worship other than Catholic worship, or who, publicly, do not observe the laws of the Church. Pius IX teaches thus that the State governs in a better way when it recognizes that it has the function of repressing the public practice of the erroneous cults, for the sole reason that they are erroneous, and not simply to safeguard the public peace; on the exclusive grounds that they go against the Christian and Catholic order of the City, and not only because the public peace or morality would be affected by them.

This is why it must be said that the "limits" fixed by the Council onto religious liberty are only dust in the eyes, concealing the *radical defect* from which they suffer and which is *not to take into consideration the difference between truth and error!* Against all justice they pretend to attribute the same right to the true religion and to the false ones, and they then strive artificially to limit the damages by barriers which are far from satisfying the requirements of Catholic doctrine. I would readily compare "the limits" of religious liberty to the security guard-rails on the highways, which serve to contain the swervings of the vehicles whose drivers have lost control. In the very first place, it would still be a question of reminding the drivers of their duty to follow the traffic laws!

---

1 PIN. 39; Denz. 1690.

Falsification of the Temporal Common Good

Let us go on now to the most basic flaws in religious liberty. The conciliar argumentation rests in reality upon a false personalistic conception of common good reduced to the sum of private interests, or, as it is said, to respect for the rights of persons—to the detriment of the common work to be accomplished for the greater glory of God and the good of all. John XXIII' in *Pacem in terris* already tends to adopt this partial and therefore warped view. He writes:

> In contemporary thought, the common good resides especially in the safeguarding of the rights and of the duties of the human person.[1]

Pius XII, confronted by the contemporary totalitarianisms, no doubt legitimately contrasted with them the fundamental rights of the human person;[2] but this does not mean that Catholic doctrine limits itself to that. By dint of mangling the truth in a personalistic sense, one ends up by entering into the game of frantic individualism that the liberals have succeeded in introducing into the Church. As Charles de Koninck (*De la primauté du bien commun contre les personnalistes*) and Jean Madiran (*Le principe de totalité*) have emphasized, it is not by exalting the individual that one genuinely fights against totalitarianism, but by recalling that the true temporal common good is not an end in itself but is ordained positively, even if indirectly, for the good of the city of God here below and in Heaven! Let us not make ourselves accomplices of the personalists in their secularization of right!

In other terms and concretely, before bothering to find out whether the Moslems, the Krishna people, and the Moonies are not overly bullied by the law, the State (I am not speaking about non-Christian countries) must be vigilant to safeguard the Christian soul of the country, which is the essential element of the common good in a nation that is still Christian. Some would say that this is a question of emphasis! No! It is a basic question: is the all-

---

1 April 11, 1963; n. 61 of the Encyclical.
2 Cf. Especially the radio message of Christmas 1942.

Inclusive idea of the Catholic city a Catholic doctrine, yes
or no?

Ruin of the Public Law of the Church

The worse thing, I would say, about the religious liberty of Vatican II is the consequences: the ruin of the
Church's public Law, the death of the social reign of Our
Lord Jesus Christ, and finally the religious indifferentism of
individuals. According to the Council, the Church can still
enjoy in fact a special recognition on the part of the State;
but it does not have a natural and primordial *right* to this
recognition, even in a nation that has a great Catholic
majority: it is all finished for the *principle* of the confessional Catholic State, which had created the happiness of
the nations that have remained Catholic. The clearest application of the Council has been the suppression of the
Catholic States, their laicization by virtue of the principles
of Vatican II and at the request even of the Vatican. All
these Catholic nations (Spain, Colombia, etc.) have been
betrayed by the Holy See itself in application of the Council! The separation of Church and State was vaunted as the
"ideal system" by Cardinal Casaroli and by John Paul II, at
the time of the reform of the Italian concordat!

The Church finds itself reduced on principle to the common right recognized by the State for all religions.
Through a nameless impiety, it finds itself on the same
footing of equality as heresy, treachery, and idolatry. Its
public right is thus radically wiped out.

Nothing stands, in doctrine and in practice, of what
had been the system of public relations of civil society with
the Church and the other religions, which can be summed
up in these words: recognition of the true religion, possible
and limited tolerance of the other religions. Thus, the *Fuero
de los Españoles*, the basic charter of the rights and the
duties of the Spanish citizen, wisely foresaw in its article 6,
before the Council:

> The profession and the practice of the Catholic
> religion, which is the religion of the Spanish State, will
> enjoy official protection. No one will be disturbed, either
> for his religious beliefs, or in the private exercise of his

worship. There will not be permitted either external ceremonies or demonstrations other than those of the State religion.[1]

This very strict non-tolerance of the dissident cults is perfectly justified: on the one hand, it can be imposed onto the State in the name of its *cura religionis*, its duty to protect the Church and the faith of its members; on the other hand, the religious unanimity of the citizens in the true faith is a precious and irreplaceable good, which it must protect at any cost, no matter what, for the temporal *common good* itself of a Catholic nation. This is what the schema on the relations between the Church and the State written up for the Council by Cardinal Ottaviani expressed. This document simply set forth the Catholic doctrine on that question, a doctrine wholly applicable in a Catholic nation:

> Hence, therefore, the same as the civil authority considers that it has the right to protect public morality, likewise, in order to protect the citizens against the seductions of error, in order to keep the City in the unity of faith, which is the supreme good and the source of manifold, even temporal benefits, the civil power can, of itself, regulate and moderate the public manifestations of other cults and defend the citizens against the diffusion of the false doctrines which, in the judgment of the Church, put their eternal salvation in danger.[2]

The Confusions that Are Kept Up Reveal the Hidden Apostasy!

The *Fuero de los Españoles*, as we have seen, tolerates the *private* practice of the erroneous cults; but it does not allow their *public* manifestations. That is a completely classical distinction that *Dignitatis humanæ* refused to apply. The Council defined religious liberty as a right of the person in religious matters, "*in private as in public*, alone or associated with others." And the conciliar document justified this refusal of all distinction: "The social nature of man indeed

---

1 Quoted by Cardinal Ottaviani, *The Church and the City*, Vatican Polyglot Press, 1963, p. 275.
2 See the whole text of this document in the appendix of the present work.

itself requires that he express externally the internal acts of religion, that in religious matters he has to have give-and-take with others, that he profess his religion *in a communcal form*" (DH.3).

Beyond any doubt, *religion* is an assemblage of acts not only interior to the soul (devotion, prayer) but exterior (adoration, sacrifice), and not only private (family prayer) but also public (religious functions in the buildings of worship—let us say the churches—processions, pilgrimages, etc.). But that is not the problem. The issue is to know with *what* religion we are dealing: whether it is the true one or a false one! In regard to the true religion, it has the right to practice all the above-mentioned acts "with a prudent liberty," as Leo XIII says,[1] that is to say, within the limits of public order, in a not unseasonable fashion.

But the acts of the erroneous cults must be carefully distinguished from one another. Acts that are purely *internal* avoid all human power by their nature itself.[2] The *private external* acts, in return, can be sometimes subject to the regulation of a Catholic State if they disturb the Catholic order: for example, prayer meetings of non-Catholics in private apartments. Finally, the *public* acts of worship fall by themselves under the power of the laws which aim at forbidding, if necessary, all advertising to the erroneous cults. But how was the Council able to agree to make these distinctions, since it refused at the outset to distinguish the true religion from the false ones and likewise to distinguish between the Catholic State, the confessional non-Catholic State, the Communist State, the pluralist State, etc. On the contrary, Cardinal Ottaviani's schema did not fail to make all these absolutely indispensable precise points. But precisely, and here the inanity and impiety of the conciliar scheme are understood, Vatican II intended to define a right which could suit all forms and shapes, independently of the truth! This is what the Freemasons had asked for. Thus you had there a hidden apostasy from the Truth, which is Our Lord Jesus Christ!

---

1 *Libertas*, PIN. 207.
2 If the power of the Church over its subjects is excepted, a power that is not purely human.

Death of the Social Reign of Our Lord Jesus Christ

Now, if the State no longer recognizes in itself a singular duty towards the true religion of the true God, the common good of civil society is no longer ordered to the heavenly city of the blessed; and the City of God on earth, that is to say, the Church, finds itself deprived of its beneficial and unique influence on all of public life! Whether one wants it or not, social life is organized outside the truth, outside the divine law. Society becomes atheistic. This is the death of the social Reign of Our Lord Jesus Christ.

This is indeed what Vatican II did, when Bishop De Smedt, chairman of the schema on religious liberty, asserted on three occasions: *"The State is not a competent authority to pass a judgment of truth or falsity in religious matters."*[1] What a monstrous declaration, that Our Lord no longer has the right to reign, to reign alone, to permeate all the civil laws with the law of the Gospel! How many times had Pius XII not condemned such a *juridical positivism*,[2] which claimed that the juridical order must be separated from the moral order, because the distinction between the true and the false religions could not be expressed in juridical terms! Read the *Fuero de los Españoles* again!

Furthermore, unsurpassable blasphemy, the Council intended that the State, freed of its duties towards God, become for the future the guarantee that no religion *"be prevented from freely manifesting the particular efficacy of its doctrine in organizing society and enlivening all human activity."*[3] Vatican II thus invites Our Lord to come and organize and enliven society, in concert with Luther, Mohammed, and Buddha! This is what John Paul II wanted to bring about at Assisi! An irreligious and blasphemous plan!

Formerly, the union between the Church and the Catholic State had as its fruit the Catholic City, the perfect realization of the social Reign of Our Lord Jesus Christ.

---

1 *Relatio de reemendatione schematis emendati*, May 28, 1965, document 4, SC.
2 Pius XII, Letter of October 19th, 1945, for the Nineteenth Social Week of Italian Catholics, AAS. 37, 274; Allocution "Con vivo compiacimento," of November 13th, 1945, to the Tribunal of the Rota, PIN. 1064, 1072.
3 *Dignitatis humanæ* 4.

Today, the Church of Vatican II is married to the State which it wants to be atheistic; the fruit of this adulterous union is pluralistic society, the Babel of religions, the indifferentist City, object of all the desires of Freemasonry!

The Reign of Religious Indifferentism

"To each his religion!" it is said. Or, "The Catholic religion is good for the Catholics, but the Moslem one is good for the Moslems!" Such is the motto of the citizens of the indifferentist City. How do you expect them to think otherwise, when the Church of Vatican II teaches them that other religions "are not devoid of significance and of value in the mystery of salvation"?[1] How do you expect them to consider the other religions differently, when the State grants to all of them the same liberty? Religious liberty fatally breeds the indifferentism of individuals. Pius IX was already condemning in the *Syllabus* the following proposition:

> It is false that the civil liberty of all forms of worship, and the full power left to all to manifest all their thoughts openly and publicly, more easily throw the peoples into corruption of morals and of the mind, and propagate the pestilence of indifferentism.[2]

This is what we are living: since the declaration on religious liberty, the great majority of Catholics are convinced that *"men can find the path to eternal salvation and obtain salvation, in the worship of any religion whatever."*[3] There again the plan of the Freemasons is accomplished; they have succeeded, by means of a Council of the Catholic Church, in *"giving credence to the great error of the present time, which consists in... putting all the religious forms onto the same footing of equality."*[4]

All those conciliar Fathers who gave their vote to *Dignitatis humanæ* and proclaimed religious liberty with Paul VI, did they realize that they had in fact uncrowned Our Lord Jesus Christ by tearing away the crown of His social

---

1 Decree on ecumenism, *Unitatis redintegratio*, n. 3.
2 Proposition 79.
3 *Syllabus*, condemned proposition no. 17.
4 Leo XIII, Encyclical *Humanum Genus* on the Freemasons, April 20, 1884.

royalty? Did they grasp that they had very concretely dethroned Our Lord Jesus Christ from the throne of His divinity? Did they understand that, making themselves the echo of the apostate nations, they were making those abominable blasphemies rise up towards His throne: "We do not want him to rule over us"[1]; "We have no king but Cæsar"? [2]

But He, making light of the confused murmur that rose up from this assembly of senseless people, withdrew from them His Spirit.

---

1 Luke 19:14.
2 John 19:15.

Chapter XXIX

A Pacifist Council

The dialogue and the free searching advocated by the Council, of which I spoke to you before, are clearly marked symptoms of the Liberalism of Vatican II: they wanted to invent new methods for the apostolate among the non-Christians by dropping the principles of the missionary spirit. You can re-read there what I called *the apostasy of principles*, which characterizes the liberal spirit. But the Liberalism which penetrated the Council went much farther; it went as far as *betrayal*, by making peace with all the enemies of the Church. They wanted to make a pacifist council.

Recollect how John XXIII, in his opening address at the Council, set forth the new attitude that the Church must have from then on with regard to the errors which threaten its doctrine: recalling that the Church had never failed to be opposed to the errors, that it had often condemned them with the utmost severity, the Pope made the most of the fact, Wiltgen tells us,[1] that it preferred now *"to use the remedy of mercy rather than the weapons of rigor*, and judged it opportune, in the present circumstances, amply to lay out the strength of its doctrine rather than have

---

1 Op. cit., p. 15.

recourse to condemnations." Now, these were not only deplorable words, showing moreover a very blurred thinking; they were a whole program that expressed the pacifism which was that of the Council.

It was said: we have to make peace with the Freemasons, peace with the Communists, peace with the Protestants. So we must finish off with these perpetual wars, this permanent hostility! This is furthermore what Msgr. Montini, then Substitute to the Secretariat of State, said to me when I asked him, during one of my visits to Rome during the 1950s, for the condemnation of *Moral Rearmament*. He answered me, "Oh, we must not always condemn, always condemn! The Church is going to look like a cruel mother!" That is the expression that Msgr. Montini used, the Substitute of Pope Pius XII. I can still hear it! So, no more condemnations, no more anathemas! Let us at last get along together.

The Triple Pact

"*Freemasons, what do you want?* What do you ask of us?" Such is the question that Cardinal Bea went to ask the B'nai B'rith before the beginning of the Council. The interview was announced by all the newspapers of New York, where it took place. And the Freemasons answered that what they wanted was "religious liberty!"—that is to say, all the religions put on the same footing. The Church must no longer be called the only true religion, the sole path of salvation, the only one accepted by the State. Let us finish up with these inadmissible privileges. And so, declare religious liberty. Well, they got it: it was *Dignitatis humanæ.*

"*Protestants, what do you want?* to satisfy you, so that we can pray together?" And the answer was this: "Change your worship, take out from it what we cannot admit!" Good! they were told, we will even have you come, when we work out the liturgical reform. You will formulate your wishes, and we will draw up our worship according to you! Well, that happened; it was the constitution on the liturgy,

Sacrosanctum concilium, the first document promulgated by Vatican II, which gave the principles and the detailed program of this liturgical alignment with the Protestants;[1] and then the *Novus Ordo Missæ* promulgated by Paul VI in 1969.

"Communists, what do you desire? in order that we may have the happiness of having some representatives of the Russian Orthodox Church at the Council, some emissaries of the KGB!" And the condition put down by the Patriarchiate of Moscow was this: "Do not condemn Communism at the Council; do not speak of it!" (I would add: "Especially do not amuse yourselves by consecrating Russia to the Immaculate Heart of Mary!"). And then, "Show openness and dialogue with us." And the agreement[2] was concluded, the betrayal completed: "Good! We will not condemn Communism." That was executed to the letter: I myself carried, along with Bishop de Proença Sigaud, a petition with 450 signatures of conciliar Fathers, to the Secretary of the Council, Bishop Felici, asking that the Council declare a condemnation of the most appalling technique of slavery in human history, which is Communism. Then, since nothing was happening, I asked how it was going with our request. Someone looked, and finally answered me with an astounding off-handedness, "Oh, your request has been mislaid in a drawer...."[3] And Communism was not condemned; or, rather, the Council, which had given itself the responsibility of discerning the "signs of the times," was condemned by Moscow to keeping silence on the most obvious and the most monstrous of the Signs of this time!

It is clear that there was, at the Second Vatican Council, an agreement with the enemies of the Church, so as to finish off with the existing enmity towards them. But this is an agreement with the Devil!

---

1 The principles of the liturgical revolution were indeed there, but formulated in such a manner as to pass unnoticed by the non-initiated.
2 Between Cardinal Tisserant, the authorized agent of Pope John XXIII, and Bishop Nicodemus, concluded at Metz in 1962 (cf. *Itinéraires*, April, 1963; February, 1964; July-August, 1984).
3 Cf. Wiltgen, op. cit., pp. 269-274.

The Church Converted to the World

The pacifist spirit of the Council seems to me very well characterized by Pope Paul VI himself in his speech to the last public session of Vatican II, December 7, 1965. The Church and modern man, the Church and the world—these are the themes approached by the Council with a new look that Paul VI here wonderfully defines:

> The Church of the Council, it is true, has not contented itself with pondering over its own nature and over the relations that unite it to God; it has been very much occupied with man, with man such as in reality he presents himself in our time: the living man, the man entirely occupied with himself, the man who makes himself not only the center of all that concerns him, but who dares to assert himself as the principle and the ultimate reason for all reality...

There then follows a whole enumeration of the miseries of man without God and of his false grandeurs, which concludes thus:

> ...man the sinner and the holy man; and so on.

I truly wonder what *the holy man* is going to do at the end of this accumulation of uncleannesses! Especially as Paul VI sums up what he has just described, by mentioning *secular and profane humanism:*

> Secular and profane humanism has finally appeared in its awful stature and has, in a certain sense, challenged the Council. The religion of God, who became man, has met with the religion (for it is one of them) of Man, who makes himself god. What has happened? A shock, a fight, an anathema? That could have happened: but it did not take place. The old story of the Samaritan has been the model of spirituality for the Council. A sympathy without limits has completely overrun it. The discovery of human needs (and they are so much greater as the son of the earth becomes more grown-up) absorbed the attention of our synod. Grant at least this merit to it, you, the modern humanists; and know how to recognize our new humanism: we also, *we more than anyone, we have the cult of man.*

There you have it then, explained, in an ingenuous and lyrical manner, but clearly and terribly, what was not the spirit, but the *spirituality* of the Council: a "sympathy without limits" towards the secular man, for the man without God! Still, if it had been for the purpose of lifting up this fallen man, of revealing his mortal wounds to him, of dressing them for him with an effective remedy, of healing him and bringing him into the bosom of the Church, of submitting him to his God.... But no! It was to be able to say to the world, "You see, the Church also has the cult of man."

I do not hesitate to affirm that the Council brought to reality the conversion of the Church to the world. I leave it to you to reflect who the moving spirit of this spirituality was: it is enough for you to remember the one whom Our Lord Jesus Christ calls the Prince of this World.

Chapter XXX

Vatican II, Triumph of Catholic Liberalism

I do not think that anyone can accuse me of exaggeration when I say that the Council was the triumph of liberal ideas. The preceding topics have sufficiently displayed the facts: the liberal tendencies, the tactics and the successes of the Liberals at the Council, and finally their pacts with the enemies of the Church.

Besides, the Liberals themselves, the liberal Catholics, proclaim that Vatican II was their victory. In his conversation with Vittorio Messori, Cardinal Ratzinger, former "periti" of a liberal mind at the Council, explains how Vatican II posed and resolved the problem of the assimilation of liberal principles by the Catholic Church; he does not say that that led to an admirable success, but he affirms that this assimilation was done, was realized:

> The problem of the 1960s was *to acquire* the best expressed values of two centuries of "liberal" culture. These are in fact values which, even if they were born outside the Church, can find their place—purified and cor-

rected—in its vision of the world. This is what has been done.[1]

Where was this done? At the Council, to be sure, which ratified the liberal principles in *Gaudium et spes* and *Dignitatis humanæ*. How was this done? By an attempt dedicated to failure, a squaring of the circle: to marry the Church to the principles of the Revolution. This is precisely the aim, the illusion of the liberal Catholics.

Cardinal Ratzinger does not boast too much of this undertaking; he even judges the result with some severity:

> But now the climate is different; it has indeed grown worse in comparison with the one which justified an optimism that was no doubt ingenuous. A new balance now must be sought.[2]

The balance therefore has not yet been found, twenty years later! But it is still being sought: this is indeed forever the liberal illusion!

Other liberal Catholics, in contrast, are not so pessimistic; they openly celebrate victory: the Council is our victory. Read for example the work of Mr. Marcel Prélot, senator from Doubs, on the history of liberal Catholicism.[3] The author begins by contrasting two quotations, one from Paul VI, the other from Lamennais, the comparison of the two being significant. Here is what Paul VI says in his conciliar message to the governors (I believe that I have already quoted this text to you), on December 8, 1965:

> What does it ask of you, this Church, after almost two thousand years of vicissitudes of all sorts in its relations with you, the powers of the earth; what does it ask of you today? It has told you in one of the major texts of this Council: it asks of you only liberty.

And here is what Lamennais wrote, for a prospectus intended to make his newspaper *L'Avenir* known:

> All the friends of religion should understand that it needs only one single thing: liberty.

---

1 *Gesu*, November, 1984, p. 72.
2 Ibid.
3 Armand Colin Ed.

Thus, you see: with Lamennais, as at Vatican II, it is the same liberal principle of *"liberty alone"*: no privilege for the truth, for Our Lord Jesus Christ, for the Catholic Church. No! The same liberty for all: for error as for the truth, for Mohammed as for Jesus Christ. Is this not the profession of the purest Liberalism (called Catholic)?

And Marcel Prélot next recalls the history of this Liberalism right up to its triumph at Vatican II:

> Catholic Liberalism... knows victories; it pierces with the circular letter of Eckstein in 1814; it flashes with the soaring of *l'Avenir* in the autumn of 1830; it knows victories, alternating with crises; until the message of Vatican II to the governors marks its end: its fundamental claims, put to the test and purified, were accepted by the Council itself. Therefore it is possible today to contemplate liberal Catholicism, as it is in itself at last, changed over the ages. It avoids the confusions which have obstructed its course, which, at certain times, have nearly ended it. It seems thus that it was really not a series of pious illusions, professed by diaphanous and ghostly shadows, but like a powerful thought, having, in the course of a century and a half, taken its hold on the minds and on the laws, before receiving the final welcome of that Church which it had so well served, but by which it had been so often unappreciated.

This confirms exactly what we are saying: Vatican II is the council of the triumph of Liberalism.

The same confirmation is to be had by reading the book of Mr. Yves Marsaudon, *Ecumenism Viewed by a Traditional Freemason*, written during the Council. Marsaudon knows what he is saying:

> The Christians must not forget, for all that, that every path leads to God... and continue in this courageous idea of freedom of thought, which—one can now speak of revolution, setting out from our Masonic lodges—has expanded itself gloriously above the dome of Saint Peter's.

He triumphs. As for us, we weep! And he adds these lines, terrible but still true:

> When Pius XII decided to direct the very important ministry of Foreign Affairs himself, the Secretary of State, Msgr. Montini was elevated to the extremely burdensome post of archbishop of the largest diocese in Italy, Milan;

but he did not receive the purple. It became not impossible canonically, but difficult from tradition, that at the death of Pius XII he should accede to the supreme Pontificate. It is for this reason that a man came who, like the Precursor, was called John; and everything began to change.

And this man, a Freemason and therefore Liberal, spoke the truth: all their ideas, for which they had struggled a century and a half, were confirmed by the Council. These liberties—liberty of thought, of conscience, and of worship—were written down at this council, with the religious liberty of *Dignitatis humanæ* and the objection of conscience of *Gaudium et spes*. Now, this has happened not by chance but thanks to men, infected themselves with Liberalism, who have ascended to the See of Peter and have made use of their power to impose these errors onto the Church. Yes, truly, Vatican II Council is the ratification of liberal Catholicism. And when it is remembered that Pope Pius IX, eighty-five years earlier, said and repeated to those who were visiting him in Rome, "Be careful! There are no worse enemies of the Church than the liberal Catholics!"—then can be measured the catastrophe that such liberal Popes and such a council represent for· the Church and for the reign of Our Lord Jesus Christ!

Chapter XXXI

Paul VI, Liberal Pope

Y ou will perhaps wonder: how is it possible, this triumph
of Liberalism through Popes John XXIII and Paul VI,
and through a Council, Vatican II? Is this catastrophe
reconcilable with the promises made by Our Lord to Peter
and to His Church: "The gates of hell shall not prevail over
it"[1]; "I am with you all days, even to the end of the
world."[2] I do not think that there is any contradiction. Indeed, to the extent that these Popes and the Council
neglected or refused to make use of their infallibility, to appeal
to that charism which is guaranteed to them by the Holy
Ghost provided that they indeed intend to use it, well, they
were able to commit doctrinal errors or, a fortiori, to let the
enemy penetrate into the Church by reason of their
negligence or their complicity. To what degree were they
accomplices? Of what faults were they culpable? To what
extent was their office itself compromised?

It is indeed obvious that some day the Church will
judge this council, will judge these Popes; it will certainly
be necessary. How will Pope Paul VI, in particular, be
judged? Certain people assert that he was a *heretic, schis-*

---

1 Matthew 16:18.
2 Matthew 28:20.

matic, and apostate; others believe that they can demonstrate that Paul VI could not have had the good of the Church in view, and that therefore he was not the Pope: this is the thesis of the *Sedes vacans.* I do not say that these opinions do not have some arguments in their favor. Perhaps, you will tell me, in thirty years things that were hidden will be discovered; basic principles that should have been self-evident to contemporaries will be better perceived, assertions of that Pope absolutely contrary to the tradition of the Church, etc. Perhaps. But I do not think that it is necessary to have recourse to these explanations; I think that it is even an error to follow these hypotheses.

Others think, in a simplistic fashion, that there were then two Popes: one, the true one, was imprisoned in the cellars of the Vatican, while the other, the impostor, the double, sat on the throne of Saint Peter, to the misfortune of the Church. Books have appeared on *the two Popes,* supported by the revelations of a person possessed by the demon and by the so-called scientific arguments that assert, for example, that the voice of the double is not that of the true Paul VI!

Finally, others think that Paul VI was *not responsible for his acts,* prisoner as he was of his entourage, even drugged, which seems to become visible from several pieces of evidence showing a Pope physically exhausted, that had to be held up, etc. This is still too simple a solution, in my opinion; for in that case we would have only had to wait for the next Pope. Now we have had (I do not speak of John Paul I, who reigned only a month) another Pope, John Paul II, who has invariably pursued the line traced by Paul VI.

*

Now, the real solution seems to me to be another one, much more complex, painful, and sorrowful. It is supplied by a friend of Paul VI, Cardinal Daniélou. In his *Memoirs,* published by a member of his family, the Cardinal says explicitly: "It is obvious that Paul VI is *a liberal Pope.*"

And this is the solution that seems the most probable historically: because this Pope is like a fruit of Liberalism;

all of his life was impregnated with the influence of the men who surrounded him or whom he took as teachers and who were Liberals.

He did not hide his liberal sympathies: at the Council, the men whom he appointed as *moderators* in the place of the presidents named by John XXIII, those four moderators were, along with Cardinal Agagianian, a Curia cardinal without personality, Cardinals Lercaro, Suenens, and Döpfner, all three of them Liberals and his friends. The presidents were relegated to the rear, to the table of honor; and it was these three moderators who directed the proceedings of the Council. Likewise Paul VI throughout the Council supported the liberal faction which was opposed to the tradition of the Church. This is known. Paul VI repeated—I have quoted this for you—the words of Lamennais, verbatim, at the end of the Council: "*The Church asks only for liberty*"; a doctrine condemned by Gregory XVI and Pius IX!

It cannot be denied that Paul VI was very strongly marked by Liberalism. This explains the historical evolution lived by the Church in these last few decades, and it characterizes very well the personal behavior of Paul VI. The Liberal, as I have told you, is a man who lives perpetually in contradiction: he asserts principles, but does the contrary. He is permanently incoherent.

Let me quote for you some examples of these thesis-antithesis binomials which Paul VI excelled in posing as so many insoluble problems which reflected his anxious and paradoxical mind. The Encyclical, *Ecclesiam Suam*, of August 6, 1964, which is the charter for his pontificate, supplies an illustration of this:

> If the Church, as We were saying, truly is conscious of what the Lord wants it to be, there rises up in it a singular fullness and a need for expression, with the clear consciousness of a mission that goes beyond it and of the good news to be spread. This is the obligation to evangelize. It is the *missionary mandate*. It is the duty of the apostolate... We know this well: "Go therefore, teach all nations," is the last commandment of Christ to His apostles. These men define their unimpeachable mission by the very name of apostles.

This is the thesis. And right away here is the antithesis:

In relation to this interior impulse of charity which tends to translate itself into an exterior talent, We will use the name, which today has become the usual one, of *dialogue*. The Church must enter into dialogue with the world in which it lives. The Church makes itself the word; the Church makes itself the message; the Church makes itself conversation.

Finally, there comes the attempt at synthesis, which does nothing but to consecrate the antithesis:

Even before converting the world, indeed better, in order to convert it, we must approach it and speak to it.[1]

More serious and more characteristic of the liberal psychology of Paul VI are the words by which he declared, after the Council, the suppression of Latin in the liturgy. After having recalled all the benefits of Latin: a sacred language, a fixed language, a universal language, he asks, in the name of adaptation, for the *"sacrifice"* of Latin, even while admitting that this will be a great loss for the Church! Here are the very words of Pope Paul VI, reported by Louis Salleron in his work, *The New Mass:*[2]

On March 7, 1965, he declared to the faithful massed in Saint Peter's Square:

It is a sacrifice that the Church is making by renouncing Latin, a language that is sacred, beautiful, expressive, elegant. It has sacrificed centuries of tradition and of unity of language for an even greater aspiration towards universality.

And on May 4, 1967, this "sacrifice" was accomplished, through the Instruction *Tres abhinc annos*, which established the use of the common language for the recitation, aloud, of the Canon of the Mass.

This "sacrifice," in the mind of Paul VI, seems to have been definitive. He explains himself on this again, on November 26, 1969, while presenting the new rite of the Mass:

---

1 *Pontifical documents of Paul VI*, 1964; ed. St. Augustin, Saint-Maurice, pp. 677-679.
2 Collection *Itinéraires*, NEL, 2nd edition, 1976, p. 83.

It is no longer Latin, but the current language, that will be the principal language of the Mass. For whoever knows the beauty, the power of the Latin, its aptitude in expressing sacred things, this will certainly be a great sacrifice, to see it replaced by the current language. We are losing the language of the Christian centuries; we are becoming like intruders and outsiders in the literary domain of sacred expression. We are thus losing to a great extent that admirable and incomparable artistic and spiritual richness that is the Gregorian chant. We have reason, to be sure, to feel regrets and almost a confusion over this.

Everything should have thus dissuaded Paul VI from bringing about this "sacrifice" and persuaded him to keep the Latin. But no; taking pleasure in his "confusion" in a singularly masochistic fashion, he is going to act contrary to the principles that he has just enumerated, and to decree the "sacrifice" in the name of the "understanding of the prayer," a specious argument that was only the pretext of the Modernists.

Never was the liturgical Latin an obstacle to the conversion of the infidels or to their Christian education; indeed, on the contrary, the simple peoples of Africa and of Asia love the Gregorian chant and that one and sacred language, the sign of their belonging to Catholicism. And experience proves that where Latin was not imposed by the missionaries of the Latin Church, there the germs of future schisms were deposited. Paul VI then pronounces the contradictory sentence:

The response seems banal and prosaic, but it is good, because it is human and apostolic. *The understanding of prayer* is more precious than the decrepit silk garments with which it has been royally adorned. More valuable is the participation of the people, of this people of today that wants *to be spoken to* clearly, in an intelligible manner that it can translate into its secular language. If the noble Latin language cut us off from children, from the youth, from the world of labor and of business, if it was an opaque screen instead of being a transparent crystal, would we be making a good calculation, we, fishers of souls, by keeping for it the exclusive rights in the language of prayer and of religion?

What mental confusion, alas! Who is stopping me from praying in my language? But liturgical prayer is not a private prayer; it is the prayer of all the Church. Furthermore, another lamentable confusion, the liturgy is not an *instruction* addressed to the people, but the worship directed by the Christian people to God. The catechism is one thing, the liturgy another! It is a question, for the people assembled at the Church, not of "being spoken to clearly," but of this people's being able to praise God in the most beautiful, the most sacred, the most solemn manner there is! "To pray to God from beauty"—such was the liturgical maxim of Saint Pius X. How right he was!

*

You see, the liberal mind is one that is paradoxical and confused, distressed and contradictory. Such indeed was Paul VI. Mr. Louis Salleron explains this quite well, when he describes the physical look of Paul VI: he says *"He has a double face."* He is not speaking of duplicity, for this term expresses a perverse intention to deceive which was not present in Paul VI. No, it is a double person, whose contrasted countenance expresses a duality: now traditional in his words, now Modernist in his acts; now Catholic in his premises, his principles, and now progressive in his conclusions, not condemning what he should condemn and condemning what he ought to preserve!

Now, through this psychological weakness, this Pope offered a dreamed-of occasion, a considerable opportunity for the enemies of the Church to take advantage of him: all the while keeping one face (or half a face, as you will) Catholic, he did not hesitate to contradict tradition. He showed himself favorable to change, baptized mutation and progress, and went thus in the direction of all the enemies of the Church, who encouraged him. Did we not see, one day in the year 1976, *Izvestia*, the organ of the Soviet Communist Party, demand from Paul VI, in the name of Vatican II, my condemnation and that of Ecône? Likewise the Italian Communist newspaper *L'Unita* expressed a similar request, reserving a whole page for it, at the time of the sermon that I gave at Lille on August 29,

1976, furious as it was over my attacks against Communism! "Be conscious," it had written, addressing itself to Paul VI, "be conscious of the danger that Lefebvre represents. And continue the magnificent movement of approach begun with the ecumenism of Vatican II." It is a little embarrassing to have friends like those, don't you think? A sad illustration of a rule that we have already remarked: Liberalism leads from compromise to betrayal.

Our Attitude Towards Such a Pope

The psychology of such a liberal Pope is rather easily conceivable, but it is more difficult to uphold! It puts us indeed into a very delicate situation vis-à-vis such a head, whether it be Paul VI or John Paul II. In practice our attitude should be based on a previous discernment, rendered necessary by these extraordinary circumstances of a Pope won to Liberalism. This discernment is this: when the Pope says something that is consistent with tradition, we follow him; when he says something that goes contrary to our faith, or he encourages or lets something be done that harms our faith, then we cannot follow him! The fundamental reason for this is that the Church, the Pope, and the hierarchy are *at the service of the faith*. It is not they who make the faith; they must serve it. The faith is not being created, it is unchangeable, it is transmitted.

This is why we cannot follow those acts of these Popes that are done with the goal of confirming an action that goes against tradition: by that very act, *we would be collaborating in the autodemolition of the Church*, in the destruction of our faith!

Now, it is clear that what is unceasingly asked of us: complete submission to the Pope, complete submission to the Council, acceptance of all the liturgical reform—this goes in a direction contrary to tradition, to the extent that the Pope, the Council, and the reforms carry us far away from tradition, as the facts prove more every year. Consequently, to ask this of us is to ask us to collaborate in the disappearance of the faith. Impossible! The martyrs died to defend the faith; we have the examples of Christians imprisoned, tortured, sent to concentration camps for their faith! A grain of incense offered to the pagan god, and immediately they would have saved their lives. Someone once advised me, "Sign, sign, that you accept everything; and then you continue as before!" No! One does not play with his faith!

Chapter XXXII

A Suicidal Liberalism: the Post-conciliar Reforms

Loyal and somewhat clearsighted souls speak of "the crisis of the Church" to designate the post-conciliar epoch. Of old, people had spoken of "the Arian crisis," of "the Protestant crisis," but never of "the crisis of the Church." But, unfortunately, not everyone is in agreement in assigning the same causes to this tragedy. Cardinal Ratzinger, for example, indeed sees the crisis, but totally exonerates the Council and the post-conciliar reforms. He begins by recognizing the crisis:

> The results that have followed the Council seem cruelly opposed to the expectation of all, to begin with that of Pope John XXIII, then that of Paul VI.... The Popes and the conciliar Fathers were expecting a new Catholic unity and, on the contrary, we have gone towards a dissension which, to take again the words of Paul VI, appears to have passed from self-criticism to self-destruction. A new enthusiasm was expected, and too often it has ended on the contrary in weariness and discouragement. There was expected a leap forward, and we have found ourselves on

the contrary faced with an evolutionary process of decadence....[1]

Next we have the explanation for the crisis, given by the Cardinal:

> I am convinced that the damages that we have suffered in these last twenty years are due not to the "true" Council but to the setting in motion, inside the Church, of latent aggressive and centrifugal forces; and on the outside, they are due to the impact of a cultural revolution in the West: the assertion of an upper middle class, the new "bourgeoisie of the tertiary period," with its liberal-radical ideology of an individualistic, rationalistic, hedonistic type.[2]

And again a little bit farther on, Cardinal Ratzinger denounces what is, according to him, the true "interior" reponsible one for the crisis: an "anti-spirit of the Council":

> Already at the time of the sessions, then more and more during the period that followed, a pretended "spirit of the Council" opposed itself which, in reality, is a true "anti-spirit" of it. According to this pernicious Konzils-Ungeist, everything that is "new" (or presumed to be such: how many ancient heresies there are in these years, presented as novelties!) would be always, however it may be, better than that which was or that which is. It is the anti-spirit according to which the history of the Church should begin at Vatican II, considered as a kind of zero point.[3]

Then the Cardinal proposes his solution: come back to the true Council, by considering it not "as a point of departure from which one goes away running, but indeed rather as a base on which it is necessary to build solidly."

*

I certainly want to consider the external causes of the crisis of the Church, particularly a liberal and pleasure-seeking mentality that has spread over society, even Christian society. But precisely what did Vatican II do to oppose

---

1 *Conversation on the Faith*, Fayard, Paris, 1985; pp. 30-31.
2 Op. cit., pp. 31-32.
3 Op. cit., pp. 36-37.

this? Nothing! Or rather, Vatican II only pushed in this direction! I will make use of a comparison: What would you think if, in the face of a threatening tidal wave, the Dutch government decided one fine day to open its dikes in order to avoid the shock? And if it excused itself afterwards, after the total inundation of the country: "We had nothing at all to do with it, it was the tidal wave!" Now that is exactly what the Council did: it opened all the traditional barriers to the spirit of the world by declaring *the opening to the world*, by religious liberty, by the pastoral Constitution "The Church in the Modern World" *(Gaudium et spes)*, which are the very *spirit* of the Council and not the anti-spirit!

As for *the anti-spirit*, I indeed admit its existence at the Council and after the Council, with the completely revolutionary opinions of the Küngs, Boffs, etc., who left the Ratzingers, Congars, etc., well behind. I concede that this antispirit completely corrupted the seminaries and universities; and there, Ratzinger the academic and theologian indeed sees the damage: this is his domain.

But I assert two things: what Cardinal Ratzinger names "anti-spirit of the Council" is only the extreme materialization of the theories of theologians who were experts at the Council! Between *the spirit* of Vatican II and the so-called *anti-spirit*, I see only a difference of degree; and it seems to me inevitable that the anti-spirit exerted influence on the very spirit of the Council. On the other hand, the spirit of the Council, this liberal spirit which I analyzed above at length[1] and which is at the root of almost all the conciliar texts and of all the reforms that have followed, must be put itself under accusation.

In other words, *"I accuse the Council"* seems to me the necessary response to the *"I excuse the Council"* of Cardinal Ratzinger! I explain myself: I maintain, and I am going to prove, that *the crisis of the Church comes down essentially to the post-conciliar reforms emanating from the most official authorities of the Church and by application of the doctrine and the directives of Vatican II.* There is, thus, nothing mar-

---

1 Chapter XXV.

ginal or underground in the essential causes of the post-conciliar disaster! Let us not forget that it was the same men and especially the same Pope, Paul VI, who made the Council and who afterwards applied it the most methodically and officially of all people, by making use of their hierarchical authority: thus the new missal of Paul VI was "*ex decreto sacrosancti œcumenici concilii Vaticani II instauratum, auctoritate Pauli PP. VI promulgatum.*"

*

Thus it would be an error to say, "But the reforms do not have their source in the Council." Without a doubt, on certain points, the reforms have gone beyond the letter of the Council; for example, the Council did not ask for the suppression of Latin in the liturgy; it only requested the introduction of the common language. But as I have said to you, in the mind of those who opened this little door, the goal was to arrive at radical change. But definitively, it suffices to report that all the reforms refer officially to Vatican II: not only the reform of the Mass and that of all the sacraments, but also those of the religious congregations, the seminaries, the episcopal assemblies, the creation of the Roman synod, the reform of relations between the Church and the States, etc.

I will limit myself to three of these reforms: the suppression of the Holy Office, the openly pro-Communist politics of the Vatican, and the new concordat between the Holy See and Italy. What was the spirit of these reforms?

The Suppression of the Holy Office

I am not making this up; I asked the question myself of Cardinal Browne, who was at the Holy Office a long time: "Is the change of the Holy Office into 'the Sacred Congregation for the Doctrine of the Faith' an accidental, superficial change, a change of label only; or is it a profound, radical change?" The Cardinal replied to me, "An *essential* change, this is evident." Indeed, the tribunal of the faith has been replaced by an *office of theological research*. They will say whatever they want, but this is the reality. The two instructions on the theology of liberation, to take this example, far from leading concretely to a clear condemnation of this "theology" and of its supporters, had as their clearest result to encourage them! And why: all this because the tribunal has become essentially an office for research. This is a radically different spirit, a Masonic spirit: there is no truth that is possessed, we are always in search of the truth. One gets lost in discussions among the members of a commission of theologians from the world over, which end up only by producing interminable texts whose haziness reflects the incoherence of their authors.

In practice they no longer condemn, they no longer designate the disapproved-of doctrines, they no longer stamp the heretics with the red-hot iron of infamy. No. These are asked to be quiet for a year, and it is said, "This teaching is not worthy of a professorship of Catholic theology"; that is all. In practice the suppression of the Holy Office is characterized, as I wrote to the Holy Father,[1] by the *free propagation of errors*. The flock of the sheep of Our Lord Jesus Christ is delivered without defense to the ravenous wolves.

The Pro-Communist Politics of the Holy See

The "Ostpolitik," or politics of the hand held out to the East, does not date from the Council, alas. Already under Pius XI and Pius XII, contacts were established, with or without the knowledge of these Popes, which led to catastrophes, fortunately limited ones.[2] But on the occasion of the Council and since then, we are seeing actual agreements: I have told you how the Russians purchased the silence of the Council on Communism.[3] After Vatican II, the Helsinki accords were patronized by the Vatican: the first and the last discourse were given there by Bishop Casaroli, who was consecrated archbishop for the event. The Holy See soon manifested a hostility towards all the

---

1 Open letter of Archbishop Lefebvre and of Bishop de Castro Mayer to John Paul II, November 21, 1983.

2 Cf. Brother Michel of the Trinity, *All the Truth on Fatima*, Tome II, *The secret and the Church*, pp. 353-378; Tome III, *The Third Secret*, pp. 237-244; G. de Nantes, editor.

3 Chapter XXIX.

anti-Communist governments. In Chile, the Holy See supported the Communist revolution of Allende[1] from 1970 to 1972. The Vatican acted thus through its nunciatures and by the nomination of cardinals, such as Tarancon (Spain), Ribeiro (Portugal), Aramburu (Argentina), Silva Henriquez (Chile), in agreement with the pro-Communist politics of the Holy See. Now the weight of such cardinals, archbishops of metropolises, is considerable in those Catholic countries! Their influence is determining over the episcopal conferences, which, through the nominations of revolutionary bishops, these too, arrive at being in the majority favorable to the politics of the Holy See, and opposed to the governments. What then can a Catholic government do against the majority of the episcopate that works against it? This is an appalling situation! We are present at an incredible overturning of forces. The Church is becoming the principal revolutionary force in the Catholic countries.

The New Concordat with Italy

The liberal politics of the Holy See, by virtue of the principles of Vatican II, has aimed at the suppression of the States still Catholic. This is what has been concretized by the new concordat between the Holy See and Italy. Having matured during twelve years of discussions, and this is no small business, this text was adopted by the Italian Senate, as the newspapers of December 7, 1978, related it, after having been approved by the commission designated by the Italian State, as well as by the commission of the Vatican. Rather than analyze this act for you, I will read to you the declaration of President Andreotti made on that day to present the document:

...Here is a disposition of principle. The new text of the first article solemnly establishes that the State and the Catholic Church are, each in its own order, independent and sovereign.

1 Cf. Léon de Poncins, *Christianity and Freemasonry*, 2nd edition, DPF, 1975; pp. 208 ff.

That is already quite false: "sovereign"; yes, it is true, that is what Leo XIII teaches in *Immortale Dei;*[1] but "independent," no! "It is necessary," says Leo XIII, "that there be between the two powers a system of well-ordered relations, not without analogy with that which in man constitutes *the union* of the soul and the body." Leo XIII says "union"; he does not say "independence"! I refer you to the conference where I covered the relations between the Church and the State.[2] But here is what follows in the text of the discourse of the Italian President:

> In principle, it is the surrender, concluded in a reciprocal manner, of the concept of the confessional State, according to the principles of the Constitution[3] and in harmony with the conclusions of **Vatican Council II.**[4]

Thus there can be no more Catholic State, confessional State, that is to say, a State that professes a religion, that professes the true religion! This is decided by principle, in application of Vatican II. And next, as a consequence of this principle, the legislation on marriage is overturned, as well as religious instruction.[5] All this is stuffed with means for making religious instruction disappear. As for Church goods, agreements were made beforehand between the State and the Methodist, Calvinist, and Hebrew religions. All of them will be on the same footing.

*

I would like to emphasize that this willingness to suppress all the Catholic institutions from civil life is a willingness in principle. It is asserted, whether it be on the lips of this Italian President, or on those of Cardinal Casaroli or of John Paul II, or on those of theologians like Cardinal Ratzinger, as definitively in the text of the conciliar declaration

---

1 Cf. Chapter XIII (PIN. 136: "the two powers").
2 Chapters XIII and XIV.
3 The new Italian Constitution, which has abolished its first article, which recognized the Catholic religion as the religion of State.
4 The President here is indicating the Declaration on Religious Liberty.
5 With the new concordat, it is the State which proposes the professors of religious instruction for the acceptance of the Church. A reversing of roles! Furthermore, if the teachers in primary school refuse to teach religion, liberty of conscience being given, they cannot be obliged to do so.

238

on religious liberty, that there should no longer be Catholic "bastions." This is a resolution in principle. In particular there must no longer be any Catholic States.

It would be something else to say: "We agree to accept the separation of Church and State, because the situation in our country has completely changed through the malice of men, the nation is no longer Catholic in the majority, etc.; therefore we are disposed to undergo a corresponding reform of the relations between Church and State, under the pressure of events. But we are not in agreement with the principle of laicization of the State and of public institutions." That would be perfectly legitimate to say, in the countries where the situation has truly changed.

But to say all-inclusively that in our era, in all countries, the system of union between the Church and the civil institutions is outmoded, this is absolutely false. Firstly, because no principle of Catholic doctrine is ever "outmoded," even if its application has to take account of circumstances; now the system of union is a principle of Catholic doctrine, as immutable as this itself.[1] And then there were, at the time of the Council and after the Council, States still entirely Catholic (Spain, Colombia, the Swiss Valais) or almost entirely so (Italy, etc.), which it would be perfectly unjustified to want to laicize.

*

Now, to take an example, Cardinal Ratzinger says exactly the opposite in his book *The Principles of Catholic Theology*:[2]

Almost no one disputes any more today that the Spanish and Italian concordats were seeking to preserve much too many things from a concept of the world which has not corresponded for a long time to the real data.

Likewise almost no one can question that to this attachment to an *out-of-date concept* of the relations between Church and State corresponded similar anachronisms in the realm of education.

---

1 On the immutability of the principles of the Church's public Law, see Chapter XIV.
2 Téqui, Paris, 1985; pp. 427 and 437.

Neither embraces nor the *ghetto* can lastingly resolve
for the Christian the problem of the modern world. It
remains that the *"dismantling of the bastions"* which Urs
von Balthasar demanded in 1952 was actually a *pressing
duty.*

It was necessary [for the Church] to separate itself
from many things which up to then assured its security
and belonged to it as proceeding almost from itself. It had
to demolish the old bastions and to rely on the sole protection of the faith.

As you can verify, these are the same liberal banalities
that we have already taken up from the pen of John
Courtney Murray and of Yves Congar:[1] the doctrine of the
Church in this matter is reduced to a "concept of the
world" tied to an age that is ended. And the evolution of
mentalities towards apostasy is affirmed as being an indifferent thing, unavoidable and completely general. Finally,
Joseph Ratzinger has only contempt or indifference
towards the rampart which the Catholic State and the institutions that flow from it constitute for the faith.

One sole question can be asked: are those people still
Catholic, if for them the social Kingship of Our Lord Jesus
Christ is an out-of-date concept? And, a second question
that I will pose to you: am I wrong in saying that Christian
and Catholic society, and definitively the Church, is dying,
not so much from the attacks of the Communists and of the
Freemasons, as from the betrayal of the liberal Catholics,
who, having made the Council, afterwards brought the
post-conciliar reforms into reality? So, admit with me,
having the facts before your eyes, that the conciliar
Liberalism is now leading the Church to the grave. The
Communists are certainly clearsighted, as the following
fact shows. In a museum in Lithuania, dedicated in part to
atheistic propaganda, there is found a large photo of "the
exchange of instruments" at the time of the signature of
the new Italian concordat between the president and Cardinal Casaroli; the photo is accompanied by this caption:
"The new concordat between Italy and the Vatican, a great

1 Cf. Chapter XIX.

victory for atheism." Any commentary seems to me super-
fluous.

Chapter XXXIII

The Remedy for Liberalism: "to Restore All in Christ"

For great evils, great remedies! But what is it that will be able to heal the cancer or the AIDS in the Church? The reponse is clear: the remedies must be applied which the Popes have proposed against the modern errors; namely Thomist philosophy, sound theology, and the Law which flows from the two first sciences.

Sound Philosophy—that of Saint Thomas Aquinas

You understand that, in order to combat the subjectivism and the rationalism which are at the basis of the liberal errors, I will not appeal to the modern philosophies, infected precisely with subjectivism or with rationalism. It is neither the *subject*, nor its knowledge, nor its love, that the philosophy of all time, and metaphysics in particular, takes as its object. It is the very being of things; it is *that which is*. It is indeed *being*, with its laws and its principles, that our most spontaneous knowledge uncovers. And at its peak, the natural wisdom that is philosophy leads, through theodicy or natural theology, into the Being *par excellence*, the Being subsisting by itself. It is indeed this first Being that common sense, supported, strengthened, and elevated by the data of the faith, prompts us to place at the summit of the real, according to the revealed definition: *Ego sum qui sum*—"I am He Who am."[1] You know indeed that to Moses, who was asking Him His name, God answered: "I am He Who am," which means: I am He Who is through Himself, I possess being through Myself.

Let us then ponder this Being who subsists by Himself, Who has not received existence but who has it through Himself. He is *"ens a se"*: being by itself, in opposition to all other beings, who are *ens ab alio*: being through another, through the gift that God has given them of existence! We can meditate on this for hours, it is so striking, unimaginable. To have being through oneself, this is to live in eternity; it is to be eternal. He who has being through himself can never have been without having it; being could never have left him. He always is, he always will be, he always has been. On the contrary, he who is *"ens ab alio,"* a being through another, he has received being from another; therefore he has begun to be at a given moment: he has begun!

How this consideration should keep us in humility! Penetrate us with the *nothing* that we are in God's eyes! "I am He Who is, you are she who is not," Our Lord was saying one day to a holy soul. How true that is! The deeper man penetrates into this principle of the simplest philosophy, the better he puts himself into his true place before God.

The mere fact of saying: I am *"ab alio,"* God is *"ens a se"*; I have begun, God is forever, what a piercing contrast! What an abyss! So it is this little being *"ab alio,"* who receives his very being from God, who would have the power to limit the glory of God? He would have the right to say to God, "You have the right to this, but no more"! "Reign in hearts, in the sacristies, in the chapels, yes; but in the street, in the city, no!" What conceit! Likewise, would it be this being *"ab alio"* who would have the power to reform the plans of God, to make things be other than what they

<hr>

1 Exodus 3:14.

are, other than what God has made them? And the laws that God, in His wisdom and His omnipotence, has appointed for all beings and especially for man and for society, these laws, the wretched being *"ab alio"* would have the power to remake them at his caprice by saying, "I am free"! What pretension! What absurdity, this revolt of Liberalism! Behold how important it is to possess a sound philosophy and thus to have a thorough knowledge of the natural, supernatural, social, and political order. And for this, the teaching of Saint Thomas Aquinas is irreplaceable. I will not resist quoting for you Leo XIII in his Encyclical, *Æterni Patris*, of August 4, 1879:

> The Angelic Doctor considered the philosophical conclusions in the reasons and the *very principles of things*: now the extent of these principles and the innumerable truths that they contain in germ supply the teachers of subsequent ages with ample material for useful developments, which will be produced at the opportune time. In using as he does this same process in the refutation of errors, the great doctor arrived at this double result, of repulsing by himself all the errors of earlier times, and of supplying invincible arms in order to dispel those that will not fail to rise up in the future.

And it is especially to the modern errors of Liberalism that Leo XIII wishes the remedy of Thomistic philosophy to be applied:

> The immense peril into which the pestilence of perverse opinions has thrown the family and civil society is obvious to all of us. To be sure, both of them would enjoy a much greater peace and security if, in the academies and the schools, a doctrine more sound and more consistent with the teaching of the Church were given, a doctrine such as is found in the works of Thomas Aquinas. What Saint Thomas teaches us on the true nature of liberty, which, in our time, is degenerating into license; on the divine origin of all authority; on laws and their power; on the paternal and just government of sovereigns; on the obedience due to the highest powers; on the mutual charity which must reign among all men—what he tells us on these subjects and others of the same kind has an immense, invincible force to overturn all these principles

of the new law, full of dangers, it is known, for good order and the public welfare.

The Sound Theology, also that of Saint Thomas

In addition to the natural wisdom that is sound philosophy, he who wants to protect himself against Liberalism will have to know the supernatural wisdom that is theology. Now, it is the theology of Saint Thomas that the Church recommends among all others in order to acquire a thorough knowledge of the supernatural order. It is the *Summa Theologica* of Saint Thomas Aquinas that the Fathers of the Council of Trent "determined that in the midst of the holy assembly, along with the book of the divine Scriptures and the decrees of the supreme Pontiffs, on the altar itself, be deposited, open, so that advice, reasons, oracles could be drawn up from it."[1] It is at the school of Saint Thomas that the Council of Trent dispelled the first clouds of nascent naturalism.

Who, better than Saint Thomas, has shown that the supernatural order goes infinitely beyond the capacities and the very requirements of the natural order? He shows us (here below this can be only in the obscure light of the faith) how Our Lord, through His Redeeming Sacrifice, by the application of His merits, has elevated the nature of the redeemed ones, by sanctifying grace, by baptism, by the other sacraments, by the holy sacrifice of the Mass. It is by knowing this theology well that we will increase in ourselves *the spirit of faith*, that is to say, the faith and the attitudes which correspond to a life of faith.

Thus, in divine worship, when one truly has the faith, he has the gestures that flow from it. Precisely what we reproach the entire new liturgical reform with, is that it gives us attitudes which are no longer attitudes of faith; that it imposes on us a naturalistic and humanistic worship. It is in this way that people are afraid to make genuflections, they no longer want to manifest the adoration that is due to God, they want to reduce the sacred to the profane. This is the most sensitive thing for the persons

---

1 Leo XIII, *Aeterni Patris*.

who have contact with the new liturgy: they reckon that it is flat, that it does not raise them up, that in it there are no longer found any mysteries.

It is sound theology as well which will fortify in us this conviction of faith: Our Lord Jesus Christ is God; this central truth of our faith: the divinity of Our Lord. Then we will serve Our Lord as God, and not as a mere man. Beyond a doubt it is by His humanity that He has sanctified us, through the sanctifying grace which filled up His holy soul; this is to tell of the infinite respect that we must have for His Holy Humanity. But today the danger is to make of Our Lord a mere man, an extraordinary man, to be sure, a superman, but not the Son of God. On the contrary, if He truly is God, as the faith teaches us, then everything changes; for from that moment on, He is the Master of all things. In this case all the consequences flow from His divinity. Thus, all the attributes that theology has us acknowledge in God: His omnipotence, His omnipresence, His permanent and supreme causality in regard to everything, to all things that exist; for He is the source of being—all this is applied to Our Lord Jesus Christ Himself. He thus has supremacy over all things; by His own nature He is King, King of the universe; and no creature, individual or society, can escape His sovereignty, His sovereignty of power and His sovereignty of grace:

> It is in Him that all things have been created, those that are in the heavens and those that are on the earth... all has been created by Him and for Him... all things subsist in Him... God... has willed to reconcile all things to Himself through Him, those which are of the earth and those which are in the heavens, by making peace by the blood of His cross.[1]

Therefore, from this first truth of faith, the divinity of Our Lord Jesus Christ, is derived this second truth of faith: His Royalty, and especially His Kingship over societies, and the obedience which societies must have to the Will of Jesus Christ, the submission which the civil laws must bring about with regard to the law of Our Lord Jesus

---

[1] Col. 1:16-21.

Christ. Indeed more, Our Lord wants souls to be saved, doubtless indirectly, but effectively, through a Christian civil society, fully submissive to the Gospel, which lends itself to His redeeming design, which will be the temporal instrument for this. From that moment on, what could be more just, more necessary, than civil laws which comply with the laws of Jesus Christ and punish with the coercion of penalties the transgressors of the laws of Our Lord in the public and social domain? Now precisely, religious liberty, that of the Freemasons, like that of Vatican II, wants to suppress this restraint. But that is the ruin of the Christian social order! What does Our Lord want, if not that His redeeming sacrifice permeate civil society! What is Christian civilization, what is Christendom, if not the incarnation of the Cross of Our Lord Jesus Christ in the life of an entire society! That is what is called the social reign of Our Lord. Therefore, this is the truth which we must preach with the most vigor today, faced with Liberalism.

And next, a second consequence of the divinity of Jesus Christ is that His Redemption is not optional for eternal life! He is the Way, the Truth, and the Life! He is the door. He says Himself:

> I am the door of the sheep. All those who have come before Me are robbers and thieves; but the sheep have not listened to them. I am the door: if anyone enters through Me, he will be saved; he will come in, and he will go out, and he will find the pastures.[1]

He is the only way of salvation for every man. St. Peter proclaims:

> Salvation is in no other, for there is under heaven no other name which has been given to men, by which we must be saved.[2]

Now, this truth is the one that must be reaffirmed the most today, in the face of the false ecumenism of a liberal nature, which assures us that there are values for salvation in all religions and that it is a question of developing them. If that were true, what good would missionaries be? It is

---

1 John 10:7-9.
2 Acts 4:12.

exactly because there is no salvation in any other than Jesus Christ that the Church is animated with the missionary spirit, with the spirit of conquest, which is the very spirit of the faith.

The Law

In addition to philosophy and theology, it is necessary that a third science come to reduce the great truths of the natural order and of the supernatural order into *juridical rules*. Liberalism, indeed, even in its most moderated forms, proclaims the rights of man without God. There is nothing more indispensable, therefore, for the Catholic jurist than to base anew the rights of men living in society upon their duties towards God, upon the rights of God. Of the rights of man, in truth, there are none except those which help him to submit to the rights of God! The same truth is expressed by saying that the positive law, civil law, must be founded on the *natural law*. Pope Pius XII insisted on this principle, against the error of juridical positivism, which makes of the arbitrary will of man the source of the law.

Then, there is the supernatural law: the rights of Jesus Christ and of His Church, the rights of the souls redeemed by the blood of Jesus Christ. These rights of the Church and of Christian souls vis-à-vis the State form what we have called the **public Law of the Church.** This is a science that is practically annihilated by the conciliar declaration on religious liberty, as I have tried to show you.[1] There is nothing more urgent still, therefore, than teaching afresh the public Law of the Church, which gives the great principles that govern the relations between Church and State.[2] On this subject I recommend especially the reading of the *Institutiones juris publici ecclesiastici*, of Cardinal Ottaviani, and of the work *Ecclesia et status, fontes selecti*, by Giovanni Lo Grasso, S.J. This latter work, in particular, supplies all the documents most misappreciated or thrown into oblivion by the Liberals, from the fourth to the twentieth century.

---

1 See Chapter XXVIII.
2 See Chapter XIII.

Let us not forget, finally, that inexhaustible source of Church law that is **ecclesiastical history**: it is thus that the attitude of the first Christian emperors, placing the temporal sword at the service of the spiritual power of the Church in the fourth century, and constantly praised afterwards by the Church, or indeed the courageous resistance of the bishops and Popes against the princes usurping the spiritual power in the sequence of ages, is quite simply dogma reduced to practice and represents the most fundamental refutation of all the Liberalisms: the Liberalism of the revolutionary persecutors of the Church, just as the much more perfidious Liberalism of the so-called liberal Catholics.

Chapter XXXIV

To Rebuild the Catholic City

L*iberalism, it is for thee that I die,"* says the Church today in its death-throes. It can say like Jesus addressing those who came to arrest Him: "It is your hour, and the power of darkness."[1] It is there at Gethsemani, but it could not die. It has the look of a city occupied by the enemy, but the Resistance to the liberal sect is organizing and strengthening itself.

This sect, we saw it rise up in the sixteenth century, from the Protestant revolt, then become the instigator of the Revolution. For a century and a half of struggle without truce, the Popes have condemned the principles and the points of application of Liberalism. In spite of that, the sect has pursued its path. We have been present at its penetration into the Church, under pretense of an acceptable Liberalism, with the idea of reconciling Jesus Christ with the Revolution. Then we learned, with amazement, of the plot of penetration of the Catholic hierarchy by the liberal sect; we have seen its progress, right up to the

---

1 Luke 22:53.

highest posts, and its triumph at the Second Vatican Council. We have had liberal Popes. The first liberal Pope, the one who scoffed at the "prophets of doom," convoked the first liberal council in the history of the Church. And the gates of the sheepfold have been opened, and the wolves have come into the flock; and they have massacred the sheep. There came the second liberal Pope, the double-faced Pope, the humanist Pope; he overturned the altar, abolished the Sacrifice, profaned the sanctuary.[1] The third liberal Pope has come on the scene, the Pope of the rights of man, the ecumenist Pope, the Pope of the United Religions; and he has washed his hands, he has veiled his face in front of so many heaped-up ruins, in order not to see the bleeding wounds of the Daughter of Sion, the mortal injuries of the immaculate Spouse of Jesus Christ.

*

As for me, I will not resign; I will not content myself with being present, my arms dangling, at the death-throes of my Mother the Holy Church. To be sure, I do not share the smug optimism of the soothing sermons of the kind: "We are living in an exalting period of time. The Council is an extraordinary renewal. Long live this age of cultural overthrow! Our society is characterized by religious pluralism and free ideological competition. Beyond a doubt this 'advance' of history is accompanied by some 'losses,' no religious practice, dispute of all authority, Christians become once more a minority. But see what advantages there are! Christians are the leaven hidden in the dough, the soul of the vitally Christian pluralistic City in gestation, the mover of the ideals of the new world that is being built, more fraternal, more peaceful, more free!"

I cannot understand such a blindness otherwise than as the fulfillment of the prophecy of Saint Paul concerning the apostates of the last times: God Himself, he says, "will send them a power of incoherence so that they believe in the lie."[2] What chastisement more terrible than a hierarchy

1 Cf. Daniel 9:27; Matt. 24:15.
2 2 Thessalonians 2:10.

that has lost its direction! If we can believe Sister Lucy on this, that is what Our Lady predicted in the third part of the Secret of Fatima: the Church and its hierarchy will undergo a *"diabolical disorientation."*[1] And, still according to Sister Lucy, this crisis corresponds to what the Apocalypse tells us of the combat of the Woman against the Dragon. Now, the Most Holy Virgin assures us that at the end of this struggle, "her Immaculate Heart will triumph."

If this is how things are, you will understand that, in spite of everything, I am not a pessimist. The Holy Virgin will have the victory. She will triumph over the great apostasy, the fruit of Liberalism. One more reason not to twiddle our thumbs! We have to fight more than ever for the social Reign of Our Lord Jesus Christ. In this battle, we are not alone: we have with us all the Popes up through Pius XII inclusively. All of them combatted Liberalism in order to deliver the Church from it. God did not grant that they succeed, but this is no reason to lay down our weapons! We have to hold on. We have to build, while the others are demolishing. The crumbled citadels have to be rebuilt, the bastions of the faith to be reconstructed: firstly the holy sacrifice of the Mass of all times, which forms saints; then our chapels, which are our true parishes; our monasteries; our large families; our enterprises faithful to the social doctrine of the Church; our politicians determined to make the politics of Jesus Christ—this is a whole tissue of Christian social life, Christian customs, Christian reflexes, which we have to restore, on the scale that God wants, at the time God wills. All that I know, the faith teaches us; it is that Our Lord Jesus Christ must reign here below, now, and not only at the end of the world,[2] as the Liberals would have it!

While they are destroying, we have the contentment of rebuilding. A still greater happiness: generations of young priests are participating with zeal in this task of reconstruction of the Church for the salvation of souls.

---

1 Brother Michael of the Trinity, *The Whole Truth On Fatima*, Tome III, *The Third Secret*, p. 507.
2 This is what the conciliar liturgy would have us believe, which pushes the feast of Christ the King symbolically back to the last Sunday of the liturgical cycle.

Our Father, Thy Kingdom come! Long live Christ the King! Holy Ghost, fill the hearts of Thy faithful! O Mary, be our Queen, we belong to Thee!

Appendix

Central Pontifical Commission
preparatory to the Second Vatican Council

"Constitution on the Church"
A Schema Proposed by the Theological Commission

Second Part

Chapter IX

On the Relations Between the Church
and the State and On Religious Tolerance

Most Eminent and Reverend
Cardinal Alfredo Ottaviani, Chairman

N.B. The doctrinal schema presented by Cardinal Ottaviani comprised in its original Latin version seven pages of text and sixteen pages of references, going from Pius VI (1790) to John XXIII (1959). It was set aside, from the first session of the Council, to the benefit of the schema drawn up by the Secretariat for Christian Unity under Cardinal Bea. This latter schema, which was intended to be pastoral, extended to fourteen pages, *without any reference* to the magisterium that preceded it.

The Ottaviani schema does not enjoy a magisterial authority, but it represents the state of Catholic doctrine on the question on the eve of Vatican II and expresses substantially the doctrine that the Council would have had to propose if it had not been turned away from its purpose by the *coup d'Etat* of those who made of it the "States general of the people of God," a second 1789! Let us add finally that the Council would have been able to bring to this statement all useful points of precision or improvements.

l. Principle: Distinction between the Church and civil Society, and subordination of the goal of the City to the goal of the Church.

Man, destined by God for a supernatural end, needs both the Church and civil Society in order to attain his full perfection. Civil Society, to which man belongs because of his social character, must watch over earthly goods and act in such a way that, on this earth, the citizens can lead a "calm and peaceful life."[1] The Church, into which man must incorporate himself because of his supernatural vocation, has been founded by God in order that, always expanding more and more, it may lead its faithful by its doctrine, its sacraments, its prayer, and its laws, to their eternal end.

Each of these two societies is rich with the necessary resources to accomplish its own mission as it should. Each is also perfect, that is to say, supreme in its class and thus independent of the other, holding the legislative, judicial, and executive powers. This distinction of the two cities, as a constant tradition teaches it, rests on the words of the Lord: "Render therefore to Cæsar what is Cæsar's, and to God what is God's."[2]

Nevertheless, as these two societies exercise their power over the same persons and often with regard to one same object, they cannot ignore each other. They must even proceed in perfect harmony, in order to flourish themselves, no less than their common members.

---

1 1 Tim. 2:2.
2 Matt. 22:21.

The Holy Council, with the intention of teaching which relations must exist between these two powers, according to the nature of each of them, declares in the very first place the firm obligation of holding that both the Church and civil Society have been instituted for the usefulness of man; that temporal happiness, entrusted to the care of the civil Authority, nevertheless is worth nothing for man if he is going to lose his soul.[1] And that therefore the end of civil Society must never be sought by excluding or by endangering the ultimate end, namely, eternal salvation.

2. *The power of the Church and its limits; the duties of the Church towards the civil Authority.*

As the power of the Church thus extends to everything that leads men to eternal salvation; as that which concerns only temporal happiness is placed, as such, under the civil authority; it follows from this that the Church is not concerned with temporal realities, except to the extent that they are ordered to the supernatural end. As for the acts ordered to the end of the Church as well as to that of the City, like marriage, the education of children, and other similar things, the rights of the civil Authority must be exercised in such a way that, in the judgment of the Church, the higher goods of the supernatural order do not undergo any injury. In the other temporal activities which, divine law remaining unharmed, can be considered or accomplished legitimately and in diverse manners, the Church does not interfere in any way. Guardian of its own rights, perfectly respectful of the rights of others, the Church does not reckon that there belongs to it the choice of a form of government, or that of the institutions proper to the civil domain of the Christian nations: of the diverse forms of government, it does not disapprove of any, on the condition that religion and morals are safe. Likewise, indeed, as the Church does not renounce its own liberty, in the same way it does not prevent the civil Authority from freely making use of its laws and its rights.

---

1 Cf. Matt. 16:26; Mark 8:36; Luke 9:25.

What great benefits the Church procures for civil Society while accomplishing its mission, the heads of nations should recognize. Indeed, the Church itself cooperates in the citizens' becoming good by their virtue and their Christian piety. And if they are such as Christian doctrine prescribes, in the testimony of Saint Augustine,[1] beyond any doubt, great will be the public welfare. The Church also imposes onto the citizens the obligation of complying with legitimate orders "not only through fear of chastisement, but from a motive of conscience."[2] As for those to whom the government of the country has been entrusted, it warns them of the obligation to exercise their function, not through the desire for power, but for the good of the citizens, as having to render an account to God,[3] of their power received from God. Finally, the Church inculcates the observance as well of the natural laws as of the supernatural ones, thanks to which all civil order, and order among citizens and among the nations, can be realized in peace and in justice.

3. Religious duties of the civil Authority.

The civil Authority cannot be indifferent with regard to religion. Instituted by God in order to help men acquire a truly human perfection, it must not only supply its subjects with the possibility of procuring temporal goods for themselves, either material or intellectual, but besides favor the abundance of spiritual goods, permitting people to lead a human life in a religious manner. Now, among these goods, nothing is more important than to know and to recognize God, and then to fulfill one's duties towards God: here indeed is the foundation of all private and, still more, public virtue.

These duties towards God oblige, towards the divine Majesty, not only each one of the citizens but also the civil Authority, which, in its public acts, incarnates civil Society. God is indeed the author of civil Society and the source of all the goods which flow down through it to all its members. Civil Society must therefore honor and serve God. As

---

1 Ep. ad Marcellinum, 138, 15
2 Romans 13:5.
3 Cf. Hebrews 13:17.

for the manner of serving God, this can be no other, in the present economy, than that which He Himself has determined, as obligatory, in the true Church of Christ; and this not only in the person of the citizens, but equally in that of the Authorities who represent civil Society.

That the civil Authority has the power to recognize the true Church of Christ is clear from the manifest signs of its divine institution and mission, signs given to the Church by its divine Founder. The civil Authority also, and not only each of the citizens, has the duty of accepting the Revelation proposed by the Church itself. Likewise, in its legislation, it must conform itself to the precepts of the natural law and take a strict account of the positive laws, both divine and ecclesiastical, intended to lead men to supernatural happiness.

Just as no man can serve God in the manner established by Christ if he does not know clearly that God has spoken through Jesus Christ, likewise civil Society itself cannot do this, if the citizens do not have at first a sure knowledge of the fact of Revelation, just like the civil Authority, to the extent that it represents the people.

It is thus in a very particular way that the civil Authority must protect the full liberty of the Church and not prevent it in any way from integrally carrying out its mission, either in the exercise of its sacred magisterium, or in the arrangement and performance of its worship, or in the administration of the sacraments and the pastoral care of the faithful. The freedom of the Church must be recognized by the civil Authority in everything that concerns its mission, especially in the choice and the formation of its aspirants to the priesthood; in the election of its bishops; in the free and mutual communication between the Roman Pontiff and the bishops and the faithful; in the foundation and the government of institutes of the religious life; in the publication and propagation of writings; in the possession and administration of temporal goods; as also, in a general way, in all those activities which the Church, without disregarding civil rights, judges appropriate for leading men towards their ultimate end, not making an exception of secular education, social works, and so many other miscellaneous resources.

Finally, it devolves seriously upon the civil Authority to exclude from legislation, government, and public activity everything which it would judge to be capable of impeding the Church from attaining its eternal end; indeed further, it must apply itself to facilitating the life which is founded on principles that are Christian and consistent at their highest point with this sublime end for which God has created men.

4. General principle of application of the doctrine set forth.

That the ecclesiastical authority and the civil Power maintain different relations according to the manner in which the civil Authority, personally representing the people, understands Christ and the Church founded by Him—this is what the Church has always recognized.

5. Application in a Catholic City.

The whole doctrine, put forth above by the Holy Council, cannot be applied except in a city where the citizens not only are baptized but profess the Catholic faith. In this case it is the citizens themselves who freely choose that civil life be formed according to Catholic principles and that thus, as Saint Gregory the Great says, "The road to Heaven be more widely opened." [1]

Nevertheless, even in these fortunate conditions, the civil Authority is not permitted in any way to compel consciences to accept the faith revealed by God. Indeed the faith is essentially free and cannot be the object of any constraint, as the Church teaches by saying, "That no one be compelled to embrace the Catholic Faith unwillingly."[2]

Still, this does not prevent the civil Authority from having to procure the intellectual, social, and moral conditions required in order that the faithful, even those less versed in knowledge, be able to persevere more easily in the faith received. Thus then, in the same way that the civil Authority judges that it has the right to protect public morality, likewise, in order to protect the citizens against

---

1 *Ep. 65, ad Mauricium.*
2 Code of Canon Law, Canon 1351.

the seductions of error, in order to keep the City in the unity of faith, which is the supreme good and the source of manifold, even temporal, benefits, *the* **civil authority** *can*, by itself, regulate and moderate the public manifestations of other cults and defend its citizens against the spreading of false doctrines which, in the judgment of the Church, put their eternal salvation at risk.

6. *Religious tolerance in a Catholic city.*

In this safeguarding of the true faith, one must proceed according to the requirements of Christian charity and of prudence, in order that the dissidents be not alienated from the Church through terror, but rather drawn to it; and that neither the City nor the Church undergo any damage. Therefore, both the common good of the Church and the common good of the State always have to be considered, by virtue of which a just tolerance, even sanctioned by laws, can, according to the circumstances, be imposed onto the civil Authority. This, on the one hand, would be in order to avoid greater evils, such as scandal or civil war, a hindrance to conversion to the true faith, and other evils of this kind; on the other hand, in order to obtain a greater good, like civil cooperation and the peaceful coexistence of citizens of different religions, a greater freedom for the Church, and a more effective accomplishment of its supernatural mission, and other similar goods. In this question, there must be taken into consideration not only the good of national order, but the welfare of the universal Church besides (and of international civil welfare). By this tolerance the Catholic civil Authority imitates the example of divine Providence, which permits evils from which it draws greater goods. This tolerance is to be observed chiefly in the countries where, for centuries, there have existed non-Catholic communities.

7. *Application in a Non-Catholic City.*

In the cities where a great part of the citizens do not profess the Catholic faith or do not even know the fact of Revelation, the non-Catholic civil Authority must, in matters of religion, conform at least to the precepts of the natural law. Under these conditions, this non-Catholic Authority should concede civil liberty to all the forms of worship that are not opposed to natural religion. This liberty is not opposed in such a case to Catholic principles, it being given that it suits the good of the Church as well as that of the State. In the cities where the Authorities do not profess the Catholic religion, the Catholic citizens have above all the duty to bring it about, through their virtues and civic actions. By means of these, united with their fellow citizens, they promote the common good of the State, that there be granted to the Church the full freedom to accomplish its divine mission. From the free action of the Church, indeed, the non-Catholic city also suffers no harm and even derives numerous and remarkable benefits. In this way, then, the Catholic citizens must do their best so that the Church and the civil Authority, although still separated juridically, lend each other a mutual benevolent aid.

In order not to harm either the Church or the State through unconcern or imprudent zeal, the Catholic citizens, in the defense of the rights of God and of the Church, must submit to the judgment of the ecclesiastical authority: to it belongs judgment on the good of the Church, according to the diverse circumstances, and the directing of Catholic citizens in the civil actions intended to defend the altar.

8. Conclusion.

The Holy Council recognizes that the principles of the mutual relations between the ecclesiastical authority and the civil authority must not be applied otherwise than according to the rule of conduct given forth above. Nevertheless, it cannot permit these same principles to be obscured by some false laicism, even under pretext of the common good. These principles, indeed, rest on the absolutely firm rights of God; on the unchangeable constitution and mission of the Church; also on the social nature of man, which, remaining always the same, across all the centuries, determines the essential purpose of civil Society itself, not-

withstanding the diversity of political systems and the
other vicissitudes of history.[1]

---

1 Translated from a French translation drawn up with the valuable cooperation of
Professor Gabriel Chabot. N.B. We have omitted the numerous notes which this
document carried. If anyone wants to become familiar with these, let him refer to
the original Latin text.

Bibliography

I. PONTIFICAL TEACHINGS

La Paix Intérieure des Nations, Documents Pontificaux, text and tables by the Monks of Solesmes, Desclée et Cie, 1962. (In the footnotes, this book is referred to as "PIN.")

II. LIBERALISM

Billot, Cardinal L., S.J. *De Ecclesia Christi,* T. II. Ed. Gregor., Rome, 1929, *de habitudine Ecclesiæ ad civilem societatem.*

Constantin, C. *Le libéralisme catholique,* in DTC. T. IX. col. 506-629.

Meinvielle, Abbé Julio, *De Lamennais à Maritain,* la Cité Catholique, Paris, 1956.

Ousset, Jean, *Pour qu'il règne,* la Cité Catholique, Paris, 1959, new edition CLC. Paris, without date, with a letter of His Exc. Mgr. Marcel Lefebvre, Archbishop of Dakar.

d'Assac, Jacques Plonard, *L'Eglise occupée,* DPF. 1975.

Roussel, Abbé A., *Libéralisme et catholicisme,* conferences given to the *"la Semaine catholique,"* Rennes, 1926.

Saint-Just, P. Theotime de, O.M.C. *La Royauté Sociale de N.S. Jésus-Christ d'après le cardinal Pie,* Beauchesne, Paris, 1925, 2d Edition.

III. THE PUBLIC LAW OF THE CHURCH

Lo Grasso, Giovanni, S.J. *Ecclesia et Status, Fontes selecti,* Univ. Greg., Romæ, 1952.

Ottaviani, Cardinal Alfredo. *Institutiones Juris publici ecclesiastici,* Imp. Polygl. Vatic., 1958-1960.
—*L'Eglise et la Cité.* Imp. Polygl. Vatic., 1963.

Roul,Abbé A. *L'Eglise catholique et le droit commun*, Doctrine et Vérité, Casterman, 1931.

IV. RELIGIOUS LIBERTY OF VATICAN II

André-Vincent, Ph., O.P. *La liberté religieuse droit fondamental*, Paris, Téqui 1976.

Le Courrier de Rome, N. 157 (May 1967), 162 (Oct. 1976). Articles of Michel Martin and R. Tévérence.

Lefebvre, His Excellency, Archbishop Marcel
—*I Accuse the Council*, The Angelus Press (1981).
—*Mgr. Lefebvre et le Saint-Office*, revue *Itinéraires*, n. 233, May 1979.
—*Open Letter to Confused Catholics*, The Angelus Press (1987).

Lumière et vie, n. 69, July-October 1964. *La liberté religieuse*, — Articles of A.F. Carillo de Albornoz, R.C. Gerest, O.P., G.M.M. Cottier, O.P., etc.

Tolérance et communauté Humaine. Casterman. 1959, Articles of Roger Aubert, Louis Bouyer, Yves Congar O.P., André Molitor, etc.

Vatican II. *La liberté religieuse*, collection *Unam Sanctam*, n. 60, Paris. Cerf. 1967. Articles of John Courtney-Murray, Jérôme Hamer O.P., Pietro Pavan, etc...

Index